PRAISE FOR *MY*

"Fresh, dynamic, and balancing are just a few words that describe this much needed book on the Holy Spirit. Mark does a wonderful job of personalizing the wonderful relationship we can all have with the 3rd person of the Trinity."

-Troy Maxwell, Senior Pastor, Freedom House Church, Charlotte, NC USA

"*My Friend, the Holy Spirit* provides life changing insight into the person of the Holy Spirit and His gifts, it will help you understand who the Holy Spirit is, what He does and how you can develop a more intimate friendship with Him"

-Dr. Phil Pringle, Senior Minister, C3 Oxford Falls, Founder C3 International, Sydney AUS

"Mark Peterson is a man full of faith and the Holy Spirit. In *My Friend, the Holy Spirit*, he relates depth and insight from life experience and the Word of God. This book is practical, profound, and powerful. You will be encouraged and equipped to know your Friend in a newfound way".

-John Reeve, Associate Pastor, The Cause Community Church, Brea, CA USA

"I believe that this book will inspire you to reach higher, dig deeper and go further into a dimension of supernatural Christian living like you have never experienced before".

-Jurgen Matthesius, Lead Pastor, C3 Church, San Diego, CA USA

MY FRIEND, THE HOLY SPIRIT

Who **He** Is, What **He** does, and How **HE** can change your life

Mark D. Peterson

My Friend, the Holy Spirit
Copyright © 2011 Mark D. Peterson

Details in some anecdotes and stories have been changed to protect the identities of the persons involved.

ISBN: 978-0-557-69782-3

Unless otherwise indicated all Scripture quotations are from:
The Holy Bible, New King James (NKJV) © 1984 by Thomas Nelson Inc.

All Rights reserved.
No Part of this publication may be reproduced, stored in a retrieval system, or transmitted in any form or by any means – electronic, mechanical, photocopying, recording or otherwise for commercial gain or profit without the prior permission of the Author. Using short quotations in reviews or occasional page copying for personal or group study is permitted and encouraged.

Printed in the United States of America
2011 – First Edition

Editing by Melissa O'Reilly and Samantha Rios
Front Cover by Paul Churchward

We want to hear from you.
Please send your comments about this book to us in care of info@myfriendtheholyspirit.com.

Dedicated to the Holy Spirit, for bringing me

Jesus, the gift of Salvation,
My beautiful wife, Summer, and
My daughters Charlize Faith and Bella Grace.

CONTENTS

Foreword by Jurgen Matthesius	9
Chapter 1: Your Friend, the Holy Spirit	11
Chapter 2: Who is the Holy Spirit?	15
Chapter 3: Necessity for the Baptism of the Spirit	31
Chapter 4: Introduction to the Gifts	47
Chapter 5: Facts about the Gifts	52
Chapter 6: Ministry Gifts vs. Spiritual Gifts	59
Chapter 7: Functions of the Gifts of the Spirit	62
Chapter 8: Word of Wisdom	69
Chapter 9: Word of Knowledge	73
Chapter 10: Gift of Faith	79
Chapter 11: Gifts of Healings	86
Chapter 12: Working of Miracles	103
Chapter 13: Gift of Prophecy	112
Chapter 14: Gift of Discerning of Spirits	121
Chapter 15: Gift of Various Kinds of Tongues	127
Chapter 16: Gift of Interpretation of Tongues	144
Chapter 17: Receiving the Baptism of the Holy Spirit	147
Chapter 18: Moving in the Gifts of the Spirit	162
Chapter 19: Hearing the Voice of God	175
Chapter 20: Closing Challenge	193

FOREWORD

The Prophet Joel declared that "In the last days, I will pour out my Spirit on all flesh, says the LORD, your sons and daughters shall prophesy, old men shall dream dreams, and your young men shall see visions. Even on my menservants and on my maidservants will I pour out my Spirit!"

Since Christ's resurrection I believe we have been living in the 'last days' and when we study the book of Acts which documents in detail the activities of the early church, we see a church vastly different to what most people experience today. We see a church that is baptized in the Spirit of God, manifest with the operation of signs, wonders, miracles and demonstrations of the power of God! What has happened to our churches today? Where has the power gone?

Survey the titles of the Christian books occupying the shelves at your local Christian book store and most deal with issues of struggle, lack and defeated living, there are few that explain how to live and operate in a dimension of power and victory available to us through the giftings of the Holy Spirit. I am so glad that Mark Peterson has undertaken the task to write a book on such a vital topic in the world today. Our television networks and cinemas are filled with programs and movies either containing or focused upon supernatural spiritual phenomena, however most if not all of them highlight the occult as the source of 'great power.' Whether it be by way of mediums, Psychics, tarot card readers or magicians, God has certainly been removed from the arena of supernatural spiritual power. This has got to change! Remember the bible teaches that the anti Christ would perform 'counterfeit' signs and wonders, in other words God is the real deal and the devil a cheap copy.

Mark has been involved in ministry in three nations, New Zealand, Australia and the USA for the better part of two decades and has always been passionate about the gifts and power of the Holy Spirit. I have personally seen the presence and power of the Gifts of the Holy Spirit in operation through Mark Peterson's life, whether it was by way of a life changing powerful prophetic word, or a significant miracle of healing and deliverance, wherever Mark has ministered there the Holy Spirit turned up and shook the place. What he is writing about is what he is experiencing in his daily walk with the LORD.

I believe that this book will inspire you to reach higher, dig deeper and go further into a dimension of supernatural Christian living like you have never experienced before. We are called to 'come up higher' just like the apostle John in Revelation where we will see and experience

MY FRIEND, THE HOLY SPIRIT

things on a whole other dimension. The disciples operated in power, and the same Spirit that empowered them seeks to empower a new generation of believers today.

I would encourage you as you read this book to open your heart, take notes, and let it become more than a book, but rather let it become a life changing manual to take you to a place in God where you have never been before! A place where God desires you to be, and where the devil is terrified of you accessing. Go for it, become a nightmare to the devil and a delight to the kingdom of heaven.

"Fasten your seatbelts Dorothy, cause Kansas is going Bye Bye!"

Jurgen Matthesius

Lead Pastor, C3 Church San Diego
Author – P U S H, God in Hollywood, Walk on water.

CHAPTER 1:

Your Friend, the Holy Spirit

I dropped out of church in sixth grade. Based on the fact that I thought all of those kid and youth programs were boring, I had quit and decided I wasn't going back. I am guessing this isn't the typical comment you hear from a pastor. The thing was, my mom had moved to several different churches while I was growing up, so I hadn't been to only one church, I'd been to too many. And no matter what church I had attended, it all felt the same to me—stale. I wanted something real. Something fresh.

"God spoke to Moses face to face as a man speaks to his friend" (Exodus 33:11).

The Message translation says, *"The Friend, the Holy Spirit whom the Father will send at my request"* (John 14:26).

I hadn't yet understood those scriptures. I hadn't yet learned that God wants to be our friend. I hadn't yet realized that He created fellowship with us through His son Jesus' death on the cross for our sins, but He communicates with us through His Spirit, the Holy Spirit. Most people think of the Holy Spirit as a thing, force or power. But the Holy Spirit is a person. And He wants to speak to us and spend time with us.

In John 16:13, it's written that the Holy Spirit will show or tell us of things to come. Jesus even told his disciples (also in John 16) that His leaving was to their advantage so that the Spirit could come. If Jesus considered the Holy Spirit to be an advantage, shouldn't we? But how we miss that crucial advantage in our day.

I was seventeen years old when I found the "fresh something" I had been looking for in church. It was March of 1991, and after watching a football match with some friends, we all headed over to McDonald's on Queen Street in New Zealand. Walking in, I saw Michelle, a friend from school sitting at a table. A flyer next to her hand caught my eye, but when I wandered over to talk to her, she conspicuously slid it underneath her tray. There are two things you should know about me: I am competitive and curious. So Michelle had really done it, because now I had to see what was so mysterious about that flyer.

I patiently hung around waiting for her to finish her meal, but Michelle ate excruciatingly slow. Finally she stood from the table, discreetly pinning the flyer underneath her fingers, told me she'd see me at school, and then disposed the contents on her tray (and with it the flyer) into the trash. No one saw this but me. She threw the baited flyer away. And there was only one thing to do. Fish it out of the garbage can.

But remember, my friends were a table away. I couldn't let them see me dumpster diving in the middle of McDonald's. So I waited and watched as more and more trash piled on top of the flyer, hoping my friends would collectively go away for a few minutes so that they wouldn't see what I was waiting to do. And then it happened, my lucky break—a bathroom break. Could it have been conceivable they all had to go at once? I coolly offered to hang back and guard our table, but once they disappeared, I plunged my hand into the trashcan. Simply not one of my finer moments, especially once I realized I had dug through the trash just for a flyer about church.

Church! The very thing I'd given up five years earlier. I stuffed the piece of paper into my pocket and didn't give it another thought until I got home.

That night in my bedroom, I studied the simple flyer, still smelling a bit of French fries and Big Macs. It was nothing showy. Just a picture of a man with the name Bill Subritzky and the words "Healing Evangelist" printed beside the photo. Apparently this Bill Subritzky, healing evangelist, was conducting some sort of meeting in a school auditorium on the North Shore in Auckland. Healing Evangelist? What in the world was that? What did they do? Heal people? I had never seen someone get healed before.

About a week later, thanks to my never-ending curiosity, there I was by myself driving 45 minutes away to one of these meetings. I talked myself out of going about a dozen times on the way there. I asked myself if I was nuts. I decided another scavenger hunt through the garbage would be more fashionable. I was wrong. That night was life changing.

For the first time, I learned that church wasn't boring. Nothing about God could be boring, not with His power to heal and do magnificent things. I witnessed with my very own eyes one of the gifts of the Spirit functioning when a man's withered hand stretched out and became useful again.

Your Friend, the Holy Spirit

Then right in the middle of this meeting, Bill Subritzky walked off the stage without saying another word. I watched him swiftly, silently walk down the aisle, leaving the auditorium and exiting through the door. I wasn't sure what was happening. I wondered if the meeting was over or if something was wrong. Moments later when he returned with a young couple, I realized what had happened. His exit was a response to a word from God through the Holy Spirit.

Obeying, he had gone outside to talk to this couple that had been watching some kids play basketball. He'd been given a word of knowledge and had gone to share it with them. He'd told them that God had spoken to him and that he understood the reason they were watching and not playing was because they both had bad backs.

Both of them that night were healed and saved right before my eyes. With tears flowing down the girl's face, she started jumping up and down and running laps around the building--two things she had not done for over fifteen years.

Until that night, I had never seen the Gospel preached with signs following like the Bible teaches. I remember thinking, "This is what I was born for. A relationship with a God who is alive and is all-powerful!" But when the salvation alter call was given, I grew confused over the terminology used to invite people to come forward and accept Christ as their Savior. He kept talking about backsliders. Was I a backslider? What was a backslider? I wasn't sure if I was meant to go forward and give my life to Jesus then or was this invitation just for the backsliders?

Confused, I silently prayed, "God if you want me to go forward and give my life to you tonight, then you tell the man up front (Bill Subritzky) to tell me to come forward." I didn't know any better. I just knew I wanted a real relationship with God. I wanted this God in my life. I'd never known God to be so magnificent. I had figured if I'd seen God talk to this man all night long, then surely God could tell him my dilemma? Surely he could explain to this healing evangelist that I wanted to respond.

At that precise moment, Bill Subritzky looked up and said, "There is a 17-year-old young man here. You have been running from God and God wants you to know tonight that He wants you to come forward."

My heart pounded fiercely. I knew without a doubt Bill Subritzky was talking to me. That was a direct answer to my prayer. I was so amazed that I went forward right then and became a Christian. As I was leaving the building, I saw the healing evangelist surrounded by at least a hundred people. I wished that I could talk to him and have him pray for me and all of my friends who did not know God. After experiencing what I had that night, I wanted the whole world to know God. But I figured those people's needs were far more important than mine.

MY FRIEND, THE HOLY SPIRIT

Then this voice inside of me said, "Stop. Wait." I froze. I don't know how I knew but I just knew this was a voice I had not heard before. Deep down I knew it was God speaking to me through His Holy Spirit. Not in an audible voice, but rather a voice in my thoughts. I listened as His voice said, "Look."

I turned around. Bill Subritzky was looking right at me. He pointed at me and waved his hand, signaling me to come over. As I walked toward him, people parted on the left and right like the Red Sea to let me through. Immediately he asked me, "What would you like me to pray for?"

I left that night never having been more astonished in my entire life. I knew I had heard the Holy Spirit's voice and had personally experienced God's response to me when I listened, when I paid attention, when I responded back.

Just as God spoke with Moses as a friend, He desires our friendship the same. Through His Holy Spirit, He comes along our side, as any great friend does, and stands alongside us through any circumstance whether good or bad. Think of it in terms that we can understand as in the concept of a business partnership. When two or more people get together to form a business, they must have very close contact with each other in order for the business to be successful.

When you are partners with the Holy Spirit and in close contact, allowing him to be the senior partner as he should be, you will experience nothing short of miracles, power, intercession, counsel, and spiritual gifts.

The Holy Spirit is our friend, our truest friend and comforter. It's probably safe to say that most of us only turn to the Holy Spirit in times of trouble. But the key is learning to walk with the Holy Spirit as a natural way of life, every day, as a friend. Each day we can say, Holy Spirit let's read together this word you wrote, let's walk together today; it's going to be an amazing day. Whether we realize it or not, we actually live with the Holy Spirit. He is with us in our sleep, filling our dreams with hope and visions. He is with us when we eat, when we pray, when we work. Fellowship with the Holy Spirit happens when we acknowledge He is with us, when He is a part of our day and when we choose to commune with Him. We then can build the friendship that He desires and we gain the benefit of spiritual gifts for God's glory.

CHAPTER 2:

Who is the Holy Spirit?

Who exactly is this Spirit of God? He is part of the Trinity. Three separate persons complete the Trinity, the Father, Son and Holy Spirit. Therefore He is "God on Earth" and equal to the Father and the Son. The Holy Spirit is the point at which the Trinity becomes personal to the believer. It is through the Holy Spirit that we experience God, feel His presence, and hear His voice.

The Holy Spirit created the heavens and the earth by the will of God as the Bible reports in Genesis 1:3, *"The earth was without form, and void; and darkness was on the face of the deep. And the Spirit of God was hovering over the face of the waters. Then God said, 'Let there be light'; and there was light."*

Not only did the Holy Spirit create the heavens and earth, but also creates and gives life.

Job 33:4 says, *"The Spirit of God has made me, and the breath of the Almighty gives me life."*

And from what we read in Job 26:13, *"By His Spirit He adorned the heavens; His hand pierced the fleeing serpent,"* we learn that the Holy Spirit has been with the Father and Son since the beginning.

The Holy Spirit has been with God from the beginning, and the Bible says that the Holy Spirit will be with us forever. *"And I will pray the Father, and He will give you another Helper, that He may abide with you forever."* John 14:16

In 2 Corinthians 3:17 we read, *"Now the Lord is the Spirit and where the Spirit of the Lord is there is liberty."* Note that it is written that the Lord is the Spirit. This shows us that the Holy Spirit is part of the Trinity.

In Acts 5:3-4, Peter *attests to the fact that the Holy Spirit is God, "But Peter said, 'Ananias, why has Satan filled your heart to lie to the Holy*

MY FRIEND, THE HOLY SPIRIT

Spirit and keep back part of the price of the land for yourself? While it remained, was it not your own? And after it was sold, was it not in your own control? Why have you conceived this thing in your heart? You have not lied to men but to God." In this passage Peter tells Ananias he had lied to the Holy Spirit and in the same sentence that he had lied to God. Peter's words proved that the Holy Spirit is indeed God.

We can see the same sort of examples, which I will expand upon more below, in a number of different scriptures: Acts 28:25-26; 1 Corinthians 12:4-6; Matthew 28:19.

Acts 28:25-26: *"So when they did not agree among themselves, they departed after Paul had said one word: 'The Holy Spirit spoke rightly through Isaiah the prophet to our fathers, saying, "Go to this people and say: 'Hearing you will hear, and shall not understand; And seeing you will see, and not perceive."*

Note that Paul gives the Holy Spirit credit for speaking through Isaiah. In the book of Isaiah it is noted that it was God who spoke, but when Paul quotes the verse (Isaiah 6:8-10), he interchanges God for the Holy Spirit, which again shows that the Holy Spirit and God are one.

1 Corinthians 12:4-6 says, "There are diversities of gifts, but the same Spirit. There are differences of ministries, but the same Lord. And there are diversities of activities, but it is the same God who works all in all."

The Holy Spirit, the Lord Jesus Christ, and God are all mentioned here together as one. Spirit, Lord (Jesus) and God.

Matthew 28:19 says, *"Go therefore and make disciples of all the nations, baptizing them in the name of the Father and of the Son and of the Holy Spirit."*

Genesis 1:26 states, *"Let us make man in our image"* and Genesis 3:22 *"the man has become like one of us"*. Notice plural terms are used, the Trinity communicates to one another.

God the Father is fully God as is the Son and the Holy Spirit. There is nothing that God is that the Holy Spirit is not.

An example of how the Trinity works in prayer is this. We pray to the Father, in the name of the Son (Jesus Christ), by the power and instruction of the Holy Spirit (Romans 8:26).

One of my favorite ways of understanding the Trinity and how it functions is by thinking of it in the terms of the sun. God the Father is like the actual sun, the Son is like the rays of the sun, and the Holy Spirit is like the warmth you feel on your arm. But they are all the sun.

As is God, the Holy Spirit is also:

- Eternal - Without beginning or end, always existing, lasting forever (Hebrews 9:14).
- Omniscient - Having complete and unlimited knowledge, there is nothing that God does not know (1 Corinthians 2:10-11).
- Omnipotent - All-powerful, infinite and unlimited, there is nothing God cannot do (Luke 1:35).
- Omnipresent - Present everywhere at the same time, there is nowhere that God does not exist (Psalm 139:7-8).

The Holy Spirit is a person

As they ministered to the Lord and fasted, the Holy Spirit said, *"Now separate to Me Barnabas and Saul for the work to which I have called them"* (Acts 13:2).

The Holy Spirit speaks; He speaks because He is a person, not a force or some special power. However, He has power because He is God. The Bible uses personal pronouns when talking or referring to the Holy Spirit as in the following scriptures.

John 15:26: *"He will testify of Me."*

John 16:8: *"And when He has come, He will convict the world of sin, and of righteousness, and of judgment."*

John 16:13-14: *"However, when He, the Spirit of truth, has come, He will guide you into all truth; for He will not speak on His own authority, but whatever He hears He will speak; and He will tell you things to come. He will glorify Me, for He will take of what is Mine and declare it to you."*

To say that someone is a person, they must have personality traits. The characteristics of personality are: knowledge, feeling, emotion and will. The Holy Spirit has a personality because He is a person. Let's explore these three characteristics through scripture.

Knowledge

"But God has revealed them to us through His Spirit. For the Spirit searches all things, yes, the deep things of God" (1 Corinthians 2:10).

1 Corinthians 2:9-10: *"But as it is written: 'Eye has not seen, nor ear heard, Nor have entered into the heart of man The things which God has prepared for those who love Him.' But God has revealed them to us through His Spirit. For the Spirit searches all things, yes, the deep*

things of God." The Holy Spirit interprets his own knowledge for us, and then imparts power to discern and appreciate what he has revealed to us.

God is a God of hide and seek. He hides things from us so we will seek Him out. When we seek Him the Holy Spirit reveals to us the things God has prepared for us.

Proverbs 25:2: *"It is the glory of God to conceal a matter, But the glory of kings is to search out a matter."*

The Holy Spirit is the author of the Bible and is ready at our side to interpret its meaning to us every time we open the book. We have a divine teacher, the Holy Spirit.

Psalm 119:18: *"Open my eyes that I may see wondrous works from your law."*

Have you ever been reading the Bible and a verse that you may have read 100 times just pops out to you and speaks to you in a way that it never has before? That's the Holy Spirit bringing revelation and life to the Bible as you read it, imparting guidance and truth from God's Word for you each day!

Feeling and emotion

"Now hope does not disappoint, because the love of God has been poured out in our hearts by the Holy Spirit who was given to us" (Romans 5:5).

God pours out his love on us by the Holy Spirit. This means the Holy Spirit expresses the emotion of the love of God upon our hearts.

"And do not grieve the Holy Spirit of God, by whom you were sealed for the day of redemption" (Ephesians 4:30).

Grief is an emotion. Watching the wrong kinds of movies and TV programs can grieve the Holy Spirit and letting the wrong kinds of words come out of our mouths grieves the Holy Spirit.

Have you ever left a conversation because what the person was saying put you off? What they were saying negatively affected you. In the same way we can grieve the Holy Spirit.

Isaiah 63:10: *"But they rebelled and grieved His Holy Spirit; So He turned Himself against them as an enemy, And He fought against them."*

Hebrews 10:29: *"...insulted the Spirit of grace".*

Acts 7:51: *"'You stiff-necked and uncircumcised in heart and ears! You always resist the Holy Spirit; as your fathers did, so do you."*

Who is the Holy Spirit?

You can only, insult, rebel, resist and grieve a person, not a mere influence or power. He desires fellowship; otherwise He can be grieved. You can talk to Him like you speak to your closest friend, or as a husband speaks to his wife, talking and listening, involving Him in your everyday activities and decisions. Who wiser than the Holy Spirit to help you through life, making great decisions?

Burdens

Romans 8:26: *"Likewise the Spirit also helps in our weaknesses. For we do not know what we should pray for as we ought, but the Spirit Himself makes intercession for us with groanings which cannot be uttered."*

He pours out the love of God, He can be grieved, and groans. He has all these emotions because the Holy Spirit is not a force but a personal God who wants to be your friend.

Love of the Spirit

Romans 15:30: *"Now I beg you, brethren, through the Lord Jesus Christ, and through the love of the Spirit, that you strive together with me in prayers to God for me".*

We think often about the Father's love. How often have we thought or meditated on the love of the Spirit?

When I was in darkness and despair, lost without Christ, and I had persistently turned a deaf ear to His promptings, the Holy Spirit pursued me until at last I opened my heart and my life and He opened my eyes to the powerful saving grace of Jesus Christ. If it had not been for the love of the Spirit, patiently and persistently drawing me to Jesus, I still would be lost.

Will

The Holy Spirit makes decisions. The Holy Spirit is a leader; He leads and directs.

Acts 8:29: *"The Holy Spirit said to Philip, 'Go over and walk along beside the carriage.'"* NLT

"But one and the same Spirit works all these things, distributing to each one individually as He wills" (1 Corinthians 12:11).

"Now when they had gone through Phrygia and the region of Galatia, they were forbidden by the Holy Spirit to preach the word in Asia. After

MY FRIEND, THE HOLY SPIRIT

they had come to Mysia, they tried to go into Bithynia, but the Spirit did not permit them" (Acts 16:6-7).

"So, being sent out by the Holy Spirit, they went down to Seleucia, and from there they sailed to Cyprus" (Acts 13:4).

He is a commander who has authority. Paul recognizes this and they instantly submitted. The Holy Spirit is in charge, because He is God.

"Or do you not know that your body is the temple of the Holy Spirit who is in you, whom you have from God, and you are not your own?" (1 Corinthians 6:19).

We pray for Him to come into our hearts and our churches, but what would He find there if He should come there? The Holy Spirit is available each day to help guide us and lead us in everything we do. Each day when I get up in the morning to pray, I lift my hands and invite the Holy Spirit to be with me and to help and guide me in every part of my day.

Many people have already made their own plans and decisions and then ask the Holy Spirit to bless them. They are not allowing the Holy Spirit to lead them; sadly, they are doing their own leading.

"For as many as are led by the Spirit of God, these are sons of God" (Romans 8:14).

We also know from scripture that the Holy Spirit is the one by whom we can cast out devils, so He has authority.

"But if I cast out demons by the Spirit of God, surely the kingdom of God has come upon you" (Matthew 12:28).

Other Functions

There are several other functions the Holy Spirit has. For example, through Him, we know we have become children of God.

We learn this through Romans 8:15-17, *"For you did not receive the spirit of bondage again to fear, but you received the Spirit of adoption by whom we cry out, 'Abba, Father.' The Spirit Himself bears witness with our spirit that we are children of God, and if children, then heirs—heirs of God and joint heirs with Christ, if indeed we suffer with Him, that we may also be glorified together."*

The Holy Spirit also magnifies Jesus. We would never understand Christ nor see His glory unless the Holy Spirit reveals Him to us. Along with that, the Holy Spirit also testifies and glorifies Jesus as we read in the book of John: *"But when the Helper comes, whom I shall send to you from the Father, the Spirit of truth who proceeds from the Father,*

He will testify of Me. And you also will bear witness, because you have been with Me from the beginning" (John 15:26).

"He will glorify Me, for He will take of what is Mine and declare it to you" (John 16:14).

The Holy Spirit causes people to be born again

"Jesus answered, 'Most assuredly, I say to you, unless one is born of water and the Spirit, he cannot enter the kingdom of God. That which is born of the flesh is flesh, and that which is born of the Spirit is spirit" (John 3:5-7).

Regeneration is the impartation of a new nature--God's own nature to the one who is born again. Regeneration (salvation) brings eternal life.

Titus 3:5 states *"not by works of righteousness which we have done, but according to His mercy He saved us, through the washing of regeneration and renewing of the Holy Spirit".*

The Holy Spirit convicts of sin

The great news is we don't have to convict the world of sin. Some Christians believe that this is their job, but it is not. Our job is to share the "good news" of Jesus Christ and let the Holy Spirit do the convicting of sin.

The Holy Spirit brings conviction and salvation. The Holy Spirit renews men, or makes men new. The Holy Spirit is the only one who can convince men of sin and cause men to be born again.

John 16:7-9,11: *And when He has come, He will convict the world of sin, and of righteousness, and of judgment: of sin, because they do not believe in Me...of righteousness, because I go to My Father and you see Me no more; of judgment, because the ruler of this world is judged.*

His various names

Jesus says in John 7:16, *"My doctrine is not Mine, but His who sent Me,"* and in John 8:26, *"I have many things to say and to judge concerning you, but He who sent Me is true; and I speak to the world those things which I heard from Him."*

So Jesus declared in the above verses that "My doctrine is not Mine but His who sent Me".

So there is a clear order in the Trinity. Each person of the Trinity has different functions. Functions are communicated by name. In the Bible,

MY FRIEND, THE HOLY SPIRIT

names communicate character and function. As far as the Holy Spirit goes, the names most commonly used are Holy Spirit, Comforter and Spirit of Truth. Let's explore His different names.

His primary name is the Holy Spirit as we see in the following scripture:

"For God did not call us to uncleanness, but in holiness. Therefore he who rejects this does not reject man, but God, who has also given us His Holy Spirit" (1 Thessalonians 4:7-8).

Sometimes we become so familiar with a name that we neglect to weigh its significance. He is not only Holy but imparts Holiness to others, which is why one of His names is also the Spirit of Holiness. Holiness means being set apart from sin and being in agreement with God.

Romans 1:4 states he is the Spirit of Holiness: *"and declared to be the Son of God with power according to the Spirit of holiness, by the resurrection from the dead."*

No one buys water that says "98% pure, 2% sewage". The Holy Spirit has been poured out so we can walk in holiness; we don't need to settle for less than God's best.

Comforter

Comforter is the other name that is most commonly used for the Holy Spirit. The word "comforter" in the Greek is paraclete, which means: comforter, counselor, helper, intercessor, advocate, strengthener, standby or one who is called to another's side. Wow, what a friend we have!

In our lives, we need great friends to give us great counsel in making life's most important decisions. Not all friends give good advice; just ask Job!

So what better counsel than the counsel of God? Making life's difficult decisions is much easier when we seek God's advice before jumping ahead. We should always seek to have mentors in our world, godly men and women from whom we can learn and glean, but the greatest teacher/mentor we can have is the Holy Spirit.

"But the Comforter (Counselor, Helper, Intercessor, Advocate, Strengthener, Standby), the Holy Spirit, Whom the Father will send in My name [in My place, to represent Me and act on My behalf], He will teach you all things. And He will cause you to recall (will remind you of, bring to your remembrance) everything I have told you" (John 14:26, Amplified).

The Message translation says, *"The Friend, the Holy Spirit whom the Father will send at my request."*

Who is the Holy Spirit?

And in John 14:16 it is written, *"And I will pray the Father, and He will give you another Helper, that He may abide with you forever."*

Notice that in scripture it is written that God said He would send the helper to abide with us; He did not say He would send "The Punisher." Some people relate holiness to legalism, but legalism does not produce holiness. God is not mad at you, but mad about you. He is so mad about you that He did not want you to receive the punishment for your sins, so He sent Jesus to take them in our place and sent the Holy Spirit to empower us for the righteous living that Christ made available for us by His death and resurrection. It is the devil that accuses (Revelation 12:10: "*...the accuser of our brethren*"), not the Holy Spirit.

God has not sent the Holy Spirit to keep an eye on you so that the moment you step out of line, He is ready to punish you. Rather, the Holy Spirit is here to help guide you in the way you should go when you begin to veer to the right or left.

Not long ago, my wife Summer was away at a conference, and I was left alone to fend for myself with my beautiful, but at times challenging, girls. I'd been struggling to get the girls to bed, when finally I got Bella to fall sleep. Charlize, however, was a different story. She wanted more songs from Daddy, more cuddles, more crackers, and more ice (she has to have ice in her water). Finally, I firmly told Charlize that the next time she got out of bed and left her room would result in the consequence of a smacked bottom.

Assured my firmness did the trick, I headed to my room and was just drifting off to a serene sleep when at my door I see the small shadow of my 2-year-old, Charlize. Before I can say a word, she says, "Be gentle, Daddy." I was in a dozy state of sleep, so I replied, "What?" With big doe eyes, she said, "Be gentle, Daddy, when you smack my bottom." She ran to the bed, jumped up, and said, "I love you, Daddy. I only wanted cuddles."

I was in a tough spot since I had told her there would be consequences if she left her room one more time to risk being in the presence of her father. Do you know what I did? I extended grace. Charlize knew already what the consequence of her action was going to be, but she was prepared to risk the punishment as she deemed it was worth the relationship connection (cuddles) with me. She deserved punishment but received grace (at least this one time!).

We likewise deserve to be punished, but God extended grace to us by sending Jesus to take our punishment so we could be in the presence of the Father. The Bible says that we can "*come boldly to the throne of Grace*" (Hebrews 4:16). God sent Jesus to take the punishment, and then Jesus sent the Comforter to help us walk in that grace.

MY FRIEND, THE HOLY SPIRIT

Spirit of Truth

The third most common name for the Holy Spirit is Spirit of Truth. John 16:13 reads, *"However, when He, the Spirit of truth, has come, He will guide you into all truth; for He will not speak on His own authority, but whatever He hears He will speak; and He will tell you things to come."*

"And I will pray the Father, and He will give you another Helper, that He may abide with you forever— the Spirit of truth, whom the world cannot receive, because it neither sees Him nor knows Him; but you know Him, for He dwells with you and will be in you" (John 14:16-17).

Jesus calls the Holy Spirit the "Spirit of truth". The devil is described in John 8:44 as being a "liar" and the "Father of it". Think of this, mankind's turmoil began with Adam and Eve being deceived by the serpent (the devil), and today the greatest power the enemy tries to exert over us is through lies and deception; his tactics have not changed because his character has not changed. But Jesus introduces us to the "Spirit of truth" so we can be empowered to live a life free from deception and lies, walking in truth because we have the Spirit of truth. Not only will the Spirit of truth cause us to walk in truth but He will tell us of "things to come".

Ten Dollars

I find it incredible that the Holy Spirit (AKA: Spirit of Truth) will show us God's plan for us, "When He the Spirit of truth has come"...He will tell you things to come". He did just that for my wife and me with a ten-dollar bill.

When Summer and I were newly married and living in Sydney, Australia (land down under), I had preached one Sunday in a town called Geelong. Summer and I had gone to lunch at a nearby restaurant with one of the pastors after the service.

Before lunch, however, the pastor, inspired by the Holy Spirit, had some money exchanged into US currency. I remember thinking as I watched her lay an American ten-dollar bill on the table, "That's really strange. I'm pretty sure this restaurant will not accept American money for payment, will it?"

While Summer and I sat staring in bewilderment at the money on the table, the pastor proceeded with a prophetic word about the ten dollars. She explained that it wasn't payment for the lunch tab. It was an investment into our future. Little did she know—or anyone else, for that matter—that we were praying and considering a move to the United States, which we actually did a short sixteen months later.

Who is the Holy Spirit?

Another beautiful example of this scripture is when Summer and I were trying for our first child. During a time of prayer, I felt the Holy Spirit show me that Summer was pregnant.

That morning I shared this with her. So she nervously walked into the bathroom with her first pregnancy test. The five minutes it took for those results to occur (plus sign for pregnant, minus for not) lasted an eternity.

She came out of the bathroom a hundred years later with a disappointed look on her face. I told her, "It's OK, Summer, you're pregnant." The next day, she took a second test. Another five horrifically long minutes later, she walked out with a long face, holding up the test stick. I peered at its tiny window and saw the minus sign. According to that stick, she wasn't pregnant. I again affirmed that God had spoken to me and she was indeed pregnant. On the third day after I had initially felt the Holy Spirit's prompting, Summer took one more pregnancy test. It was positive!

Shortly after, God spoke to me again through His Spirit, revealing that we would have a baby girl. During our 20-week ultrasound, we anxiously awaited as the technician struggled for an hour to determine the gender of our baby. Finally, our baby moved into the right position. Can you guess? That's right, a girl!

Now sure, there's a 50/50 chance of getting it right, you might say. And while that is true, God had shown me so clearly that I know this was no lucky guess.

When we thought Summer might be pregnant with our second child, I had a dream. I saw a girl in the womb and doctors with a syringe. Then I saw the baby being shaken and falling out of the womb. I woke up so disturbed about this, but I soon learned there were three things the Holy Spirit was showing me:

1. Summer was pregnant.
2. Our second baby was also a girl.
3. A warning for protection, which I didn't fully comprehend until a week later.

You see, we had to have compulsory vaccinations done for our Green Card application for U.S. residency. Standing in the doctor's office, waiting our turn, the dream I'd had a week earlier came to mind. I immediately asked the doctor that if by chance Summer was pregnant, could any of these injections harm the baby. "Yes," he replied. I realized then God had given us a warning so that our baby would not be potentially harmed. We have our two beautiful, healthy girls, Charlize Faith and Bella Grace, and they were both shown to me in dreams.

MY FRIEND, THE HOLY SPIRIT

Why did the Holy Spirit do this? Because God's word told us that He would. *"He will tell you things to come"* (John 16:13), and that this is what He is here to do. Jeremiah 33:3 says, *"Call to me and I will show you great and mighty things which you do not know."*

All we have to do is wait on Him, converse with Him, fellowship with the Spirit of Truth and lessen our attention to all the things that clutter our hearts and our thinking in order to hear Him speaking to us.

He will tell us of things to come, just like He did for me with my two daughters. His guidance is far greater than any Taro card reader or Horoscope prediction (demonic practices that they are). The Holy Spirit will guide us into the truth and tell us about the great future God has for us, and it will not even cost you $3.99 per minute.

Ephesians 2:10 says, *"For we are His workmanship, created in Christ Jesus for good works, which God prepared beforehand that we should walk in them."*

God has sent the Holy Spirit to help us, counsel us, guide us and empower us to walk in those good things He has already planned and prepared for us! Imagine if every day we started with that kind of a positive mindset!

His plans are perfect

Have you ever planned something great for someone special? I once tried doing this for my wife. A surprise birthday party. However, it was not very well organized. I had a whole day of fun activities planned, including a car show in the morning in the city, but because she had no idea about the surprise party on the beach (over an hour's drive from the car show) and we were having such a good time that I lost track of the hour, we ended up arriving two hours late to the surprise party.

Most of the people had left, the majority of the food had been eaten and the faithful few remained only for enough time to sing happy birthday and eat the cake. It was a disaster, and the disaster was compounded when I chose a cheesecake for her birthday (she hates cheesecake). Not a good day for me, but the point is I planned something for Summer ahead of time for her to walk in and the plan didn't quite work out because I'm not perfect, but God is.

His plans are perfect and you only make plans for people that you love deeply, but that is what God is doing all the time for us--preparing good works for us beforehand that we should walk in them. And even when we mess up, He is working all things (including mess-ups) to work together for good! What an amazing God!

Romans 8:28: *"And we know that all things work together for good to those who love God, to those who are the called according to His purpose."*

He goes back to the drawing board to create new good works for us to walk in even when we get it wrong, and He is continually doing this for us. You have to believe this and speak this in faith. No matter what has happened, God will work it for good, but you must believe in order for this passage of scripture to function in your life. The promises of God do not just happen automatically, they must be accessed by faith.

Some of the other names of the Holy Spirit and their corresponding scripture references are below. Each of these names describes something about the personality or characteristics of the Holy Spirit, as names describe character we can learn about the Holy Spirit and His functions as a person.

Spirit of Intercession

"Likewise the Spirit also helps in our weaknesses. For we do not know what we should pray for as we ought, but the Spirit Himself makes intercession for us" (Romans 8:26).

I find this thought particularly reassuring. When we find it difficult to pray, when we don't feel like praying, the Holy Spirit is interceding for us. He is praying for us, cheering for us, praying that we will get back up, that we will have strength for the day. That we will overcome. That we will win!

Spirit of Wisdom and Understanding

"The Spirit of the LORD shall rest upon Him, the Spirit of wisdom and understanding, the Spirit of counsel and might, the Spirit of knowledge and of the fear of the Lord" (Isaiah 11:2).

Spirit of Life

"For the law of the Spirit of life in Christ Jesus has made me free from the law of sin and death" (Romans 8:2).

"It is the Spirit who gives life; the flesh profits nothing. The words that I speak to you are spirit, and they are life" (John 6:63).

"Who also made us sufficient as ministers of the new covenant, not of the letter but of the Spirit; for the letter kills, but the Spirit gives life" (2 Corinthians 3:6).

MY FRIEND, THE HOLY SPIRIT

Spirit of the living God

"Clearly you are an epistle of Christ, ministered by us, written not with ink but by the Spirit of the living God, not on tablets of stone but on tablets of flesh, that is, of the heart" (2 Corinthians 3:3).

Spirit of Lord Jehovah

"The Spirit of the Lord GOD is upon Me, because the Lord has anointed Me to preach good tidings to the poor; he has sent Me to heal the brokenhearted, to proclaim liberty to the captives, and the opening of the prison to those who are bound" (Isaiah 61:1-3).

Spirit of Christ and the Spirit of God

"But you are not in the flesh but in the Spirit, if indeed the Spirit of God dwells in you. Now if anyone does not have the Spirit of Christ, he is not His" (Romans 8:9).

Spirit of His Son

"And because you are sons, God has sent forth the Spirit of His Son into your hearts, crying out, "Abba, Father!" (Galatians 4:6).

Spirit of Promise

"And being assembled together with them, He commanded them not to depart from Jerusalem, but to wait for the Promise of the Father, which he said, 'You have heard from Me; for John truly baptized with water, but you shall be baptized with the Holy Spirit not many days from now'" (Acts 1:4-5).

Spirit of Knowledge and Fear of the Lord

"The Spirit of knowledge and of the fear of the Lord" (Isaiah 11:2).

Spirit of Grace

"Of how much worse punishment, do you suppose, will he be thought worthy who has trampled the Son of God underfoot, counted the blood of the covenant by which he was sanctified a common thing, and insulted the Spirit of grace?" (Hebrews 10:29).

Spirit of Supplication

"And I will pour on the house of David and on the inhabitants of Jerusalem the Spirit of grace and supplication; then they will look on Me whom they pierced. Yes, they will mourn for Him as one mourns for his only son, and grieve for Him as one grieves for a firstborn" (Zechariah 12:10). Note: True effective prayer has both the Spirit of grace and supplication.

Eternal Spirit

"How much more shall the blood of Christ, who through the eternal Spirit offered Himself without spot to God, cleanse your conscience from dead works to serve the living God?" (Hebrews 9:14).

Blaspheming the Holy Spirit

I have prayed with many people who feel they may have lost their salvation because they felt they blasphemed the Holy Spirit.

"Therefore I say to you, every sin and blasphemy will be forgiven men, but the blasphemy against the Spirit will not be forgiven men. Anyone who speaks a word against the Son of Man, it will be forgiven him; but whoever speaks against the Holy Spirit, it will not be forgiven him, either in this age or in the age to come" (Matthew 12:31-32).

So what is the unpardonable sin? It is the total rejection of Jesus Christ, the work of salvation and the Holy Spirit who brings the conviction for salvation. If you have accepted Jesus then you have not blasphemed the Holy Spirit or committed the unpardonable sin.

Symbols of the Holy Spirit

Whereas names communicate specific characteristics, symbols are exactly that, symbolic of the Holy Spirit. There are many symbols in the Bible representing the Holy Spirit; the following are a few of the most common ones used in scripture: dove, wind or breath of God, fire, water, rain, and oil.

Probably the most recognized symbol of the Holy Spirit is the dove as shown in John 1:32, *"And John bore witness, saying, 'I saw the Spirit descending from heaven like a dove, and He remained upon Him.'"*

The dove is the symbol of peace. When God brought a flood to the earth and Noah rescued mankind in the ark, the first evidence to show peace had come to the earth and the judgment and wrath of God had passed away was a dove. Likewise, the Holy Spirit brings peace and assurance in our hearts that we are Christ's, that the judgment of God was taken on the cross by Jesus. So this is symbolic that we are no longer under the judgment of God, but peace has returned to the earth.

To recap who the Holy Spirit is, He is our faithful friend who God sent to us to do everything that the word declares that He will do. He is a comforter, counselor, a standby. You can talk to Him as a person, you can ask Him, or invite Him to be part of your day every day, to take the lead in all the decisions you must make each day. He watches over the needs and situations of every area of our lives. He is the best one to give us guidance. The Holy Spirit is a person, He is your friend and He is God.

CHAPTER 3:

Necessity for the Baptism of the Spirit

Jesus told us that He would be with us, in us and upon us. How can Jesus do all these things when we know He ascended into heaven and is no longer physically on Earth? Through the Holy Spirit. By sending the Holy Spirit, Jesus broke the limitations of having to be in one place at one time. In the book of Luke, when the disciples were desiring political power, Christ responded to this by telling them of a more important power they would receive after Pentecost. Jesus was talking of the Holy Spirit.

The Holy Spirit is:

1. With us to convict at salvation.
2. Inside of us so we can experience salvation and live with God.
3. On us to empower us for service and bear witness of Christ.

In salvation there is impartation of life by the Spirit's power, and the one who receives it is saved. In baptism with the Holy Spirit, there is impartation of power, and the one who receives it is empowered for service.

The Holy Spirit is available to help us in ministry of preaching the gospel:

- As we pray: Romans 8:26-27
- As we study the word: John 14:26
- As we do personal work: Acts 8:29
- As we preach and teach: 1 Corinthians 2:4
- As we are tempted: Romans 8:2
- As we leave this world: Acts 7:54-60

MY FRIEND, THE HOLY SPIRIT

Charles Finney said, "The great commission has been given to the whole church. And that every member of the church is under obligation to make it his lifework to convert the world. I then raise two inquiries:

1. What do we need to secure success in this great work, and
2. How can we get it?
Answer: We need the endowment of power from on high."

When we receive the Holy Spirit (baptism in the Holy Spirit), we receive power and boldness to witness through signs and wonders! Miracles! How would you like to give "absolute evidence and miraculous proof" of the resurrection of Jesus Christ? Wouldn't that be amazing? And yet, this power is available to us, each of us.

Luke 9:1-2 states, "*Then He called His twelve disciples together and gave them power and authority over all demons, and to cure diseases. He sent them to preach the kingdom of God and to heal the sick*" and again in Matthew 10:1, "*And when He had called His twelve disciples to Him, He gave them power over unclean spirits, to cast them out, and to heal all kinds of sickness and all kinds of disease.*"

The word "power" in Greek is exousia. Meaning privilege, authority, force, capacity, competency, freedom, mastery, superhuman, delegated influence, liberty, power. What this means is that what is controlling the world no longer controls us because we have been given exousia!

In Acts 4:31 we read, "*And when they had prayed, the place where they were assembled together was shaken; and they were all filled with the Holy Spirit, and they spoke the word of God with boldness.*"

The baptism in the Holy Spirit converts cowards into heroes. After the baptism of the Holy Spirit, the same Peter who had denied Christ three times was no longer afraid before the very council that had condemned Jesus to death, rulers of people and elders of Israel.

As Acts 4:8-12 reports,

> "*Then Peter, filled with the Holy Spirit, said to them, 'Rulers of the people and elders of Israel: If we this day are judged for a good deed done to a helpless man, by what means he has been made well, let it be known to you all, and to all the people of Israel, that by the name of Jesus Christ of Nazareth, whom you crucified, whom God raised from the dead, by Him this man stands here before you whole. This is the stone which was rejected by you builders, which has become the chief cornerstone Nor is there salvation in any other, for there is no other name under heaven given among men by which we must be saved.'*"

Necessity for the Baptism of the Spirit

Peter boldly proclaimed Christ to the very same people to whom he had also denied Christ.

"But Peter and the other apostles answered and said: "We ought to obey God rather than men" (Acts 5:29-32)

Jesus also told the disciples in Luke 24 that they should not depart to undertake the work of God that had been commissioned until they received the promise of the Father, the baptism of the Holy Spirit.

Were they not equipped for the work? No they were not equipped, there is preparation that is absolutely necessary for effective work that you must not go one step further until you receive it.

"Behold, I send the Promise of My Father upon you; but tarry in the city of Jerusalem until you are endued with power from on high" (verse 49). The word "tarry" means to sit down. In essence, preachers should sit down until they have received the baptism of the Holy Spirit. Every candidate for the ministry must first be baptized in the Holy Spirit. This is not just true for ordained ministers but also for every Christian.

The importance of this baptism was the reason Paul was so adamant in Acts 19:1-6,

> *"And it happened, while Apollos was at Corinth, that Paul, having passed through the upper regions, came to Ephesus. And finding some disciples he said to them, 'Did you receive the Holy Spirit when you believed?' So they said to him, 'We have not so much as heard whether there is a Holy Spirit.' And he said to them, 'Into what then were you baptized?' So they said, 'Into John's baptism.' Then Paul said, 'John indeed baptized with a baptism of repentance, saying to the people that they should believe on Him who would come after him, that is, on Christ Jesus.' When they heard this, they were baptized in the name of the Lord Jesus. And when Paul had laid hands on them, the Holy Spirit came upon them, and they spoke with tongues and prophesied."*

When Paul found out they had not received the Holy Spirit, the first thing he did was teach them that they should receive the Holy Spirit before they went on to reach the city.

The Bible declares this in Acts 1:8, *"But you shall receive power when the Holy Spirit has come upon you; and you shall be witnesses to Me in Jerusalem, and in all Judea and Samaria, and to the end of the earth."* The Amplified version states it even better: *"You shall receive virtue, miracle ability, supernatural energy after the Holy Ghost has come upon you for a specific purpose, to enable you to give absolute evidence and miraculous proof of my resurrection."*

MY FRIEND, THE HOLY SPIRIT

Sometimes we think that our great words and arguments will win a world for Christ. While words are important, words without the Spirit are just the letter of the law. The Bible says in 2 Corinthians 3:6b, *"The letter kills but the Spirit gives life."* Because we have removed the power from the Church, we have become so good at "words" but so poor with "demonstration."

When the power of God is replaced by arguments something is wrong. When cancer is healed and blind eyes are opened, then no argument is needed. A person receiving a touch from the Holy Spirit is enough proof that Jesus is who He says He is.

Being clothed in the natural feels great, but being clothed with God's power in the Supernatural far surpasses it! Clothing in biblical times generally covered your entire body (head included), I think this is what it means when we are "clothed with power from on high," head to toe we carry the anointing of the Holy Spirit for a specific purpose of changing lives and bringing reformation to our cities.

I have heard some say that when we get up to minister with no anointing, it is like getting up to minister with no clothes on; so the anointing, "power from on high", is the clothing of the Spirit. When Christ gave the great commission to convert the world, he also told the disciples to wait in Jerusalem until they were endued with power from on high. He furthermore told the disciples not to embark on this work of converting the world until they had received this power from on high. The disciples then continued in prayer until they received the baptism of the Holy Spirit for the great work of converting the world.

The word Baptism comes from Bapto, which means complete immersion. The word Power comes from the Greek word dunamis, from which we get dynamite. So Jesus intended the Christian experience to be complete immersion in dynamite kind of power.

Why was it called the Day of Pentecost when the Holy Spirit was poured out? Because Jesus appeared to the disciples over a period of 40 days, the disciples then went to Jerusalem for another 10 days, so the Holy Spirit fell 50 days after Jesus rose from dead.

We have two great needs, one is forgiveness, the other is empowerment. The first need was answered via salvation, the second need was answered on the day of Pentecost when the Holy Spirit was poured out.

Jesus and the Holy Spirit

"He who says he abides in Him ought himself also to walk just as He walked" (1 John 2:6).

Necessity for the Baptism of the Spirit

Jesus Christ is our pattern. Whatever was available for Jesus through the Holy Spirit is available for us today! The baptism of the Holy Spirit is so important that Jesus did not enter His public ministry until He was baptized with the Holy Spirit. In fact, Jesus didn't perform a single miracle until the Holy Spirit had descended upon Him.

"When all the people were baptized, it came to pass that Jesus also was baptized; and while He prayed, the heaven was opened. And the Holy Spirit descended in bodily form like a dove upon Him, and a voice came from heaven which said, 'You are My beloved Son; in You I am well pleased'" (Luke 3:21-22).

- Jesus was formed within Mary by the Spirit's power (Luke 1:35).
- Jesus led a holy and spotless life (through the Holy Spirit; Hebrews 9:14).
- Jesus was baptized by the Spirit (John 1:32-33).
- Jesus was anointed and fitted for service by the Holy Spirit (Luke 4:14,18-19)
- Jesus was led by the Holy Spirit in his movements on earth (Luke 4:1).
- Jesus was given revelation and wisdom via the Holy Spirit (Isaiah 11:2-3).
- Jesus worked miracles by the Holy Spirit (Acts 10:38).
- Jesus was resurrected by the Holy Spirit (Romans 8:11).
- Jesus is still working in the power of the Holy Spirit after resurrection (Acts 1:2).

The same Holy Spirit by which Jesus was born, is at our disposal to be born again.

The same Holy Spirit by which Jesus offered himself without spot is at our disposal so we may also offer ourselves without spot.

The same Holy Spirit by which Jesus was baptized with is also available for us to be baptized with the Holy Spirit and power.

The same Holy Spirit by which Jesus was anointed for service is available to us that we may be anointed and empowered for service.

The same Holy Spirit by which Jesus was led here on earth is available to us ready to lead us day by day.

The same Holy Spirit by which Jesus received revelation and wisdom is available to us so we can receive wisdom and revelation straight from heaven.

MY FRIEND, THE HOLY SPIRIT

The same Holy Spirit by which Jesus worked miracles is available to us so that we may work the miracle power of God.

"Nevertheless I tell you the truth. It is to your advantage that I go away; for if I do not go away, the Helper will not come to you; but if I depart, I will send Him to you" (John 16:7).

No conditions were attached. Jesus didn't say He would send the Helper to some but not to others. He simply commanded, "If I go, I will send Him."

The Bible says that the *"manifestation of the Spirit is for the profit of all"* (1 Corinthians 12:7). If we don't have the Holy Spirit and His gifts operating in our churches, then we are running at a loss.

Many churches have a theology of the Holy Spirit, but have no living consciousness or outworking of his presence and power. Theology without experience is like faith without works; it is dead.

How many churches and Christians dismiss the Bible's clear record of the Holy Spirit and His power? Many churches fail even to preach or teach on these verses; it is as though they do not exist.

Has the world and all its carnal thinking so invaded the Church that we have become evangelized and we don't even know it? Nothing in the New Testament writings says that whatever the Holy Spirit accomplished through the early Church we should just forget about today and try our best with fancy messages and human programs without the presence of God.

Hebrews 13:8 says that *"Jesus Christ is the same yesterday and today and forever"* and Malachi 3:6 states, *"I the Lord do not change"*. The God of the Bible is the same God who wants to move in power today.

The church in the book of Acts had no New Testament, no band, drums or guitars, no buildings of their own, yet they still rocked the world.

Too many Christians come to church with the attitude of "let's see what the pastor does today." There is no faith. They are relying on the pastor. They come to church not to be participators but to be spectators. They come to critique the preaching and the worship, when really they should be critiquing their own hearts before God. This kind of attitude will suffocate the power of God. We must come with faith to the house of God, not rely on the pastor's faith as so many do because unbelief and doubt paralyze the miraculous.

The real question is, why are we critiquing the worship when we should be getting lost in it? Someone commented to me that they didn't like the worship that morning; I replied, "Oh, I didn't realize it was for you." Faith comes to worship God regardless of the worship or how good the

Necessity for the Baptism of the Spirit

preaching. What makes a great service is that we are there and God is there and that we come in faith.

We never need to be embarrassed by what the Spirit does, we just need to know that it's Him. As long as you can see and know that its him then you don't always have to be able to understand it or explain it. Some people come to church afraid that God might do something that could embarrass them. God put gifts in place to help people not harm people, and sometimes these gifts have been abused by flakes, fruits, and super spiros (the super spiritual). Don't let those people ruin what God has planned for you to be great.

Having the Holy Spirit in our churches does not give license for many bizarre things to happen, like people barking like dogs or clucking like a chicken. Where is this found in scripture and how does it edify a congregation?

"But the manifestation of the Spirit is given to each one for the profit of all" (1 Corinthians 12:7).

People go forward for emotional fixes every week, and then go home and live the way they have always lived, no spiritual change, no repentance, no increase in their prayer life or Bible reading, and no fruit of the Spirit to show for their encounter. A true encounter with God changes you, doesn't just give you nice feelings, shakes or other manifestations.

Many people who see this end up saying no thank you and throw the baby out with the bath water giving no place to the Holy Spirit. But just because some imitate the moving of the Spirit or have false manifestations does not mean that God does not have the real thing for us today.

I believe that the devil's key strategy in preventing believers from experiencing a relationship with the Holy Spirit where the power and gifts are in full manifestation is to make them scared, scared of the Holy Spirit and what he may do, that they may lose control or do something really strange. Just because people may act weird or strange in church and claim it is the "Holy Spirit", does not mean it is. It is most likely just them being in the flesh and weird, and the Holy Spirit had nothing to do with it. These people were probably strange before they were saved! Nowhere in the Bible is there a record of someone who became super strange and weird after being baptized with the Holy Spirit. On the contrary, they became powerful instruments in the hands of God, moving in signs, wonders and the miraculous.

My Experience

After I was saved I went back to a meeting being held the next night,

MY FRIEND, THE HOLY SPIRIT

and after witnessing more incredible healings and another great salvation altar call, they then proceeded to talk about the baptism of the Holy Spirit. I knew I needed this to walk the life that God had called me to live. I knew I needed this to help me as I returned to school and faced the possible mockery of my classmates.

I went forward and was prayed for to receive the baptism of the Holy Spirit. I felt nothing. The ones praying for me told me that it didn't matter that I didn't feel anything but to receive by faith. Well, it mattered to me. They said that I should now speak in tongues as evidence, so I stepped out in faith and a few sounds came but nothing like what I had heard coming from some of the people beside me who were also being prayed for to receive the baptism of the Holy Spirit.

I left feeling leaving dejected but remembered their parting advice to hold on to the sounds I had and to keep praying and eventually speaking in tongues would flow more easily. All the way home I prayed in tongues. Just little sounds, and it didn't sound like a language. It didn't flow from my lips, but I just stuck at it. Every day I would get up and pray for 30 minutes before school. I had no idea what to pray for in those days, so this gift of tongues really helped me get through the long half hour.

Returning to school wasn't like I had feared. Though many people did ask what had happened and why I no longer swore, did drugs or got drunk. Even an ex-girlfriend saw the difference in my life and wanted to know about the change, and I enjoyed the opportunity to tell her I became a Christian, along with a couple of members of my tennis and football teams. Often during my lunch hour, I would open my Bible and read and many students would come and ask me questions about my faith. I found that the Holy Spirit always supplied me with the right answer.

My speaking in tongues had become more fluent and seemed to flow easier each time I prayed. But I still craved what I had seen in those meetings, where I saw the manifested presence of God in action. It wasn't until about 11 months later when I was enrolled in Bible College that I experienced this. It was at a Bible College evening event with a guest lecturer named Mal Maloney. He laid hands on me on the altar call at the end of the meeting and for the first time ever I fell to the ground under the power of God. I was suddenly on the floor, and I did not know how I got there so fast and if someone had caught me or not. All I knew was that I was down there and my entire body was filled with a pins and needles kind of electricity (without the discomforting pins and needles feeling). My entire body from head to toe felt numb, even my mouth and face, and I could not move or speak.

I did not want to move as I wanted this incredible experience to continue. I stayed there as long as I could, probably for over an hour as

Necessity for the Baptism of the Spirit

the electricity and tingling sensations slowly subsided. When I was helped up from the floor I felt dizzy, like I could not walk properly, and I had to be helped to a chair, where I sat for a short while before I could of my own ability stand and walk.

Everything was different after that day. I had the revelation that the same God who met me at that altar by his Holy Spirit was the same God who could meet with me in private in the same way.

Even though many months before I had been baptized in the Holy Spirit and was speaking in tongues each day, I realized I needed an infilling of the Holy Spirit every day. Faith came into my heart on the back of this revelation.

Every day I spent time waiting, lifting my hands and inviting the Holy Spirit to fall upon me afresh. Some days were so powerful I was brought to my knees in tears, other days in joyous laughter, other days I felt nothing. But regardless I knew the Holy Spirit was touching and changing my life in some way.

It is not that we seek after feelings, tingles or anything else, we seek after the Holy Spirit, and at different times and in different ways we experience Him. Sometimes it is overwhelming and other times we feel nothing. But by faith we receive all He has for us each day regardless of feelings.

When our first daughter Charlize was born, I had overwhelming feelings for her, but after a few sleepless nights and a truckload of poopy diapers later, those same "feelings" were not as strong as before. My love for her, however, was stronger than ever even though I didn't always have those lovey-dovey feelings.

When just the other night, Charlize prayed her first legible prayer in English, "Jesus thank you for a wonderful day, amen," there was a lot of emotion and warm fuzzy feelings, but an hour later when she still wouldn't go to bed I wasn't "feeling" so wonderful about her.

But thank God the just don't live by feelings. The Bible states that "*The just shall live by FAITH!*" (Romans 1:17)

The Holy Spirit has given me many experiences to learn the importance of a friendship with Him, along with who He really is and what function He plays in our everyday lives. My prayer life soon went into overdrive. Now I was spending time praying in tongues but was also experiencing tangible power each day. I was spending time in worship, and I could sense the waves of God's love wash over me like never before. This is what it means to be continually filled with the Spirit.

The Holy Spirit pours out grace and love into our spirits through His communion with us.

MY FRIEND, THE HOLY SPIRIT

Communion of the Spirit

"The grace of the Lord Jesus Christ, and the love of God, and the communion of the Holy Spirit be with you all. Amen" (2 Corinthians 13:14).

Communion means: communicating with or travelling together with.
Imagine on the way to work, your car stopped working. Your day would be disrupted, you would be late, you may have to pay a tow truck, your whole day would be a stress and a strain; imagine if that happened to you every day? Naturally you could not survive. Eventually you would lose your job and your whole world would come to a standstill without your method of transportation.

Likewise, the communion of the Holy Spirit, daily travelling and constant friendship and fellowship with the Holy Spirit is critical for us in our Spiritual world. Many people's walk with God have literally come to a standstill because they have neglected the method, the person, that God has provided for us to travel through life with.

The first meaning of communion means: "fellowship on the basis of intimate relationship".

The second meaning of communion is "partnership". This means to do business in partnership or to work together as partners for the same purpose. Luke 5:10 reads, *"and so also were James and John, the sons of Zebedee, who were partners with Simon. And Jesus said to Simon, "Do not be afraid. From now on you will catch men."* The work of winning souls has been virtually bankrupt across many churches. Why? Because the partnership with the Holy Spirit has been broken. Evangelism was meant to be carried out as a partnership between the Holy Spirit and us, the Holy Spirit of course being the Senior partner. Many churches today neither acknowledge the Holy Spirit or welcome Him.

You can only give what you've got. Peter and John at the gate beautiful in Acts 3 were stopped in their tracks by a man lame from birth. They raised this man up and he was healed from his infirmity, walking for the very first time in his life. The key to this miracle is found in two powerful statements (in Acts 3).

"Silver and gold I do not have" (You cannot give what you don't have).

"But what I have I give you" (You can only give what you have).

Mission Possible

Shortly after my powerful experience with the Holy Spirit and having been regularly filled on a daily basis, I was hitchhiking with a Swedish man named Torbjorn. Our Bible college had an outreach activity called

Necessity for the Baptism of the Spirit

"Mission Possible," we had to be like the 12 disciples in Jesus' day, to go out and preach the gospel without any money or change of clothes.

We were dropped off on the freeway and there we opened our envelope to discover our destination for the weekend where we would reach out to lost people. I was very excited to be on this adventure with Torbjorn as he was a brilliant evangelist much older than I. As we were dropped off by the main freeway junction, we tore open the envelope in anticipation finding our location to be Paihia, a four to five hour drive away! Well we were not discouraged, we put out our hitchhiking thumbs and waited.

First, we were picked up by a Christian schoolteacher, and she took us a few towns distance dropping us off after about an hour of driving away. Only a short while later a truck pulled over with a motorbike in the back. There were two guys in the front and only one spare seat in the cab, so I sat in the back of the truck. The plan was I would pray while Torbjorn would share the gospel with these two men.

For over two hours I sat praying in the back of the truck wondering how Torbjorn was doing. All of a sudden the truck started to slow down, pull over and came to a stop. Everyone got out, and it was clear that one of the guys was upset. Peter the driver said that they ran out of gas. His friend James pulled down the motorbike from the back of the truck and took off to go get some gas. Torbjorn quietly whispered to me that Peter was very interested in Jesus, but his friend James was very against God and had interrupted Torbjorn repeatedly while he was sharing about Jesus with them.

I knew right away that taking James out of the picture while he went for gas was a God moment. Peter was sitting in the driver's seat of the truck when we walked over and Torbjorn continued talking to him about Jesus. Peter confessed that it was too late for Jesus. His life consisted of dealing drugs and running from guys who wanted to kill him. I piped in that I had done drugs myself but that drugs were nothing compared to God. I shared my testimony with him; about how God delivered me from drugs and alcohol and that I found a power, the most high, that was the best high, an eternal high, that lasted forever, not just a short fix.

He looked up at me and asked if he could have that eternal high, if he could experience that God was truly real. Well, now the pressure was on and the only answer was to pray for him and hope that God showed up. I laid hands on him and prayed. I can't remember what I prayed or how I prayed. All I know is that God showed up in such a big way that Peter started shaking. The whole truck started shaking because of Peter's shaking. He said that he felt electricity all over his body. Right there he asked how he could know Jesus as Lord and savior. We opened up a gospel tract and shared the story with him. He prayed the prayer in that exact moment, and in fact with each page we turned he said he felt a fresh surge of God's powerful love go through his body and it physically shook him each time.

Once we were done, he wanted to keep the tract, as every time he read the scripture on the pages power surged through his body. His friend came back from the gas station with a puzzled look on his face. He was not interested in hearing what had happened, and we all jumped back into the truck and about an hour later they dropped us off.

Peter gave me his address and phone number. He was from England but was currently doing drugs in New Zealand. A few months later I called the number in England, and his parents answered. They were worried about him and had been praying for him, but they had not heard from him in quite some time. I told them the story of how he became a Christian and they cried tears of joy over the phone. I then gave them my number, and a few months later they called and said they feared the worst, as they still had not heard from him. I sadly lost that number and could not find how to contact them again. I don't know of his earthly state, whether he is alive or dead, but I know his eternal state: he is alive in God, all because of the power of God, the Holy Spirit!

So Great a Salvation

There is an astounding scripture in Hebrews where God's word clearly describes how salvation is communicated. *"How shall we escape if we neglect so great a salvation, which at the first began to be spoken by the Lord, and was confirmed to us by those who heard Him, God also bearing witness both with signs and wonders, with various miracles, and gifts of the Holy Spirit, according to His own will?"* (Hebrews 2:3-4).

Three things we learn from this passage is that the good news of Jesus Christ is to be spoken by God, spoken by man, and confirmed with signs, wonders and miracles, and gifts of the Spirit. Essentially we are to preach the gospel with signs and wonders via the gifts of the Spirit, which it states above is "according to His own will." Who's will? Ours? No, it is His will. Yet how can we preach the gospel with signs following if we have no baptism and no gifts and for the most part, no understanding or knowledge?

We can't. This can only be done through the Holy Spirit as it says in 1 Corinthians 2:1-5,

> *"And I, brethren, when I came to you, did not come with excellence of speech or of wisdom declaring to you the testimony of God. For I determined not to know anything among you except Jesus Christ and Him crucified. I was with you in weakness, in fear, and in much trembling. And my*

speech and my preaching were not with persuasive words of human wisdom, but in demonstration of the Spirit and of power, that your faith should not be in the wisdom of men but in the power of God."

"For our gospel did not come to you in word only, but also in power, and in the Holy Spirit and in much assurance, as you know what kind of men we were among you for your sake" (1 Thessalonians 1:5).

"And with great power (not great witnessing) the apostles gave witness to the resurrection of the Lord Jesus" (Acts 4:33).

Our Advantage

The power of the Spirit is so important that Jesus didn't even begin His ministry until He was baptized in the Holy Spirit (John 1:29-32). In fact, history from the Bible shows us that the church didn't start until the disciples were baptized in the Holy Spirit. How important then is it for us to be baptized in the Holy Spirit?

"Nevertheless I tell you the truth. It is to your advantage that I go away; for if I do not go away, the Helper will not come to you; but if I depart, I will send Him to you" (John 16:6-7).

Jesus actually told the disciples it was to their advantage that He go away so that the Holy Spirit could come. Can you imagine being one of the disciples, hanging out with Jesus, eating dinner, and while you are having the most incredible time of your life, He says something that sounds so absurd? How could His leaving be any advantage? He is the Messiah after all. But if Jesus said it, then it, without question, must be true, right? Jesus even told His disciples that they needed to receive the Holy Spirit before they left Jerusalem to share the gospel (Acts 1:4 - 5). I can't help but wonder if the disciples who walked, talked, and lived with Jesus needed the baptism of the Holy Spirit before they went out to reach the lost, then how much more we must need this today. I believe this is why so much of the Church's efforts of reaching the lost have been in vain, because we have not received the Baptism of the Holy Spirit.

Super Christian?

When you receive the baptism of the Holy Spirit you may be expecting to feel suddenly different, like some sort of Super Christian. Some people think if they don't feel differently after they've prayed for the Holy Spirit, then it either must have not took, their prayer wasn't good enough, or they were not a good enough person to receive such an incredible gift.

MY FRIEND, THE HOLY SPIRIT

Don't let this worry you. Trust in God when you ask Him. Take His word at face value for the promise that it is. Do you remember when you turned twelve years old and for 363 days afterward, you couldn't wait to turn thirteen? Yet when your next birthday came and went, you felt exactly the same as you did the day before. That didn't mean you did not turn a year older. It didn't mean that because you didn't feel differently that you were still in fact twelve years old. Regardless of whether you felt a year older or not, you had indeed entered your teenage years. The Bible doesn't say we walk by feelings, it says we walk by faith.

New Wineskins

Many people have asked if they have to be a Christian in order to receive the Holy Spirit. The answer is yes. Scripture says, *"And no one puts new wine into old wineskins. For the wine would burst the wineskins, and the wine and the skins would both be lost. New wine calls for new wineskins"* (Mark 2:22). This means that anyone who belongs to Christ has become a new person. *"The old life is gone; a new life has begun"* (2 Corinthians 5:17). Based on these scriptures, I believe we must be made new before we can receive the Spirit of God.

In talking with others, though, I have come to realize there is quite a bit of confusion regarding salvation, water baptism and the Holy Spirit baptism. I have been asked whether or not they are all the same thing.

Salvation, Water Baptism and Holy Spirit Baptism

I have heard some people say, "Well I am born again; I am born of the Spirit. I have the Holy Ghost already! And that's all there is to it!" Some of this confusion may come from a misunderstanding of John 20:22, *"And when He had said this, He breathed on them, and said to them, 'Receive the Holy Spirit.'"* This scripture describes the born-again experience, or the point where a person decides to follow Jesus and make Him Lord. This is where your spirit becomes born again. At this point in scripture the disciples became "born again"; this happens by the Holy Spirit because He is the one that convicts of sin and brings people to a place of relationship with God. We receive Jesus via the Holy Spirit in becoming born again. Our spirit, which was once dark in sin, is now full of the life and light of God!

How do we know that when Jesus said to them, "Receive the Holy Spirit," that He was referring to being born again and not being baptized in the Holy Spirit? Because if the disciples had received the baptism of the Holy Spirit that night, then why would Jesus tell them to wait in Acts, chapter 1 for it? It would have been absurd for Jesus to tell them to wait in Jerusalem for 10 days to receive something they

Necessity for the Baptism of the Spirit

already had. Of course they had not received the baptism of the Holy Spirit at all, which is why he told them to wait in Jerusalem for this.

Take a look at Acts 8, where these three separate experiences are talked about:

> *"But now the people believed Philip's message of Good News concerning the Kingdom of God and the name of Jesus Christ. As a result, many men and women were baptized. Then Simon himself believed and was baptized. He began following Philip wherever he went, and he was amazed by the signs and great miracles Philip performed.*
>
> *"When the apostles in Jerusalem heard that the people of Samaria had accepted God's message, they sent Peter and John there. As soon as they arrived, they prayed for these new believers to receive the Holy Spirit. The Holy Spirit had not yet come upon any of them, for they had only been baptized in the name of the Lord Jesus. Then Peter and John laid their hands upon these believers, and they received the Holy Spirit"* (verses 12-17).

Notice where it says Simon believed. This means he believed the message of Good News that Philip was sharing. This is referring to Simon's salvation. When he believed, he became a Christian. His old life was gone and his new life had begun (as noted above in 2 Corinthians).

But it also says that Simon believed and was baptized. So receiving salvation and being baptized by water are two separate experiences.

Diving deeper into these verses, we discover that the people of Samaria had received salvation and had been water baptized when Philip shared God's message with them. Then we learn that Peter and John went to Samaria and prayed with the people to receive the Holy Spirit since the saved Samarians had only been baptized by water up until that point.

This passage undoubtedly demonstrates that salvation, water baptism and baptism in the Holy Spirit are three separate experiences.

Let's look at another verse in Acts 6:3 *"Therefore, brethren, seek out from among you seven men of good reputation, full of the Holy Spirit and wisdom, whom we may appoint over this business"*. If they had to choose men that were "full" of the Holy Spirit then it meant that there were those that were "not full" of the Holy Spirit, which shows that the baptism of the Holy Spirit is a separate experience from salvation. If every believer or Christian was filled or baptized in the Holy Spirit, why would the apostles mention it as a criteria for deacons? It's obvious that the baptism of the Holy Spirit is something distinct from salvation. It was something that was clearly known.

MY FRIEND, THE HOLY SPIRIT

Receiving the baptism of the Holy Spirit doesn't necessarily make us better Christians. It's like asking a woman who's pregnant to be "better" pregnant. You can't be better pregnant, you are either pregnant or you are not. The same goes for us, you are either a Christian or you are not.

Real life change comes about when we allow the Holy Spirit to convict us of our wrong attitudes and develop our character. Change happens when we allow ourselves to be in partnership with the Holy Spirit.

CHAPTER 4:

Introduction to the Gifts of the Spirit

God commands that we should not be ignorant of spiritual gifts and that we have correct teaching and doctrine regarding the gifts of the Spirit. 1 Corinthians 12:1 reads, *"Now concerning spiritual gifts, brethren, I do not want you to be ignorant"*. Yet we find so many in the Church have little to no understanding of the gifts of the Spirit due to poor teaching or a complete lack of teaching.

"There are different kinds of spiritual gifts, but the same Spirit is the source of them all" (1 Corinthians 12:4).

There are nine gifts of the Spirit; but there are actually three different groups of gifts and ministries mentioned in the Bible as seen below. I believe it's important to understand that spiritual gifts are not to be confused with our talents. Yes, God, too, is the source of our natural talents and abilities and skills to develop. The Bible instructs us on the purpose of these gifts, their functions and what we are to do with them.

- Motivational Gifts (Referred to as the Gifts of the Father): Romans 12:6-8

- Ministry Gifts (Referred to as Gifts of the Son): Ephesians 4:11

- Gifts of the Spirit (Referred to as Gifts of the Spirit): 1 Corinthians 12:8-10

Again we see the Trinity working together and distributing different kinds of gifts in perfect harmony and unity.

In this book we are focusing on the nine gifts Paul teaches us about in 1 Corinthians 12, as these are the gifts Paul primarily centers his teaching around, giving doctrine and proper use. Before we start it is important that we always understand that character is valued far greater than gifts. Matthew 7:21-23: *"Not everyone who says to Me,*

MY FRIEND, THE HOLY SPIRIT

'Lord, Lord,' shall enter the kingdom of heaven, but he who does the will of My Father in heaven. Many will say to Me in that day, 'Lord, Lord, have we not prophesied in Your name, cast out demons in Your name, and done many wonders in Your name?' And then I will declare to them, 'I never knew you; depart from Me, you who practice lawlessness!'"

So ultimately we won't be judged on our gifts but by the fruit of our lives and we should not mistake the Gifts of the Spirit for ministry gifts or offices. *"Beware of false prophets, who come to you in sheep's clothing, but inwardly they are ravenous wolves. You will know them by their fruits. Do men gather grapes from thorn bushes or figs from thistles?"* (Matthew 7:15-16).

God rewards faithfulness, not titles, gifts or ministries. Higher titles do not receive greater rewards, just greater responsibility. *"His lord said to him, 'Well done, good and faithful servant; you were faithful over a few things, I will make you ruler over many things. Enter into the joy of your lord'"* (Matthew 25:21). Notice Jesus said Well done good and faithful "servant", not well done good and faithful preacher, or pastor, evangelist of gifted man or woman of God.

We learn about each gift in 1 Corinthians 12:7-11,

> *"But the manifestation of the Spirit is given to each one for the profit of all: for to one is given the word of wisdom through the Spirit, to another the word of knowledge through the same Spirit, to another faith by the same Spirit, to another gifts of healings by the same Spirit, to another the working of miracles, to another prophecy, to another discerning of spirits, to another different kinds of tongues, to another the interpretation of tongues. But one and the same Spirit works all these things, distributing to each one individually as He wills."*

The nine gifts of the Spirit are:

1. Word of wisdom
2. Word of knowledge
3. Faith
4. Gifts of healing
5. Working of miracles
6. Prophecy
7. Discerning of spirits
8. Different kinds of tongues
9. Interpretation of tongues

Introduction to the Gifts of the Spirit

Each of these nine gifts is significant enough to devote a chapter to each in order to fully explain them, which I will do in the upcoming chapters.

What to do with a drunken sailor?

The first memory I have of the Holy Spirit empowering me with one of His gifts was when I was visiting in Paihia, New Zealand. I was sitting outside a bar trying to tell an intoxicated sailor about Jesus. For some reason, I didn't feel like anything I was saying made a lick of sense to him. I am guessing you are not too surprised over this. Could it have been due to the ample amount of alcohol he'd consumed? However, if you know anything about me, then you know I rarely give up. Even though he kept nodding as if to say, "Yeah, yeah, I've heard it all before," I kept persisting because it just so happened I'd been learning about the gifts of the Holy Spirit in Bible college, so I knew to pray for wisdom on how to reach my new inebriated friend and wait on the Holy Spirit's response. And then I felt it. The Holy Spirit revealed to me through my thoughts that this sailor's wife had left him eighteen months earlier. Great, right? Sure, but how in the world do I share something like that? "Hey, by the way, God just told me that your wife left you eighteen months ago, and He is reaching out to you and loves you"? What if the sailor said, "But I've never been married"? What if I had it all wrong? What would I do then?

Approaching this whole matter with a great lack of faith, I finally worked up the nerve to ask, "So, are you married?" He replied, "I was, but my wife left me." Immediately I was struck with two notions, "I really should have had more faith," and "Okay, God, what do I say now?" This time, listening to the Holy Spirit with a half dram more of faith than before, I explained why I had asked if he was married and that God loved him and had a plan for his life. With my faith increasing more by the second, I said, "God told me your wife left you eighteen months ago. Is that true?" He started weeping and choked out the words, "Yes, she left me exactly eighteen months ago." After we talked a bit longer, he invited Jesus into his heart, and I am forever thankful that God used me to help him.

1 Corinthians 12:31 states, *"But earnestly desire and zealously cultivate the greatest and best gifts and graces (the higher gifts and the choicest graces). And yet I will show you a still more excellent way [one that is better by far and the highest of them all--love]"*. (AMP)

God would not say to "earnestly desire" spiritual gifts and then say, "no you can't have them", although many claim now that the gifts are no longer available. God desires us to desire the gifts because they are for us and they are for today. You cannot be apathetical about the gifts and hope to flow in them. Desiring the gifts means to seek after them, not for you own gain but for the benefit of others, the love for others. We should seek to read, study and learn from others about the gifts, and most importantly seek after the Giver of the gifts.

Gifts are to be used

Gifts are only gifts if they are given to others as instructed in Romans 12:6, *"Having then gifts differing according to the grace that is given to us, let us use them...".* When the gifts actually flow from us to the person that really needs them, like the sailor who needed a "word of knowledge" to show that there was a God and that he loved him deeply. 1 Peter 4:10-11 states, *"As each one has received a gift, minister it to one another, as good stewards of the manifold grace of God. If anyone speaks, let him speak as the oracles of God. If anyone ministers, let him do it as with the ability which God supplies, that in all things God may be glorified through Jesus Christ, to whom belong the glory and the dominion forever and ever. Amen."*

We have so much teaching committed to us from the Bible on these gifts, yet we find so little use of them. God has an expectation and command that we "use them" or "minister it", but why don't we? Why is it that many who have been saved for many years have never "used them" or "ministered it" (the gifts) that we have been freely given? The answer is you cannot minister what you do not have. The sad condition of the church is that a high percentage of Christians have not received what God has freely made available and therefore cannot give it.

Matthew 10:8 states, *"Freely you have received, freely give".*

I would like to say that my encounter with the sailor was the one and only time in which I struggled to trust God, and from that point on, I have been unhindered when the Holy Spirit grants me a gift in order to help someone for God's glory. But that wouldn't be telling the whole truth.

Despite my eagerness to be a good steward of these gifts, I have found myself worrying about what others will think of me when I use them. And even though I know that would not be a time to shrink back and worry about such trivial things, I humbly admit I have. Over the years, I've learned that most of us experience this feeling of insecurity. But it was during one of those moments that I realized something remarkable: We all are fretting over the same thing.

I was worried about other people's thoughts or judgments of me, and they were worrying about what I was thinking about them. It's silly when you think about it. Everyone is walking around concerned about everyone else's opinions. But that silliness is holding us back from

Introduction to the Gifts of the Spirit

doing what we need to do. I believe it's just another effort to distract us from doing the good God has planned for us to do. When we have fear or are controlled by what others think of us we can't receive or release the Holy Spirit.

Some people feel inadequate, they want to move in the power of God and the gifts but feel a sense of "I'm not good enough, or talented enough." But the power of God does not depend on our power, but our powerlessness. *"And He said to me, 'My grace is sufficient for you, for My strength is made perfect in weakness'"* (2 Corinthians 12:9). Weakness does not disqualify us it qualifies us.

My daughters love singing songs in the car; we put on tracks like "the wheels on the bus go round and round". One of the songs goes like this, "shake a leg, shake a leg, move your arms in the air now...". One daughter being 3, knows all the actions to all the songs and has a great time doing them all. My other daughter being 1, doesn't know all the actions; she shakes her hands when the song says to shake a leg, but she still does it anyway, and she has just as much fun.

The power is in the stepping out! Not in the holding back. The power is in the releasing, not in the worry. We are all manufacturers, we either manufacture the power of God or we manufacture, fear, doubt and unbelief. My daughters manufacture happiness; why manufacture? Because it is a choice! It is a choice to be happy, or sad, or critical or live in fear or to step out in the power of God. The anointing is there potentially, but it's not in manifestation constantly. The power of God does not come from you but it is dependent upon you to release. You don't have to be perfect or talented, just obedient. Give it a shot, shake a leg, or an arm!

We all need the baptism of the Holy Spirit to empower us to move beyond the fear of man and under the fear of God. If the apostles who walked, talked and lived with Jesus needed the Baptism of the Holy Spirit before they went out to reach the lost and make disciples, how much more do we need this today?

CHAPTER 5:

Facts About the Gifts

Love for others, the kind of love described in 1 Corinthians 13, must be our motivation in using the gifts. I have seen people use the gifts of the Spirit and power of God for their own selfish desires, for manipulating others, and for getting glory for themselves, and sadly many people have been spiritually abused this way.

Gifts are there to help people and meet their needs, not exalt ministers. Gifts are to profit the body not to destroy or tear down. We don't need to force the gifts; as we spend time each day in the presence of God, gifts will flow. Gifts should never be used to manipulate lives or situations or for monetary gain.

Judas was one of Jesus' disciples and was sent out with the power of God with the other 11 disciples, so we can see that we can be anointed by God and move in power but have the wrong motives. The Holy Spirit did not come or grant us gifts so that we could put on a show to make ourselves look great. He is here to empower us to change lives and make Jesus look great. Even before we focus on developing our gifts, we have to keep the primary focus on benefiting and loving others first and allowing the Holy Spirit to develop our character. The most important result of any manifestation of the gifts is the salvation of lost people.

The Bible says the *"Gifts and calling of God is without repentance"* (Romans 11:29).

When we receive the gifts we don't also receive great character, which explains why we have seen many men of God move in great power and gifts but then find out they have been stealing or cheating. When you receive a gift on your birthday, you will be the same person you were after you got that gift as you were before you got that gift. Getting a TV for your birthday will not change your character.

Facts About the Gifts

Gifts vs. Fruits

We must distinguish between gifts and the fruit of the Holy Spirit because we shall be judged by the fruit of the Spirit in our lives, not the gifts. Galatians 5:22-23 says, *"But the fruit of the Spirit is love, joy, peace, long-suffering, kindness, goodness, faithfulness, gentleness, self-control. Against such there is no law."* If the Holy Spirit is given control of our lives, this is the fruit that He will bear. We must realize that it is the Holy Spirit's work and it is His fruit that is displayed in and through our lives. Notice the verse says "fruit" not "fruits." Really the fruit of the Spirit is a life that is under perfect control by the power of the Holy Spirit.

In contrast, when the Holy Spirit is not in control of our lives, we reap the works of our flesh as written in Galatians 5:19-21, *"Now the works of the flesh are evident, which are: adultery, fornication, uncleanness, lewdness, idolatry, sorcery, hatred, contentions, jealousies, outbursts of wrath, selfish ambitions, dissensions, heresies, envy, murders, drunkenness, revelries, and the like; of which I tell you beforehand, just as I also told you in time past, that those who practice such things will not inherit the kingdom of God."*

If we live in the flesh this is the kind of life we will live; it is the life that is natural to us. Romans 8:5-6 says, *"For those who live according to the flesh set their minds on the things of the flesh, but those who live according to the Spirit, the things of the Spirit. For to be carnally minded is death, but to be spiritually minded is life and peace."*

The flesh cannot bear the fruit of the Spirit; this means that you cannot attain them by your own efforts. You must allow the Holy Spirit to take control of your life by submitting your whole heart under his direction. Give regard to Galatians 5:16-17, *"I say then: Walk in the Spirit, and you shall not fulfill the lust of the flesh. For the flesh lusts against the Spirit, and the Spirit against the flesh; and these are contrary to one another, so that you do not do the things that you wish."*

Constantly Feeding yourself with a diet of movies, magazines, books or TV shows that engage in and promote things of a fleshly nature will only lead to a lifestyle of walking in the flesh. This is why so many people have become dull or desensitized to the voice of God; it is according to what you "set" your mind upon that you establish in your life. What you dwell on, you dwell in.

Just like the fruit of the Spirit, the gifts of the Holy Spirit don't come from you either, they come from God. You are just the vessel God uses. Therefore gifts are not a sign of spiritual maturity. Brother John may prophesy often but he may be someone who is also gossiping and stirring up trouble dissension and division.

Ignorance is one of the most powerful weapons the enemy uses to keep the Children of God in bondage. Ignorance disempowers you. We should know what we believe and why we believe it, and we should know what the word of God says about the gifts that he has freely given to us. On the contrary, knowledge is power. The Bible says, *"My people are destroyed due to lack of knowledge"* (Hosea 4:6).

I believe the better we understand scripture in regards to the gifts, the easier we'll flow in them. Listed below are ten, although often overlooked, basic facts about the gifts of the Spirit.

1. God distributes the gifts at His will as we need them

"But one and the same Spirit works all these things, distributing to each one individually as He wills" (1 Corinthians 12:11).

When does God give us these gifts? When we need them. When we need a word of knowledge that's what we will get. When we need the gift of prophecy that is when we will get it. That's why we can speak in tongues whenever we need to just as the Bible teaches we should pray "without ceasing," or we should be "praying always" (Ephesians 6:18). One of the "various kinds of tongues" is your personal prayer language, generally referred to as just "tongues."

2. Four of the gifts are plural

Gifts of healings, workings of miracles, discerning of spirits and different kinds of tongues.

This means there are different genres of gifts within these four gifts. For example, because there are many sicknesses and diseases, I believe there are gifts of healings for every kind of sickness out there. Which is why it is called "gifts of healings" not "the gift of healing."

One vitally important thing to point out is that we administer "gifts of healings" to the sick. I have heard people in the past say, "I have the gift of healing," which I cannot see any biblical foundation for. Now it's true some people have a ministry in healing, but we will cover the differences between ministry gifts and spiritual gifts in the next chapter.

It isn't called "the word of wisdom" but "word of wisdom." There is no word "the" in the Greek language. Some people will say, "Oh, my gift is the word of wisdom," and then attempt to tell you how to run your life. The spiritual gift word of wisdom is a message for a specific moment given by God only when it's needed or asked for. It does not necessarily mean you have wisdom in everyday real life.

I have seen many "spiritual people" move incredibly in the gifts but then lack wisdom in their own lives. This is because the gifts of the Spirit are

Facts About the Gifts

exactly that, gifts. They don't stay with you always. They are there when you need them, and, most times the gift is something to share for someone else.

3. The nine gifts can be separated into three categories

While these categories aren't necessarily biblical, I think categorizing them has been generally accepted by church leaders across the globe and is helpful in understanding the way the gifts function.
   1. Revelation: word of knowledge, word of wisdom and discerning of spirits
   2. Power Gifts: faith, gifts of healings, workings of miracles
   3. Inspiration: prophecy, different kinds of tongues, interpretation of tongues

Rodney Howard Browne puts it this way, which I really like: "three of them say something, three of them do something, three of them reveal something."

4. The Greek word for gift(s) is Charisma

This is derived from the Greek word charis (grace). Now we know grace is free and cannot be earned. Charisma is grace made effective, grace made available in a particular way. We can make God's grace available to mankind through these gifts. For instance when we release the gift of healing to a person who is sick, we are effectively releasing God's grace to that person. Even though we do not deserve God's grace, He still died for us and bore our sin and our sickness so we don't have to be in sin or sickness.

Isaiah chapter 53 states that *"Surely He has borne our griefs and carried our sorrows; Yet we esteemed Him stricken, Smitten by God, and afflicted. But He was wounded for our transgressions, He was bruised for our iniquities; the chastisement for our peace was upon Him, And by His stripes we are healed"* (Isaiah 53:4-5).

5. You don't have to be a mature Christian to receive the Baptism of the Holy Spirit or to operate in the gifts

Some people believe you must be a Christian for a few years or have gone to Bible college or have some position in the Church to function in the gifts. This is not so. Paul stated of the Corinthian Church that they came behind in no gift (1 Corinthians 1:7). And then later in the letter, he called them spiritual babes (1 Corinthians 3:1). You can be newly born again and move in the gifts and the power of God.

6. You must be a connected Christian

We must find our place in the body of Christ. A ministry that is not connected to the house of God is not a ministry. We must make ourselves accountable to the house of God.

> *"For as we have many members in one body, but all the members do not have the same function, so we, being many, are one body in Christ, and individually members of one another. Having then gifts differing according to the grace that is given to us, let us use them: if prophecy, let us prophesy in proportion to our faith; or ministry, let us use it in our ministering; he who teaches, in teaching; he who exhorts, in exhortation; he who gives, with liberality; he who leads, with diligence; he who shows mercy, with cheerfulness"* (Romans 12:4-8).

I have heard people say, "Oh, Pastor, I am part of the body. I just haven't found a church that I like." But the body is the Church. So then how is someone a part of the body if they are not a part of the Church? It's like a foot that is not part of a body saying, I'm part of the body, really I am, but I haven't found a body I like. No, then you are not part of the body, you are a foot disconnected all by yourself and a foot without a body won't last very long!

This is another common comment I hear, "I watch Christian preaching on TV at home every Sunday." The Church is the people. Being a part of the church is not a lone ranger at home watching Christian Ministry on TV.

Being a Christian is about being connected to a body. The body of Christ, a body of believers. This is not just a Sunday thing. The Church should be Monday to Saturday as well. The thumb just doesn't "attend" your hand on Sundays, it is a member of your hand and your hand a member of the body. Pastor Phil Pringle uses a great analogy of a watch. A watch assembled works. A watch unassembled does not work. The Bible says do not forsake the assembling of the saints. Your life works as it was created to work when you are "assembled" with the saints.

Hebrews 10:25 says, *"...not forsaking the assembling of ourselves together, as is the manner of some, but exhorting one another, and so much the more as you see the Day approaching."*

I cannot stress enough the importance of being connected, getting involved in the house of God, and giving God your time, talent and treasure.

Facts About the Gifts

7. The gifts always benefit people

"But the manifestation of the Spirit is given to each one for the profit of all..." (1 Corinthians 12:7). When I was attending Bible college, a young man there was asked to leave. This happened because he believed that he had a gift from God to give "critical prophesies". This is not even scriptural.

At a citywide meeting, I saw this same man give an usher a piece of paper and say, "Please give this to the man of God preaching tonight." I knew this would most likely be a critical word for the minister. I went to the usher and informed him about this man. I was expecting this usher to have an extremely relieved look on his face. I mean, we, together, were going to warn the minister about a person who mistakenly was operating under the wrong influence. What I wasn't expecting was for the usher to turn to me and say, "He is my best friend and he has a powerful ministry in the prophetic." Kicking myself for not asking the usher if he knew the guy first, I replied, "But it is negative and critical."He proceeded to tell me that his friend had been given a gift by God to point out faults in others. Now I didn't bite my tongue, only because what I said was true, "Brother, you don't need a gift for that. People have been doing that for centuries!"

The gifts are meant to edify one another, help each other in our Christian walk, not tear each other apart and point out every wrong thing.

Matthew 7:3-5 says, *"And why do you look at the speck in your brother's eye, but do not consider the plank in your own eye? Or how can you say to your brother, 'Let me remove the speck from your eye'; and look, a plank is in your own eye? Hypocrite! First remove the plank from your own eye, and then you will see clearly to remove the speck from your brother's eye."*

8. Love and spiritual gifts go hand in hand

Some people think that if they have love they don't need spiritual gifts. 1 Corinthians 14:1 says, *"Pursue love and desire spiritual gifts."* It doesn't say just pursue love and you don't need spiritual gifts. One of the ways we know that we love is that we desire and are exercising spiritual gifts. By doing these together the fruit of the Spirit will be evident in our lives. Biblical love is active. It does not sit around using nice phrases. It does something.

"*For God so loved the world He gave His only begotten son*" (John 3:16). God so loved the world that He did something about it. He didn't just sit there and say it. He showed it to us. He gave us a practical demonstration of what love is!

9. Gifts are for glorifying God

"As each one has received a gift, minister it to one another, as good stewards of the manifold grace of God. If anyone speaks, let him speak as the oracles of God. If anyone ministers, let him do it as with the ability which God supplies, that in all things God may be glorified through Jesus Christ, to whom belong the glory and the dominion forever and ever. Amen" (1 Peter 4:10-11).

The gifts of the Spirit are not there to bring glory to ourselves, but to God alone. They are His gifts that flow through our lives. As my old Bible college lecturer Trevor Yaxley always said, "We are just drain pipes for Jesus."

CHAPTER 6:

Ministry Gifts vs. Spiritual Gifts

Understanding the difference between ministry and spiritual gifts is a pivotal factor in functioning in the gifts of the Spirit. In fact many of the misunderstandings about the gifts of the Spirit stem from people confusing ministry gifts with spiritual gifts (gifts of the Spirit). For instance the ministry of a prophet is vastly different than that of the gift of prophecy. The ministry of healing is again different to that of the spiritual gift, gifts of healings. We will go into great detail in this chapter regarding how ministry gifts and spiritual gifts differ. Of course ministry gifts are just as "spiritual" as spiritual gifts, so when referring to spiritual gifts we are talking about the nine gifts of the Spirit.

We gain a better comprehension of these differences by looking at 1 Corinthians 12:4-11, *"There are diversities of gifts, but the same Spirit. There are differences of ministries, but the same Lord. And there are diversities of activities, but it is the same God who works all in all."*

This scripture shows us the three areas:

1. Diversities of gifts
2. Differences of ministries
3. Diversities of activities

Diversities of gifts refers to the nine different spiritual gifts that we've been talking about: word of wisdom, word of knowledge, faith, gifts of healing, working of miracles, prophecy, discerning of spirits, different kinds of tongues, and interpretation of tongues.

The different ministries are found in Ephesians 4:8-12, *"Now this, 'He ascended'—what does it mean but that He also first descended into the lower parts of the earth? He who descended is also the One who ascended far above all the heavens, that He might fill all things. And He*

MY FRIEND, THE HOLY SPIRIT

Himself gave some to be apostles, some prophets, some evangelists, and some pastors and teachers, for the equipping of the saints for the work of ministry, for the edifying of the body of Christ." From this scripture we learn the ministries include apostles, prophets, pastors, teachers and evangelists.

While still talking about the different ministries, we find an expanded list of the ministries in 1 Corinthians 12:28, *"And God has appointed these in the church: first apostles, second prophets, third teachers, after that miracles, then gifts of healings, helps, administrations, varieties of tongues."* Notice that gifts of healings, prophecy, miracles and varieties of tongues, four of the nine gifts of the Spirit, are also listed as ministries. I'll explain what this means for us later in this chapter when I cover the differences of ministry and spiritual gifts. But first, we need to understand the third area, diversities of activities, which incorporates any work of God and the varying ways people function in their ministry or gifts. I have seen many people who move in the teaching or healing ministry, and no two are alike. How each one ministers vastly differs, which is how it should be. God does not move the same way all the time. We need all kinds of people to reach all kinds of people.

For example, I have seen some ministers anoint people with oil every time they pray, and others don't. I've seen others lay hands on people in prayer, and others don't lay hands on people at all when they pray. I've seen those that are loud and those that move more softly, which way is right? The right way is being who God has called you to be. You are unique and how you minister to people may not be the way that brother so and so does it. But God wants to use you, not you trying to be brother so and so!

God gives us these many different gifts, but what exactly is the difference between ministry gifts and spiritual gifts? How do you know which is which? It really boils down to three main differences.

1. Ministry gift is a gift Jesus gives to the Church.

A ministry gift is a person and it is a life work; whereas, spiritual gifts are a gift that is given to the person who needs it. Not making sense yet? Let me give an example, if a person needs a prophecy, then the gift of prophecy may flow through one of us to benefit the person who needs it. Same with spiritual gifts, the person has the gift flow through them most often for another person. But with ministry gifts, the gift IS the person.

2. Ministry gift is a lifework.

With a ministry gift your whole life is centered on being a pastor or an apostle. But spiritual gifts are brief, dramatic. A prophecy may last only minutes and then it is finished whereas the ministry of a prophet is a lifetime work.

3. Ministry gift cannot be divorced from one's character.

1 Corinthians 14:31 says, *"We may all prophesy."* But it doesn't say we all will be prophets.

It's vitally important to understand that prophesying does not give us the ministry of a prophet or the character that is needed for this ministry gift. In essence as your ministry gift develops and grows so should you character, because they are intrinsically connected. Otherwise your gift will take you places where your character cannot sustain.

However this is not the same with spiritual gifts. Imagine that it's Christmas time and you unwrap a brand new Sony Bravia TV with 3D viewing. It even comes with several pairs of 3D glasses. This gift is magnificent. It's one of the first-generation 3D-compatible TVs, plus it's expensive. Not everyone is going to get to unwrap as cool a gift as you did. But really no matter what the gift is, no matter how expensive, how rare it is, the very person you were before you got that gift will still be the same person you will be after you unwrap the gift. The gift does not make you a different person, even if you are watching everything in 3D.

If we think exercising a spiritual gift makes us spiritual, we should think of Balaam's donkey (see Numbers 22:22). In other words, if you were a donkey before you prophesied, guess what you will be afterward?

Matthew 7:21, a frightening passage of scripture, states, *"Not everyone who says to Me, 'Lord, Lord,' shall enter the kingdom of heaven, but he who does the will of My Father in heaven. Many will say to Me in that day, 'Lord, Lord, have we not prophesied in Your name, cast out demons in Your name, and done many wonders in Your name?' And then I will declare to them, 'I never knew you; depart from Me, you who practice lawlessness!'"*

This passage is talking about people who moved in spiritual gifts. They prophesied, they did wonders, but their personal lives were a mess. And eventually they became disconnected from God. Their relationship just became a means to use God for his "power." We must be careful that in our pursuit for spiritual gifts that we always pursue the giver of the gifts, God, first and foremost.

CHAPTER 7:

Functions of the Gifts of the Spirit

Having a greater understanding of the function of the spiritual gifts will help you function in them with greater clarity and power.

1. Gifts work together.

A lot of time there is more than one gift operating at the same time. Sometimes it is difficult to determine exactly which gift is in manifestation because they often overlap and blend together. For instance, many times the word of knowledge is used in partnership with gifts of healings. Also workings of miracles and gifts of faith are closely related.

A good example of this is raising the dead: there are three gifts working together here; the gift of faith, the working of miracles and gifts of healings; why gifts of healings also? Because once back to life, the person needs to be healed of what they died from. Note that Jesus didn't pray for every dead person to be raised back to life (example: John the Baptist).

It's wise to avoid heavy emphasis on definitions, though, because there is no point arguing about the same thing that we really are just defining or interpreting differently.

We should not try to figure out or try to classify what gifts we are moving in. If someone needs to be healed, then it doesn't matter what gift is in operation. Whether it is gift of faith, miracles, or gifts of healings, the main thing is that the person receives that gift and is healed.

2. It takes faith to use the gifts.

Without faith it is impossible to please God. You must have boldness, and you have to step out. You cannot wait until it is convenient, as quite often the moment/opportunity will have passed.

I remember a time when I was walking to the cricket pitch where I prayed and I saw a guy packing gear into the back of his car. Immediately, I felt the Holy Spirit tell me that this guy had been searching for God and that I should speak to him. Well I only had a few moments to obey, I was so fearful and wrestling in my mind and heart about it. Just as I passed him I thought, "Maybe it isn't God." (Sure, because both the Devil and my flesh wanted me to witness to this guy!) With each step that took me farther away from the guy, the more convicted I felt to speak to him, but I just kept walking.

By the time, I got around the corner to my place of prayer on the field I couldn't shake my feeling of guilt for disobeying. Here I was in my place of prayer, praying prayers like, "God use me," and here God was trying to answer those prayers! I couldn't pray without the overwhelming feeling of regret for not stopping to share with this man, so I promised God if he was still there packing gear, I would talk to him. But I felt the Holy Spirit say, "He is gone. The moment has passed." Still, I ran back anyway, but he was gone.

The next time I felt that leading to share with someone was a short time after. There I was again out on the field praying. The sun was setting, and it was getting dark and a little hard to see. Somehow I noticed a man walking across the park. I felt in my heart to share with him, but I didn't know what to say. He wasn't coming my way and was probably only in earshot of me. So I called out, "Hey you." He stopped in his tracks. "Yes," I said even louder," you." He didn't move. I blurted out, "God loves you and wants to meet with you." Still no movement. Then all of a sudden, he ran. He ran fast. He ran hard, and he kept running. I could still see him running way into the distance until he was just a small dark figure racing into the sunset.

I don't know what happened with that guy, whether God touched or convicted him that night. I am sure He did as God always blesses obedience. I know that if I wasn't saved and someone called that out to me in the middle of a field, I would remember it, and it would be on my mind as I went to sleep that night. So I always go by this saying, "you never know unless you have a go."

3. Their primary purpose is always to glorify God.

"As each one has received a gift, minister it to one another, as good stewards of the manifold grace of God. If anyone speaks, let him speak as the oracles of God. If anyone ministers, let him do it as

with the ability which God supplies, that in all things God may be glorified through Jesus Christ, to whom belong the glory and the dominion forever and ever. Amen"* (1 Peter 4:10-11).

4. The Gifts are to bring edification and profit for all.

"How is it then, brethren? Whenever you come together, each of you has a psalm, has a teaching, has a tongue, has a revelation, has an interpretation. Let all things be done for edification" (1 Corinthians 14:26).

"But the manifestation of the Spirit is given to each one for the profit of all" (1 Corinthians 12:7).

5. Love and gifts coincide.

As we learned earlier they are "grace" gifts. It is very hard to administer grace for those you don't love. The best book on love is the Bible. Two of my favorite passages on love are 1 Corinthians 13:1, *"Though I speak with the tongues of men and of angels, but have not love, I have become sounding brass or a clanging cymbal"* and also 1 Corinthians 14:1, *"Pursue love, and desire spiritual gifts."*

So although faith is a major part of operating in gifts, we must also have love; you can pray in faith but without love eventually people will just see us as a "noisy cymbal or gong". The more you love people the more evident the gifts flowing in your life will be because people will be more inclined and open to receive the gifts from someone they know deep down really loves them and cares for them.

6. Gifts are for today.

Is the Baptism of the Holy Spirit for today? Absolutely! Let's cover this by using the law of usage and the law of context.

The law of usage

When you find a word or phrase in any passage of scripture, you wish to know what it means, look up other passages of scriptures where the word is also used, and notice especially how the writer uses it in these other passages.

The law of context

When you study a passage you should not take it out of connection but

Functions of the Gifts of the Spirit

should look at what goes before it and what comes after it. On its own it could mean various things.

So let's give an example of applying these two laws.

"Then Peter said to them, "Repent, and let every one of you be baptized in the name of Jesus Christ for the remission of sins; and you shall receive the gift of the Holy Spirit. For the promise is to you and to your children, and to all who are afar off, as many as the Lord our God will call" (Acts 2:38-39).

Law of usage

If we were trying to discover what the word promise means in Acts 2:39, we would go back to Acts 1:4-5 when the word is first introduced. *"And being assembled together with them, He commanded them not to depart from Jerusalem, but to wait for the Promise of the Father, "which," He said, "you have heard from Me; for John truly baptized with water, but you shall be baptized with the Holy Spirit not many days from now."*

Let's look at another verse. Acts 2:33: *"Therefore being exalted to the right hand of God, and having received from the Father the promise of the Holy Spirit, He poured out this which you now see and hear."*

So it is evident here that the "promise" is the baptism of the Holy Spirit. If this expression means the baptism of the Holy Spirit, following the same law of interpretation in Acts 1:4-5 and Acts 2:33, can it possibly mean something different six verses further down in Acts 2:39? Of course not.

Therefore, the law of usage therefore determines that the promise of Acts 2:39 is the promise of the baptism of the Holy Spirit.

Law of context

In verse 38, we see that Peter is clearly talking about the baptism of the Holy Spirit, so this is the context in which he then goes on to talk about the promise. The promise in the correct context of this verse is the baptism of the Holy Spirit. So let's put this altogether with the understanding that Peter is talking about the promise of the Holy Spirit.

"Then Peter said to them, 'Repent, and let every one of you be baptized in the name of Jesus Christ for the remission of sins; and you shall receive the gift of the Holy Spirit. For the promise is to you and to your children, and to all who are afar off, as many as the Lord our God will call'" (Acts 2:38-39).

MY FRIEND, THE HOLY SPIRIT

Peter says:

1. "Every one" (this means all who were there.)

2. "Children" (this means that the promise of the Holy Spirit is to be passed through the generations, it was not just for those that were present.)

3. "All who are afar off" (this means the whole world; Jewish rabbis actually used that expression in speaking about foreigners/heathens.)

4. "As many as" (this relates to everyone regardless of sex, age, race, position or rank, and everyone until the end of time, when Jesus returns.)

So the "promise", the baptism of the Holy Spirit IS for today, it is for right here and right now.

Now that we understand that the "promise" is the baptism of the Holy Spirit we can clearly see the three simple steps that Peter gives as he is preaching the gospel. First, repent, second, be water baptized and third, receive the gift of the Holy Spirit.

In Old Testament times God would grant the anointing of the Holy Spirit to specially chosen vessels only; kings, priests, prophets and deliverers of Israel. Only a few people were anointed with the power of God so ordinary people could not even dream of such grace. The Old Testament saints would surely be astonished at the "promise" that we have been given and yet be even more astonished at those who acknowledge but then ignore this very same "promise".

Joel 2:28-29: *" And it shall come to pass afterward*
That I will pour out My Spirit on all flesh;
Your sons and your daughters shall prophesy,
Your old men shall dream dreams,
Your young men shall see visions.
And also on My menservants and on My maidservants
I will pour out My Spirit in those days."

God promises here to even give His spirit to humble servants and handmaids. These were prisoners taken from a foreign country and bought with money to be slaves. People who were ill-treated and despised and were the lowest position of Jewish society. This is an incredible statement, those people living back in the days of Joel must have truly wondered about this prophecy!

Then hundreds of years later Peter, after receiving baptism of Holy Spirit, claimed that what was spoken by prophet Joel was being fulfilled in front of their eyes.

Functions of the Gifts of the Spirit

Acts 2:14-18: *"But Peter, standing up with the eleven, raised his voice and said to them, 'Men of Judea and all who dwell in Jerusalem, let this be known to you, and heed my words. For these are not drunk, as you suppose, since it is only the third hour of the day. But this is what was spoken by the prophet Joel: And it shall come to pass in the last days, says God,*

> *That I will pour out of My Spirit on all flesh;*
> *Your sons and your daughters shall prophesy,*
> *Your young men shall see visions,*
> *Your old men shall dream dreams.*
> *And on My menservants and on My maidservants*
> *I will pour out My Spirit in those days;*
> *And they shall prophesy.*

When did the last days start?

We can see from above from scripture that the last days started when Jesus left (ascended to heaven) and the Holy Spirit came on the day of Pentecost. Certainly we are in the last days even now. Nothing comes after "last", if you are in a race and you are in last place then that is it, there is nothing else behind you. Peter is telling those present that what is happening right now is what was prophesied by the Prophet Joel, and what did Joel say? "And it shall come to pass in the last days..." this means we are STILL in the last days and we will still be in the last days until Jesus returns meaning the baptism of the Holy Spirit and the gifts of the Holy Spirit will still be poured out until Jesus comes back. For people to say God cannot do what he did 2000 years ago, shows me they do not know the God I know. He is the same yesterday, today and forever. My God can do anything today that he did back then. Why would he not? I mean, we need the power of God more today, so why would he withhold it now? The Baptism of the Holy Spirit is for you, for your children, for all who are afar off (everyone), for even as many as the Lord our God shall call unto them. The Baptism of the Holy Spirit and his gifts are for EVERY child of God in EVERY coming age.

7. We can operate in all gifts, but it is as He wills.

In 1 Corinthians 12:7 and 11, we learned that the same Spirit works the gifts and distributes them as He wills. God knows your capacity. He knows how you will use the gifts. Therefore He gives them as He wills.

The Holy Spirit owns the gifts, and is the giver of the gifts as we need them. Some people believe that they just get some of the gifts or one gift when they are baptized in the Holy Spirit and that is all they have for the rest of their lives. Meaning if they didn't get the gift of tongues, they will never be able to speak in tongues. The truth is you didn't get any of the gifts, the gift is actually the Holy Spirit and He distributes the gifts to us as we need them. He owns them, not us. Paul says in 1 Corinthians 14:1 that we should "pursue love", and "desire spiritual gifts" (plural) and "especially that we may prophesy". Why would God say in His word, "desire spiritual gifts," but then say, oh but you can't speak in tongues like some teach. God would not encourage you by saying "especially that we may prophecy" if it wasn't available to everybody. God never says in His word that you cannot function in all of the nine gifts, this is man's doctrine, not God's. Whenever God refers to the gifts of the Spirit it is plural and inclusive of all of the gifts, so all of the gifts are for you today. Whenever you need them is when you will receive them, as the Holy Spirit gives them freely.

8. Watch out for deception.

"Now the Spirit expressly says that in latter times some will depart from the faith, giving heed to deceiving spirits and doctrines of demons, speaking lies in hypocrisy, having their own conscience seared with a hot iron," (1 Timothy 4:1).

"But know this, that in the last days perilous times will come: For men will be lovers of themselves, lovers of money, boasters, proud, blasphemers, disobedient to parents, unthankful, unholy, unloving, unforgiving, slanderers, without self-control, brutal, despisers of good, traitors, headstrong, haughty, lovers of pleasure rather than lovers of God, having a form of godliness but denying its power. And from such people turn away!" (2 Timothy 3:1-5).

9. The Gospel should be preached with signs following.

> *"And He said to them, 'Go into all the world and preach the gospel to every creature… And these signs will follow those who believe: In My name they will cast out demons; they will speak with new tongues; they will take up serpents; and if they drink anything deadly, it will by no means hurt them; they will lay hands on the sick, and they will recover.' So then, after the Lord had spoken to them, He was received up into heaven, and sat down at the right hand of God. And they went out and preached everywhere, the Lord working with them and confirming the word through the accompanying signs. Amen"* (Mark 16:15, 17-20).

He wants to use you in the gifts. God needs all kinds of people to appeal to all kinds of people.

CHAPTER 8:

Word of Wisdom

Word of wisdom defined: This is an impression on our mind or a vision or voice of the Holy Spirit through a thought about HOW to deal with situations, both present and future. It is a tiny portion of God's total wisdom directly and supernaturally imparted by the Holy Spirit.

The word of wisdom is not the same as the everyday wisdom that God provides for us, like the kind written about in James 1:5, *"If any of you lacks wisdom, let him ask of God, who gives to all liberally and without reproach, and it will be given to him."*

So we can possess three kinds of wisdom, the first comes naturally, it comes through learning, from others, or from books or other sources of learning, so it relates to something we can be taught. But the highest wisdom comes directly from God; this is wisdom we can move in that is beyond natural or "learned" wisdom and we can operate in this constantly, but the "word of wisdom" is specific wisdom for a specific moment and in most times is used in conjunction with one or more of the other gifts. The word of wisdom enables us to know how to apply answers to any situation.

How do you start?

Humble your heart before the Lord and humbly ask the Holy Spirit for wisdom and guidance. Its only when we have entirely put away our own righteousness that we get the righteousness of God, only when we have entirely put away our own wisdom that we get the wisdom of God, emptying must proceed the filling, the self must be poured out so God can be poured in.

"Let no one deceive himself. If anyone among you seems to be wise in this age, let him become a fool that he may become wise" (1 Corinthians 3:18).

MY FRIEND, THE HOLY SPIRIT

There are two very powerful examples of the spiritual gift word of wisdom from the Bible in both the Old and New Testaments. The first one is the King Solomon Example, found in 1 Kings 3:16-28:

> *"Now two women who were harlots came to the king, and stood before him. And one woman said, 'O my lord, this woman and I dwell in the same house; and I gave birth while she was in the house. Then it happened, the third day after I had given birth, that this woman also gave birth. And we were together; no one was with us in the house, except the two of us in the house. And this woman's son died in the night, because she lay on him. So she arose in the middle of the night and took my son from my side, while your maidservant slept, and laid him in her bosom, and laid her dead child in my bosom. And when I rose in the morning to nurse my son, there he was, dead. But when I had examined him in the morning, indeed, he was not my son whom I had borne.' Then the other woman said, 'No! But the living one is my son, and the dead one is your son.' And the first woman said, 'No! But the dead one is your son, and the living one is my son.' Thus they spoke before the king. Then the king said, 'Bring me a sword.' So they brought a sword before the king. And the king said, 'Divide the living child in two, and give half to one, and half to the other.' Then the woman whose son was living spoke to the king, for she yearned with compassion for her son; and she said, 'O my lord, give her the living child, and by no means kill him!' But the other said, 'Let him be neither mine nor yours, but divide him.' So the king answered and said, 'Give the first woman the living child, and by no means kill him; she is his mother.'"*

In this example, Solomon faced a real dilemma, with no DNA testing available in those days, he had to rely on a word of wisdom to adjudicate between the two women. This word of wisdom revealed the real mother because only the real mother would rather see her son given away than die.

The second example seems so simple but yet so brilliant. It's like the scribes and Pharisees thought they had Jesus trapped. They thought for sure Jesus would not be able to wriggle his way out of that one. There has been so much conjecture to what Jesus wrote on the ground. Some say it was the details and names of certain sinners in the crowd. Some say he was just writing random things and buying time and listening to the voice of the Holy Spirit. Whatever he was writing you can bet that He was getting direction from heaven, and His answer was perfect, perfect in wisdom and in grace.

> John 8:1-7: *"But Jesus went to the Mount of Olives. Now early in the morning He came again into the temple, and all the people came to Him; and He sat down and taught them. Then the scribes and Pharisees brought to Him a woman caught in adultery. And when they had set her in the midst, they said to Him, 'Teacher, this woman was caught in adultery, in the very act. Now Moses, in the law, commanded us that such should be stoned. But what do You say?' This they said, testing Him, that they might have something of which to accuse Him. But Jesus stooped down and wrote on the ground with His finger, as though He did not hear. So when they continued asking Him, He raised Himself up and said to them, 'He who is without sin among you, let him throw a stone at her first.' And again He stooped down and wrote on the ground. Then those who heard it, being convicted by their conscience, went out one by one, beginning with the oldest even to the last. And Jesus was left alone, and the woman standing in the midst. When Jesus had raised Himself up and saw no one but the woman, He said to her, 'Woman, where are those accusers of yours? Has no one condemned you?' She said, 'No one, Lord.' And Jesus said to her, 'Neither do I condemn you; go and sin no more.'"*

Had Jesus said not to stone her, he would have been going against the law of Moses, had Jesus said to stone her, they would have said that he condoned murder and wasn't full of mercy and grace. Sometimes in life we are faced with crucial decisions, maybe not life or death scenarios like the one above, but maybe so. Whatever the decision we have to make, the word of wisdom will help us on what to say and when to say it, what to do and how and when to do it.

Works with other Gifts

Quite often the word of wisdom is crucial in using the other gifts. For example, I may have a word of knowledge about someone or a prophecy but how do I use it? Do I tell them directly? Do I ask questions? If God gives you a word for someone how is the best way to share that word, and when? This is where the word of wisdom comes in. A great example of this was a story someone told me. At our Church we were running a Gifts of the Spirit class, after each lesson we would break everyone off into groups of around 8 to practice the gifts in a small group ministry setting.

This one lady had a word of knowledge that a certain girl had a rash on her body and needed healing. To come outright and say this to the girl in front of the whole class may have embarrassed her, so she shared that she felt someone in the group had a rash and that she would pray a general prayer. Being a group of all girls the particular girl felt comfortable enough to open up and say that she was the one, and she revealed the rash that was hidden under an item of clothing that was not in an embarrassing area, invisible to people, but visible to God.

The way some people would have done it is, "Well, you, yeah lady, you have a rash. God wants to heal it. Let us pray for this rash," or perhaps a young man could be struggling with lust. "Hey, young guy over there, let's get rid of that spirit of lust and pornography off your life. Yeah, you, the one that's been watching nudie films again, stand up. Let's all reach hands out and pray for that spirit of perversion." That is an example of how not to handle it, and quite honestly you will very quickly grieve the Holy Spirit and will find the gifts stop flowing in your life.

Possible ways the Holy Spirit could lead you to deal with this scenario is do a general altar call including those who struggle with lustful spirits, as well as things like discouragement or fear, or perhaps speak to the young man privately afterwards and pray for him or book an appointment to see him and discuss and pray in a non-confrontational environment where there isn't a crowd. You may be thinking that is just common sense. However I have found that common sense is actually not that common and why rely on the flesh when we can tap into the heavenly resources and get a word of wisdom from heaven for any situation at any time.

The word of wisdom can also be powerful in helping make business decisions or how to reach out to lost loved ones and on how to counsel effectively. And obviously, the word of wisdom can be crucial to churches and church leaders. Remember though, just because you get a word of wisdom for a specific circumstance, this does not suddenly make you "wise". The beginning of wisdom is the fear of the Lord.

I've seen people who move in the gifts of the Spirit, even in the word of wisdom, but then throw thousands of dollars into an unstable business that tanks or lose their house due to laziness. Their desire for the "quick buck" or "living the dream" blinds them from the basics of hard work, good counsel, and being grounded in the Word. It's one thing to have a word of wisdom or word of knowledge for someone else, but it's entirely different to have wisdom in one's own life. James states that if anyone asks for wisdom, it will be given liberally. This wisdom is not the Spirit's gift of wisdom, but godly wisdom, wisdom for everyday living.

CHAPTER 9:

Word of Knowledge

Word of knowledge defined: This is an impression, a thought, the audible voice of the Holy Spirit, or even a vision about a situation that you had no previous knowledge of.

Word of knowledge

- deals with that which already exists that you do not know about.
- deals with past and present.
- is the impartation of a fact.
- is many times used to bring faith into operation for healing.

Through the word of knowledge we receive information we could have not gotten any other way than from the Holy Spirit. The word of knowledge is to be used with love, it is not there to expose sin. The Bible says that *"love covers all sins"* (Proverbs 10:12), not uncovers sin. Sure there may be a time that God reveals something to you and in the spirit of love you share this with the specific person.

In the Old Testament in 2 Kings 6:8-12 a nation is saved by the gift of word of knowledge.

A great New Testament example of the word of knowledge in action was when Jesus used it in John 1:48-49: *"Jesus saw Nathanael coming toward Him, and said of him, 'Behold, an Israelite indeed, in whom is no deceit!' Nathanael said to Him, 'How do You know me?' Jesus answered and said to him, 'Before Philip called you, when you were under the fig tree, I saw you.' Nathanael answered and said to Him, 'Rabbi, You are the Son of God! You are the King of Israel!'"* In this text, Jesus had a word of knowledge about Nathanael when he told Nathanael that he saw him under the fig tree before Philip called him.

MY FRIEND, THE HOLY SPIRIT

In this case, he had a vision of Nathanael, though the gift of word of knowledge is not always a vision.

Suicide

One of the most powerful words of knowledge the Holy Spirit has ever given me came one night when I was out street-witnessing with a fellow leader from church. A young girl who appeared to be intoxicated staggered towards us as we walked down the street. In truth I kind of felt this could be a divine appointment, so I didn't make any real effort to get out of the way. When her head landed in my chest, she stumbled back, and I started a conversation with her and her friend.

As I was talking to her about Jesus Christ, she started responding with some of the usual objections like, "I grew up in a Christian family "and "I go to a Christian school," which are both great things but neither makes you a Christian in as much as going to McDonalds doesn't make you a hamburger! Silently I prayed, "Lord give me something that will touch this girl's life." Then I got the word "family," so I shared with her that I felt God knew about the stuff going on in her family life and He loved her and He told me this because she was important to Him. Even though, the word I'd felt "family" was so general and could have been relevant to half the population, that was all I had been given, so that is what I shared. It must have hit home because she started to tear up. Now feeling stronger with faith, I pressed God for more. I could tell she was about to leave. Suddenly I felt another word impressed upon my heart, "suicide."

I had only moments, maybe even seconds, before she would be gone. I mustered up courage and just said out loud, "Suicide." She looked me square in the eye and tears started to well up again. Instantly words just came forth from my mouth, flowing like a river.

I had this image, like a movie playing in my mind, and I spoke what I saw. I said to her "The reason I said suicide is that God spoke to me and told me you just tried to commit suicide." I was seeing this picture of her in her room, sitting on her bed, crying out to God. I heard what she was saying as she was popping pills. Even though by all rights, she should have been dead I told her that God heard her prayer and saved her from dying that night and that He sent me to answer that cry and to tell her that she was important to Him. The more I said, the more she wept. She finally knelt to the ground on the main street of the city. People passing by were probably wondering what was going on.

We found out later that everything God had revealed was exactly what had happened earlier that week. We also learned that the reason she had tried to kill herself week was because she recently had been raped and felt she had no value. Because of the word of knowledge the Holy

Word of Knowledge

Spirit gave me, we were able to counsel to her and lead her to Christ that night.

Another compelling example from scripture of the use of the word of knowledge comes in John 4:7-19, the story about the woman at the well:

> *"A woman of Samaria came to draw water. Jesus said to her, 'Give Me a drink.' For His disciples had gone away into the city to buy food. Then the woman of Samaria said to Him, 'How is it that You, being a Jew, ask a drink from me, a Samaritan woman?' For Jews have no dealings with Samaritans. Jesus answered and said to her, 'If you knew the gift of God, and who it is who says to you, "Give Me a drink," you would have asked Him, and He would have given you living water." The woman said to Him, 'Sir, You have nothing to draw with, and the well is deep. Where then do You get that living water? Are You greater than our father Jacob, who gave us the well, and drank from it himself, as well as his sons and his livestock?' Jesus answered and said to her, 'Whoever drinks of this water will thirst again, but whoever drinks of the water that I shall give him will never thirst. But the water that I shall give him will become in him a fountain of water springing up into everlasting life.' The woman said to Him, 'Sir, give me this water, that I may not thirst, nor come here to draw.' Jesus said to her, 'Go, call your husband, and come here.' The woman answered and said, 'I have no husband.' Jesus said to her, 'You have well said, "I have no husband," for you have had five husbands, and the one whom you now have is not your husband; in that you spoke truly.' The woman said to Him, 'Sir, I perceive that You are a prophet.'"*

Notice Jesus didn't "jump in with it" straightaway, but spent time conversing with the woman and drawing her in with conversation. Gifts always flow best when we truly care and are genuinely interested in people. People don't care how much you know, until they know how much you care. Jesus cared. The Samaritan woman was so impacted that she craved what Jesus was offering, the "living water".

Jesus then used a word of knowledge to unmask her sin and need of a savior. The word of knowledge was about her past and present. She was living with a man whom she was not married to and her life was a broken mess of failed relationships. Jesus referenced another five previous husbands.

Notice how he used this information (word of knowledge). He didn't come out blazing hellfire and brimstone and accusing her by saying, "You're a sinner. You're living with a man and I know what you two unmarried people have been doing because I'm God. I know your past.

MY FRIEND, THE HOLY SPIRIT

You've been with five other men. Repent now of these things and then you will get the living water." Sadly that's how some Christians treat unbelievers. It doesn't mean that he approved of her lifestyle, but he accepted her.

Bad heart?

The word of knowledge can be used in ministering to the sick and broken like the time I was at a gifts of the spirit workshop and we had to split into small groups to practice these gifts. As we each went around the group one by one, we shared a word of prophecy or word of knowledge, either general or specific. I had a word of knowledge that someone in the group had a bad heart and needed healing. Yet when I shared this, no one responded, and I was completely embarrassed, even though I had felt confident that it was right. This was one of my first times stepping out in the word of knowledge as a young Christian, and I remember feeling so let down that I had not been able to hear God. Not to mention that I had actually felt this word strongly for a particular man in our group, but he hadn't responded at all. I even addressed the group and kind of focused my words in his direction as a subtle hint and said, "I felt REALLY sure it was for someone in the group." He however sat there unmoved. I felt that I'd got it wrong. My first attempt and I blew it.

We finished up the small group workshop and returned to the main meeting. Bill Subritzky who was running the class (I came to know Christ at his meeting) then taught on the word of knowledge and proceeded to show us how to operate in it. He started by saying, "God is speaking to me about someone in this room who has a bad heart." I was like, "What?" No one moved. He then proceeded to say, "In fact, I feel the Lord telling me it is someone on the right side of the room." Again...no one moved. He tried again, pointing to a row of chairs, "I believe it is in this section of the crowd." There I saw him, the man from our group whom I thought this word was for, shifting nervously in his seat in the same row Bill had pointed out. My eyes were glued to him as Bill continued, "And God is telling me that you are in the 5th row." This man could not contain it anymore; he shot up on his feet and said, "It's me. It's me." I wanted to say, "You dirty dog! I knew it was you. I knew it!" But I kept silent and learned a powerful lesson: don't doubt God; doubt your doubts but never doubt God.

Spit in the face

A story I will never forget is a testimony I heard a man share about himself. There was a teenage girl and an older man out sharing to the homeless, alcoholics, and drug addicted who came across him. When

Word of Knowledge

the young girl handed him a tract, he in his drunken stupor thought was money. As she handed it to him, she looked into his eyes with compassion and said, "Jesus loves you." He thought, "Wow, thank you for this money." He then looked down at what he thought was a wad of bills, but to his surprise it was a tract with writings about Jesus. He instantly cursed at the girl and spat in her face. The girl turned and ran off crying and afraid.

Later that night resting on a bench, he closed his eyes and all he could see was a vision of the girl saying, "Jesus loves you." This played over and over in his mind. He couldn't get those words or the vision of the love in the young girl's compassionate eyes out of his mind. He fumbled around in his pocket for the tract he had stuffed in there. When he found it, he pulled it out and read the story of Jesus, the story of love and salvation, and he broke down in tears and prayed the prayer at the end of the book.

The very next night he went out looking for this girl on the streets, he did not find her. But he found other Christians witnessing and he shared his story and they helped him get on his feet and become connected with a church. He would go out every night on the streets with them sharing his story with other homeless people, every night looking for that girl in hopes that he would see her again to apologize to her and to thank her for being bold enough to love him.

Before long he was sober and working in a job, and soon after that he got married and had children. But every night from the day he was saved he continued to dedicate himself to sharing the gospel to those that lived on the streets. And every night he looked and hoped he would see that young girl and thank her, but he never did. He finished his story by sharing that when he gets to heaven the first person that he was going to look for was that young girl, so he could thank her for being obedient, for stepping out. Because of that...he'd found Christ.

That girl probably went home feeling like a failure, that she had missed the mark, that being obedient and that sharing the gospel got her spat in the face. One day in heaven she will get a surprise when she learns that the man with whom she shared Jesus with actually came to Christ that night, and that in her obedience, salvation arrived.

"For our light affliction, which is but for a moment, is working for us a far more exceeding and eternal weight of glory, while we do not look at the things which are seen, but at the things which are not seen. For the things which are seen are temporary, but the things which are not seen are eternal" (1 Corinthians 4:17-18).

Things are not always as they seem. What the girl saw or felt wasn't the big picture because in the eternal realm, the invisible realm, to God

MY FRIEND, THE HOLY SPIRIT

she was a hero, an obedient girl who brought his love and salvation into a man's heart that changed his destiny!

CHAPTER 10:
Gift of Faith

Gift of faith defined: The gift of faith is God functioning in you and through you, the ability that God gives to discern and accept with extraordinary confidence the will and purposes of God on the earth.

When God gives you the gift of faith, you don't take no for an answer. Faith doesn't try, it just does. Faith doesn't have good intentions, it obtains promises. You speak and it is done. You don't have to work it, it is just there. It is faith that comes instantly, supernaturally as a gift directly from God via the Holy Spirit for a brief dramatic moment. The gift of faith can also essentially supercharge the other gifts.

People with this gift can see what God will do, even when the task seems impossible to accomplish. The gift of faith is given to you at a specific time and specific place for a specific purpose. Raising someone from the dead involves the gift of faith.

There is so much teaching in the Bible regarding faith! *"Without faith it's impossible to please God,"* Hebrews 11:6. Relatively speaking, in order to please God always, we must always have faith.

The gift of faith is not the same as saving faith or what some term as simple faith or your normal everyday faith. Which is the type of faith discussed in Romans 10:17, *"So faith comes from hearing, that is, hearing the Good News about Christ,"* which I call your natural everyday faith.

"Everyday" Faith
Joseph Thayer, in his Greek-English Lexicon, describes faith as "a firm and welcome conviction." Every "believer" has this kind of faith, by definition. He is one who believes.

MY FRIEND, THE HOLY SPIRIT

George Mueller defined such faith as follows: "Faith is the assurance that the things which God said in His Word are true; and that God will act according to what He has said in His Word. This assurance, this reliance on God's Word, this confidence, is Faith."

Natural, everyday faith is referred to in Romans 12:3, where it says, *"For I say, through the grace given to me, to everyone who is among you, not to think of himself more highly than he ought to think, but to think soberly, as God has dealt to each one a measure of faith,"* and also in Romans 12:6, *"Having then gifts differing according to the grace that is given to us, let us use them: if prophecy, let us prophesy in proportion to our faith."*

These scriptures are not talking about the gift of faith, but rather the kind of faith that God has dealt to each believer. The faith that God has given each believer is 24/7 faith, natural, everyday faith that you have to live out your God-given destiny! But the gift of faith is different; it is brief and dramatic and only lasts momentarily.

Saving Faith

Another type of faith that is mentioned in the Bible (and also differs from the gift of faith) is saving faith. One example of saving faith is found in Luke 23:42-43, *"Then one of the criminals who were hanged blasphemed Him, saying, 'If You are the Christ, save Yourself and us.' But the other, answering, rebuked him, saying, 'Do you not even fear God, seeing you are under the same condemnation? And we indeed justly, for we receive the due reward of our deeds; but this Man has done nothing wrong.' Then he said to Jesus, 'Lord, remember me when You come into Your kingdom.' And Jesus said to him, 'Assuredly, I say to you, today you will be with Me in Paradise.'"*

It was by the one criminal's faith that he would be in Paradise with Jesus. We are saved by faith as it is written in Ephesians 2:8, *"For by grace you have been saved through faith, and that not of yourselves; it is the gift of God".*

To receive salvation, it takes faith, and even though it is a gift, it must be accessed by faith. Again this type of faith is different than the gift of faith, because saving faith you only need once, when you get saved. The gift of faith is given after you have been saved and are already a believer.

How does the gift of faith work?

In two distinct ways: toward something or someone on behalf of God and toward God on behalf of someone or something.

Gift of Faith

Let's look at some examples from scripture.

In Matthew 21:18-22, we get a glimpse of the gift of faith working toward something on behalf of God, when Jesus spoke to the fig tree.

> *"Now in the morning, as He returned to the city, He was hungry. And seeing a fig tree by the road, He came to it and found nothing on it but leaves, and said to it, 'Let no fruit grow on you ever again.' Immediately the fig tree withered away.*
>
> *"And when the disciples saw it, they marveled, saying, 'How did the fig tree wither away so soon?' So Jesus answered and said to them, 'Assuredly, I say to you, if you have faith and do not doubt, you will not only do what was done to the fig tree, but also if you say to this mountain, "Be removed and be cast into the sea," it will be done. And whatever things you ask in prayer, believing, you will receive.'"*

Here we see Jesus speaking to the fig tree on behalf of God and the fig tree withers and dies. This is the gift of faith in action. It is brief and it is dramatic. This is not something that you would do daily; it is usually a one-time event.

Another scriptural example can be found in Mark 4:35-41, when Jesus spoke to the sea:

> *"On the same day, when evening had come, He said to them, 'Let us cross over to the other side.' Now when they had left the multitude, they took Him along in the boat as He was. And other little boats were also with Him. And a great windstorm arose, and the waves beat into the boat, so that it was already filling. But He was in the stern, asleep on a pillow. And they awoke Him and said to Him, 'Teacher, do You not care that we are perishing?' Then He arose and rebuked the wind, and said to the sea, 'Peace, be still.'"*

When Jesus spoke to the wind and the sea, the storm instantly stopped. Neither Jesus nor the disciples had to pray and fast for this miracle for a week. They didn't have time! This situation needed someone (Jesus) to function in the gift of faith quickly, otherwise they all may have perished.

Setback

When Summer and I were trying to organize our move from Australia to the United States, we were coming against many obstacles. For starters, we were in the middle of planning our wedding, and since we couldn't plan a wedding and a big move like that simultaneously, we picked getting married (good choice!). We then had to wait on numerous other things to fall into place with the church that was sponsoring us. When our family, close friends and leaders of our church found out that we were planning to move, we were constantly asked when we were leaving, and we always gave very vague response, "Oh we don't know...we are working on it."

Dealing with setback after setback, we thought we were finally scheduled to move in February of 2006. These plans, however, were seemingly wrecked on Christmas Day of 2005: Frustrated, I went for a walk on the beach in tears; I let God know that my wife had cried in the car on the way to Christmas dinner at her parents' home. In fact we had to sit outside in the car for a while so she could compose herself.

We talked and talked about our "mountain." We cried about it. We constantly thought about it. It kept us up at night. We talked about our mountain with friends and family. We strategized on how we could get around or over our mountain. Then one day the light came on. None of these things that we were doing were biblical.

God spoke clearly to me. Faith speaks to the mountain, and the mountain moves. Faith doesn't speak about the mountain (problem).

Mark 11:23 -24 says, *"So Jesus answered and said to them, 'Have faith in God.' For assuredly, I say to you, whoever says to this mountain, 'Be removed and be cast into the sea,' and does not doubt in his heart, but believes that those things he says will be done, he will have whatever he says. Therefore I say to you, whatever things you ask when you pray, believe that you receive them, and you will have them.'"*

That one word from God, that impartation of the gift of faith for our circumstance changed everything. I spoke to Summer about what had happened and we prayed and then heard from God that we should depart for the US in the last week of May. So we decided from now on whenever anyone would ask us or if either of us would speak to each other about our move to the US, we would tell them we were leaving the last week of May. This seemed crazy as we had just been told no, and that it may be possible in 18 months. May was only 5 months away!

Every day I would wake up, see the mountain in front of me, and declare that we were moving during the last week of May. Whenever Summer and I would talk about it, we always referred to the last week of May. Whenever we were asked by family or friends when we were leaving, we told them the last week of May. Now we weren't working this up, or moving in presumption, I got a revelation from heaven. The gift of faith through me spoke this word, and just like the fig tree shriveled and the sea and waves subsided, on May 24th 2006 our plane landed in San Diego, California.

Gift of Faith

Now let's look at some examples from scriptures of the gift of faith in operation toward God on behalf of someone else.

> *"At Joppa there was a certain disciple named Tabitha, which is translated Dorcas.... But it happened in those days that she became sick and died. ...And since Lydda was near Joppa, and the disciples had heard that Peter was there, they sent two men to him, imploring him not to delay in coming to them. Then Peter arose and went with them. When he had come, they brought him to the upper room. And all the widows stood by him weeping, showing the tunics and garments which Dorcas had made while she was with them. But Peter put them all out, and knelt down and prayed. And turning to the body he said, 'Tabitha, arise.' And she opened her eyes, and when she saw Peter she sat up. Then he gave her his hand and lifted her up; and when he had called the saints and widows, he presented her alive. And it became known throughout all Joppa, and many believed on the Lord"* (Acts 9:36-37 and 39-42).

Notice in this passage that Peter "put them all out". Why? I believe it was because of all the widows weeping. He needed to remove the emotion from the room so he could not be affected by this in his prayers to God. He operated in the gift of faith to raise Tabitha from the dead. Peter spoke to God on behalf of Tabitha, and Tabitha came back to life!

The "Apostle of Faith" Smith Wigglesworth (1859 - 1947) raised several people from the dead, including his wife Polly, a man called Mitchell, and a Baptist Pastor's wife, Mrs. Clarke.

Wigglesworth's wife had been dead for two hours. Smith declared, "She is not dead." He walked into the bedroom, pulled her up against the wall, and said, "I command you to come to me now!" And she did.

In addition to this, Smith Wigglesworth's friend and biographer Walter Hibbert claims that Smith raised a man from the dead who had been embalmed and was in a funeral parlor. In his biography he tells of a woman who was brought into a meeting in a coffin, slapped Wigglesworth's face after being raised up, stating that she had had a far better time in the hereafter. Wigglesworth claimed to have raised between three and twenty-three people from the dead.

Smith Wigglesworth would on occasion strike people who were brought to him. Lester Sumrall, the late American evangelist, knew Smith Wigglesworth and attended his meetings. Sumrall recounted in his book that at one meeting a man with stomach cancer who had been brought into the meeting on a stretcher, wearing a hospital gown. He was too weak to walk and in such poor condition that he was accompanied by a doctor. When Wigglesworth came to minister healing to him, he struck him in his abdomen with his fist, telling him in his thick colloquial accent to "be 'ealed" in Jesus name. The doctor put a stethoscope to the man's heart saying, "You killed him! You killed him!" Wigglesworth paid little attention and kept on ministering to other people. A few moments later, the sick man with stomach cancer got up off his stretcher and walked around with his backside showing through his hospital gown. He had been completely healed.

Jesus raising Lazarus from the dead is the gift of faith in operation. In John 11:39-44 (scripture below), Jesus spoke to God on behalf of someone (Lazarus), who then rose from the dead. Jesus spoke to God and it was done for Lazarus and his family.

> "Then Jesus, again groaning in Himself, came to the tomb. It was a cave, and a stone lay against it. Jesus said, 'Take away the stone.' Martha, the sister of him who was dead, said to Him, 'Lord, by this time there is a stench, for he has been dead four days.' Jesus said to her, "Did I not say to you that if you would believe you would see the glory of God?' Then they took away the stone from the place where the dead man was lying. And Jesus lifted up His eyes and said, 'Father, I thank You that You have heard Me. And I know that You always hear Me, but because of the people who are standing by I said this, that they may believe that You sent Me.' Now when He had said these things, He cried with a loud voice, "Lazarus, come forth!" And he who had died came out bound hand and foot with grave clothes, and his face was wrapped with a cloth. Jesus said to them, 'Loose him, and let him go.'"

Bible College

Another amazing experience I have had with this gift is when I felt God had called me to go to Bible College. Because I wanted to get into the finance industry and had a job lined up for this, I had disobeyed God by not enrolling in the class that I felt He wanted me to. With only a couple of months before the class began, I enquired if any spots remained open. I was told it was full but that I could send in an application at no charge in case anyone pulled out before class commenced.

I said to God, "OK, it's full. If you really want me to go, then I will apply and you will make a way. I heard nothing at all, but the day that the Bible College started, I received a call that someone had just pulled out and I could enroll for that semester if I wanted to. I could almost feel the laughter of heaven. I told them I did want to enroll because I had made a deal with God and wanted to honor my word. They asked if I could be there by 6:30 that night with the tuition fee for that year. I answered, "yes" without thinking. When I hung up the phone, I immediately thought, "What have I done?" I didn't even have the money and I knew they wouldn't accept me unless I paid upfront tonight! But where I ended, faith kicked in. Right then the gift of faith was provided. There was just a certainty that it would be done, the money would arrive in time. So I got up, showered, packed all my stuff, and had everything ready. I called my parents (who knew I had applied) and told them what I was doing and that I knew God would provide the tuition fee.

Every time my phone rang, that day, I thought it could be someone calling to tell me I had money. I checked the mailbox for a check. Every time I answered the door, I thought that maybe this was someone with my tuition check. Six o'clock rolled around, but I still didn't have the money. I had thirty minutes left to get the money or I wouldn't be able to enroll in that class. Shortly afterward, my mother came home, and someone had given my parents a check anonymously during the day. There it was! I still don't know to this day who it was, but I thanked God for them as I headed off to Bible college!

On this occasion I didn't have to speak and it was done. I acted. I made a decision and it was done. I packed and got ready to leave, I didn't say to the Bible college administrator, "Sorry I don't have the money. I'll enroll when I do." You may ask what would have happened if the money had not come? Well I wouldn't have been operating in the gift of faith, it would have been presumption. So you may ask how does one know the difference? If you have to ask yourself that question, then you are not really sure, and so you are not in faith because faith knows the answer. Faith is not trying to believe, Faith never tries. Faith Does, Faith Speaks, Faith Expects, Faith Commands, Faith Praises, Faith doesn't waver or doubt, Faith always prevails. Without faith, nothing is possible. With Faith, nothing is impossible.

CHAPTER 11:

Gifts of Healings

Gifts of healings defined: A supernatural manifestation for the healing of sicknesses or diseases without any natural source or means. Healing relieves the body or mind of disease or injury. It may be gradual or it can be instantaneous.

Doctors and medical science are a natural means of healing. Gifts of healings and other methods of divine healing are a supernatural and not natural means of healing. Paul told Timothy to take some wine for his stomach problems, so certainly healing can come through medical/natural means. 1 Timothy 5:23 *"No longer drink only water, but use a little wine for your stomach's sake and your frequent infirmities."*

Healing looks after the entire person, it caters to your physical, mental and emotional needs. In fact studies have linked many physical conditions to things like bitterness, rejection, grief and other such emotions. That's why the Bible states that a "merry heart does good, like medicine, But a broken spirit dries the bones" (Proverbs 17:22).

Sometimes what people need most is an emotional healing, obtaining a happy and healthy attitude (merry heart) is like medicine. The Holy Spirit has a gift of healing for any need that we have, that's why it is called "gifts of healings" (plural).

What is the difference between healing and miracles?

Healing is the removal of sickness or disease, whereas a miracle is creative. For example, an arm growing back would be classified as a miracle. Healing can be gradual, so just because you don't see immediate change, don't give up!

Healing along with tongues are two of the most controversial topics amongst Christians today. This is due to either poor teaching or no teaching at all on these topics. The purpose of this book is not to give a

Gifts of Healings

complete doctrinal study on healing. It would take an entire book to do this and you can certainly accomplish this by reading other books written specifically about healing, such as *Healing the Sick* by T.L Osbourne and *Christ the Healer* by F.F Bosworth. Rather, the purpose is to give an overview of this gift, answer some common questions, and give you the knowledge to apply this gift.

Below are three of many biblical examples of gifts of healings in action.

"But Simon's wife's mother lay sick with a fever, and they told Him about her at once. So He came and took her by the hand and lifted her up, and immediately the fever left her. And she served them" (Mark 1:30-31). *"Also a multitude gathered from the surrounding cities to Jerusalem, bringing sick people and those who were tormented by unclean spirits, and they were all healed"* (Acts 5:16).

Another example of the gifts of healings comes from Acts 28:7-9:

> *"In that region there was an estate of the leading citizen of the island, whose name was Publius, who received us and entertained us courteously for three days. And it happened that the father of Publius lay sick of a fever and dysentery. Paul went in to him and prayed, and he laid his hands on him and healed him. So when this was done, the rest of those on the island who had diseases also came and were healed."*

In the book of Mark it points out that signs will follow those who believe (Mark 16:18). One of those signs is healing.

There are a few important facts about this gift. First, as I've mentioned before, it's vital to realize that this particular spiritual gift is written in the Bible in the plural form, "gifts". Some people may say that they have the gift of healing. This statement is not even scriptural. Someone may have a "ministry" in healing but this is different. But as far as the nine gifts of the spirit goes it is "gifts" of healing. Gifts of healing is something that is given to the person that needs it, the person who is sick.

Why is it termed "gifts" of healing? Because that is exactly what is given to others when we pray for them. If someone has need of prayer for an ailment, then we can exercise gifts of healing on their behalf. So the gift is not for the person praying (unless the person praying is the one who needs the healing of course). Gifts of healing is for the person you are praying for.

We essentially don't even give this gift of healing (God does; He is the healer). We simply distribute "gifts of healing" to those who need it on His behalf.

MY FRIEND, THE HOLY SPIRIT

Is it God's will?

Another mental hurdle that people seem to stumble over is wondering whether or not the healing they are asking for is in God's will. In answering that, I ask you to consider this: does everyone get saved when you share the Gospel with them? Of course not. But is it His will that everyone gets saved? Of course it is (See 2 Peter 3:9). Not everyone you pray for may get healed either, just like not everyone gets saved that you share the gospel with. Still both are God's will. Should we then stop witnessing to people if not everyone we witness to get's saved? No. Likewise we should never stop praying for sick people despite the fact that not everyone we pray for will receive healing.

Healing Evangelist Andy Kubala told a great story about a radio interview that he was doing and he was asked why not everyone who he prays for gets healed. Andy replied by asking whether or not it would be powerful if he prayed for 100 people with cancer and one got healed. The interviewer answered an emphatic yes.

We too often focus on the ones that didn't get healed and let that discourage us rather than focusing on the ones that did get healed. Some people say that they have never seen anyone healed, and my question to them is, "Well, how many sick people have you prayed for?"

I have prayed for many people to be healed and not everyone that I have prayed for was healed. But the important thing to understand is that everyone can be healed. We don't know the reasons why someone may not have received healing, but we must also always keep in mind that a person's salvation is more important than their healing. I believe God would rather that both occur, but it's better to get to heaven blind than not to get to heaven at all!

"Then Philip went down to the city of Samaria and preached Christ to them. And the multitudes with one accord heeded the things spoken by Philip, hearing and seeing the miracles which he did. For unclean spirits, crying with a loud voice, came out of many who were possessed; and many who were paralyzed and lame were healed. And there was great joy in that city" (Acts 8:5-7).

Notice it says "many" were healed; if all were healed the Bible would have said so. This means that not "everyone" received healing; I think the important part of this passage is that Philip "went" and "preached Christ" and "many" who were paralyzed and lame were "healed".

That's why Jesus first taught, preached and then healed as it says in Matthew 4:23, *"And Jesus went about all Galilee, teaching in their synagogues, preaching the gospel of the kingdom, and healing all kinds of sickness and all kinds of disease among the people."* Notice with Jesus it is not "many" but "all".

Gifts of Healings

The reason I believe that not everyone gets healed is this: God uses certain people to heal different types of sicknesses and diseases. If one person could heal every sickness, then every sick person on the face of the earth would go to them. We need all members of the body of Christ moving in gifts of the spirit to distribute all different sorts of gifts of healings to all different kinds of people.

F.F. Bosworth stated: "I usually never fail to get a deaf person healed, or one who's hearing is impaired...." So I do believe that there are areas of healing that God will use you in more than others. I personally believe (and this is not backed up by any specific scripture) that if someone had a 100 percent success rate in healing, then that person would be worshipped as God. But if the Church as a whole had a 100 percent success rate in healing, then the world would worship God. I have written this book so that the whole Church would embrace healing and step out and *"lay hands on the sick"* (Mark 16:17).

Healing is God's will just as much as salvation is. In fact the word "salvation" in Greek means "sozo". It means to be delivered from both spiritual and temporal evils; protected; made whole or sound in our spirit, soul and body. In the Bible, salvation means our spirit, soul, and body are made whole. Salvation is Jesus saving you from sin and sickness! Some only receive the free gift of being saved from their sins, but salvation means that we can be saved from our sickness as well. There are many reasons people have come up with to explain why healing is not available to all, but let's apply some of these reasons to salvation and see if it makes sense.

1. Maybe it isn't God's will to heal you
   Maybe it isn't God's will to save you

2. Perhaps your sickness is for God's glory
   Perhaps your sin is for God's glory

3. Perhaps God is using this sickness to chastise you
   Perhaps God is using this sin to chastise you

4. The days of healing are past
   The days of salvation are past

Just as salvation is His will, for His glory and is for today, so is healing. In scripture you will find that healing is always connected with salvation, like in Psalm 103:1-3, *"Bless the LORD, O my soul; And all that is within me, bless His holy name! Bless the LORD, O my soul, And forget not all His benefits: Who forgives all your iniquities, Who heals all your diseases...."*

MY FRIEND, THE HOLY SPIRIT

And I love what it says in 1 Peter 2:24, *"Who Himself bore our sins in His own body on the tree, that we, having died to sins, might live for righteousness—by whose stripes you were healed."*

Healing is for today and for all as shared in 3 John 1:2, *"Beloved, I pray that you may prosper in all things and be in health, just as your soul prospers."* God wants us to prosper and be in health. The word health here means specifically to be well in your body and entire being. Here are two more of my favorite scriptures pertaining to this topic:

"Surely He has borne our griefs (sicknesses, weaknesses, and distresses) and carried our sorrows and pains [of punishment], yet we [ignorantly] considered Him stricken, smitten, and afflicted by God [as if with leprosy]" (Isaiah 53:5, Amplified).

And in Matthew 8:17 it says, *"He Himself took our infirmities and bore our sicknesses."*

The question here is that if Jesus already bore our sins on the cross, should we bear them? Of course not. If Jesus already bore your sickness, why would you have to bear it again? If that were the case, Jesus bore it for nothing. If salvation is for all as it is written in the Bible, then healing is for all. We do not tolerate sin in our lives because Jesus bore our sins. Neither should we tolerate sickness in our bodies because Jesus bore our sicknesses.

The Gospel of salvation is to touch the whole man, spirit, soul and body. The Holy Spirit helps us do this. By taking a deeper look at the origination of the word "evil," we can grasp the intended reach of God's salvation. The word "evil" found in Matthew 6:13, where it says, "Deliver us from evil," comes from the Greek word "pono," which means pain. The word "pono" comes from the root "ponos," meaning poor. So let's break this down: evil, sin = pain, sickness, and poor (poverty). But Jesus destroyed the power of sickness and poverty through his redemptive work on the cross.

Matthew 17:14-20 describes a powerful story that starts with the disciples praying for a boy and the boy not getting healed, which is a situation that has commonly occurred with many Christians across the globe. Many become discouraged and change their doctrine, making their experiences rule over what the Word of God actually states regarding healing, but Jesus did not allow the disciples to enter into false doctrine, firmly correcting them.

> *"And when they had come to the multitude, a man came to Him, kneeling down to Him and saying, "Lord, have mercy on my son, for he is an epileptic and suffers severely; for he often falls into the fire and often into the water. So I brought him to Your disciples, but they could not cure him. Then Jesus answered and said, "O faithless and perverse generation, how*

long shall I be with you? How long shall I bear with you? Bring him here to Me." And Jesus rebuked the demon, and it came out of him; and the child was cured from that very hour.

Then the disciples came to Jesus privately and said, "Why could we not cast it out?"

So Jesus said to them, "Because of your unbelief; for assuredly, I say to you, if you have faith as a mustard seed, you will say to this mountain, 'Move from here to there,' and it will move; and nothing will be impossible for you. However, this kind does not go out except by prayer and fasting."

This is a powerful story of a boy whom after being prayed for by the disciples was not healed, but when Jesus prayed for him he was healed. Today we would explain it away saying it was not God's will or that God is trying to teach him something from this sickness and that God has chosen not to heal this boy but somehow God will be glorified through the sickness. But Jesus was right there so they could not use these explanations. It was His will to heal the boy and after He did so He explained that the disciples were unsuccessful in healing him due to their unbelief or lack of faith. This wasn't the only time that Jesus rebuked the disciples for a lack of faith.

Luke 8:25 *But He said to them, "Where is your faith?" And they were afraid, and marveled, saying to one another, "Who can this be? For He commands even the winds and water, and they obey Him!"*

Mark 4:40 *But He said to them, "Why are you so fearful? How is it that you have no faith?"*

Jesus wasn't berating his disciples, he loved his disciples, but he wanted to keep them from a false thought process and theology that would destroy their faith.

Jehovah Raphah, I am the Lord that heals you

Exodus 15:26: *"I am the Lord who heals you."* This is one of God's names, the Lord that heals. Wouldn't it be strange if you went around calling yourself a doctor, but when asked what medicine you practice you said that you didn't practice any. Your title is a function of your character. I have the title Pastor, why? Because I pastor people and perform that function. Same goes if your title is CEO, Manager or Postman. You would not be called by these names if you did not perform the function associated with those names. God's name is HEALER! Why? Because He heals. God spoke those words to about three million people. All of them believed God's words were true. The result was that all of them who needed healing were made perfectly whole. *"He (God) brought them forth... and there was not one feeble person among their tribes"* (Psalm 105:37). The only reason three million Israelites were well and strong was that they believed what God had said: "I am the Lord who heals you."

Christians today have somehow failed to believe that God meant what He said, which is basically what Satan said to Adam and Eve, "God did not mean what he said." If, under the old covenant, three million of God's people could be well at one time, then how many more of God's people may be well today who are living under the New Covenant of mercy, grace, and truth, established on better promises, with a better priesthood (Hebrews 8:6), through a more excellent ministry. Until you are fully convinced that God wants you to be well, there will always be a doubt in your mind as to whether or not you or others will be healed. Bosworth said, "Don't doubt God. If you must doubt something, doubt your doubts, because they are unreliable, but never doubt God or His word." Bosworth goes on to say, "The message taught in the Gospels is one of the complete healing for the spirit and body, for all who will come to Him. Many today say, "I believe in healing, but I do not believe it is for everyone." If it is not for everyone, then how could we ever pray the prayer of faith?"

There is only one person who asked Jesus if it was His will to heal him when the leper in Mark 1:41 said, "If you will, you can." And Jesus answered, "I will".

Take careful consideration of the words in this scripture, one we all know well: Matthew 6:10, *"Your kingdom come. Your will be done on earth as it is in heaven."* Is there sickness in heaven? No. Is there poverty in heaven? No. God's will is for earth to be like heaven.

The Bible says in Hebrews 11:6, *"But without faith it is impossible to please Him."* You will never be able to please God without being fully convinced of His word, that you know for certain in faith that healing is for you, that it is for today! According to scriptures there should be no question. Because James 5:14 asks the question, *"Is any sick among you?"* Any includes you if you are sick. And Matthew 12:15 says that *"Great multitudes followed Him, and He healed them all."*

Below are three more scriptures further emphasizing that Jesus heals all and any who are sick.

"The whole multitude sought to touch Him, for power went out from Him and healed them all" (Luke 6:19).

"When evening had come, they brought to Him many who were demon-possessed. And He cast out the spirits with a word, and healed all who were sick" (Matthew 8:16-17).

"When the sun was setting, all those who had any that were sick with various diseases brought them to Him; and He laid His hands on every one of them and healed them" (Luke 4:40).

Note from these examples from scripture that the words mean exactly what they say. Because *"Jesus Christ is the same yesterday, today, and forever."* (Hebrews 13:8). Yet those who oppose that healing is for today show no biblical support for this belief. Sure, most believe God can heal, but many struggle as to whether God will heal. God can and He wills.

Stepping Out

The first person I ever saw healed was a Christian sportsman who was speaking at a Christian's athletic meeting. I had been a Christian for only six months. He had a serious knee injury. After quite a few Christian athletes had spoken and it was near the end of the meeting, I felt the Holy Spirit prompt me to stay to pray for the sportsman with the serious knee injury. I wrestled with this for what seemed a long time. The meeting finished and a lot of people wanted to talk to the athletes. So I waited and waited, and this particular guy was so great with chatting to people that in the end it was just he and I left in the auditorium.

It felt weird being there alone and wondering if he thought that I was some kind of stalker. I was only 17 at the time and newly saved. But I believed in the saying, "you never know unless you have a go!" When everyone had left and it was just the two of us left in the auditorium, I asked if I could pray for him. He complied. I prayed for healing for him right then and there. After I finished praying, he thanked me, but I felt the Lord prompt me to say to him "test it out." He replied that the only way to really test it out was by running. Again the Lord spoke to me, "ask him to run." So I asked him. He got up and ran a little bit and with a surprised look on his face, he told me it felt much better. He went on to play at least five more years at the top level, and what many experts had said may have been a career-ending injury turned into a great testimony for God's glory!

Healing is a redemptive right for all people. This was provided through Christ's atonement--the once-and-for-all perfect sacrifice. Atonement means at-one-ment with God. That is, to restore us in relationship with God and all that was lost at the fall including health. Sin and sickness is the double-curse that came to mankind, and Jesus provided a cure for both.

MY FRIEND, THE HOLY SPIRIT

Reasons Why People Don't Receive Healing

These are some of the main reasons from scripture that people fail to grasp God's great promise of healing. As stated earlier in this chapter, the goal of this book is not to give a complete doctrinal teaching on healing, but rather to cover some of the misconceptions regarding the gifts of healing while providing a basic overview and building a solid foundation of teaching for this largely misunderstood gift.

1. Unbelief

Mark 11:24 says *"Therefore I say to you, whatever things you ask when you pray, believe that you receive them, and you will have them"* The Bible also says "*whatever is not of faith is of sin*". (Romans 14:23).

A person cannot be double minded about God. He either heals today or He does not. You must decide for yourself what you believe.

Even Jesus was restricted in what miracles He could perform because of unbelief. He marveled at it and could do "no mighty work there" because of unbelief, except "he laid hands on a few sick people and healed them" (Mark 6:5-6). Think of it, Jesus the Son of God is in your midst and you turn your nose up at Him! He "could do no mighty work there" means that people who needed a mighty work, a miracle or a major healing did not get it! But He did heal a few sick people which is amazing that this would be considered something small; in most churches today a few sick people being healed would be like revival breaking out!

2. Confession against the truth

Truth planted in you can be uprooted through negative words. *"Life and Death are in the power of the tongue"* (Proverbs 18:21).

So many times I have heard people pray for someone to be healed but then straight after the prayer is finished they admit that they are not sure if the person will make it! Prayer is not limited to whatever you say in Jesus' name. Prayer is your life! You cannot pray one thing and live another way, as this renders your prayer null and void. The Bible says *"faith without works is dead"* James 2:17. Prayer is not a magic wand. Prayer (faith) must be backed up with action that correlates with that which you pray (works).

3. Lack of knowledge

Hosea 4:6 says, *"My people are destroyed from lack of knowledge."*

You need to know the truth to be set free by the truth. Sadly many people do not live God's best plan for their lives simply because they do not know everything God has made available to them. They believe healing is not for today, but not because they have searched it out for themselves (had they done so they would clearly see from scripture it is for today and it is for all).

People who believe in this misunderstanding of the truth often say things like, "But we prayed for Johnny and he didn't get healed. So it is not His will for all." But the same people who say this also witness to people who don't get saved, but you would never hear them saying, "It is not His will that everyone get's saved."

4. Not asking

"*You do not have because you do not ask*" (James 4:2)—be specific.

Matthew 7:7-8 says, *"For everyone that asks, receives."* Be specific about what you want God to do. People ask me to pray for loved ones who are sick. This is fine and I love to do this, but I find many times these people have not actually laid hands and prayed for these loved ones themselves. They don't have yet because they haven't even asked.

5. Presumption

Some people just have hope without substance – but "*faith is the substance of things hoped for*" (Hebrews 11:1). You can't just pray and hope people will be healed.

Some people believe that just because they read a book on healing or went to a healing conference, they now they have their eyes opened to how God wants to heal and they proceed to go out and pray for healing on behalf of several people, but are then disappointed when they see very little come of it.

Why? Because doubt and unbelief has dominated their minds for so long and they have become conditioned to a wrong doctrine even though the light has been turned on in their mind. The room of the mind needs to be cleaned of all the doubt and unbelief and wrong mindsets of the past. Sure the truth has set them free, but many times people step out in presumption rather than faith. The Bible says that even the demons "believe". You can believe the Bible and what it says is true, but that is just "mental assent".

Mental assent is brilliantly described in E.W. Kenyon's book *The Two Kinds of Faith*, "Mental assent agrees that the Bible is a revelation, that it came from God, and that every word is true, and yet when crisis comes it does not work. It simply recognizes the truthfulness of that wonderful book but does not act on it. Hope says, 'I will get it sometime.' Faith says, 'I have it now.'"

You may say, "But I prayed and it didn't work?" The Bible says that it is with *"Faith and patience that we inherit the promise"* Hebrews 6:12. God's time is the perfect time. He doesn't work according to your schedule but His, so let go and let God do his thing in His way and in His time. James 1:3 says, *"Let patience have her perfect work"*. In other words "Don't give up".

6. Unforgiveness

"And whenever you stand praying, if you have anything against anyone, forgive him, that your Father in heaven may also forgive you your trespasses. But if you do not forgive, neither will your Father in heaven forgive your trespasses" (Mark 11:25).

You say, "But I can't forgive." You simply must. A great way for God to work the healing work of forgiveness in your heart is to pray for those that wrongfully treated you; pray for them every day. Verbally speak that you forgive them and pray for them. You will find forgiveness take root in your heart. Make sure you that you forgive yourself for past mistakes. Many times people say but I forgive everyone, but they have not forgiven themselves. Do not let your past mistakes hold your future in captivity, you already suffered enough from the past, why let that suffering now affect your future?

7. Sin

1 John 1:8-9 says, *"If we say that we have no sin, we deceive ourselves, and the truth is not in us. If we confess our sins, He is faithful and just to forgive us our sins and to cleanse us from all unrighteousness."*

Repent of and renounce known sin, both past and present. Many times when we come to Christ, we pray a very general salvation prayer, but there are things we may have involved ourselves with in the past that need to be specifically renounced. Am I saying you are not saved until you have repented specifically of these things? Of course not! You became saved the moment you invited Jesus Christ to take control of your life. But any past ties to any cult or false religion, séances, Ouija boards, the occult and other such activities can block the blessing of God today until specifically renounced.

The key is every day we should pray like Kind David did in Psalm 139:23-24 *"Search me, O God, and know my heart; Try me, and know my anxieties; And see if there is any wicked way in me, And lead me in the way everlasting".*

Ways to Receive and Administer Healing

1. Prayer and confession of faith

Follow the examples set forth in Mark 11:23-24, *"For assuredly, I say to you, whoever says to this mountain, 'Be removed and be cast into the sea,' and does not doubt in his heart, but believes that those things he says will be done, he will have whatever he says. Therefore I say to you, whatever things you ask when you pray, believe that you receive them, and you will have them".*

Romans 4:17: *"Call those things that are not as though they were"* and Joel 3:10, *"Let the weak say, 'I am strong.'"* You need to speak faith until you have faith. Continually speaking and meditating on the promises of God brings health and healing to your life. But don't live in denial. If you have sickness, then don't pretend that you don't. Only acknowledge that the word of God and the name of Jesus has power over your sickness, that your sickness was defeated at the cross, that Jesus bore it for you. Remember that *"God sent his word and it healed them"* (Psalm 107:20). As you speak the word of God it brings healing.

"Faith filled words brought the universe into being, and faith filled words are ruling that universe today" - E.W. Kenyon

Rebuke the enemy in Jesus' name, order him to leave our bodies and thank God for your healing. When we use the name of Jesus we bring God into actual contact with our sickness.

God laid our sickness on Jesus. Jesus bore sickness already. Faith never rises above its confession. Our faith is measured by our confessions, you will always live at your level of confession; our confessions rule us. So start talking Jesus! Not sickness, disease and hopelessness.

Notice that Jesus always confessed what He was:

- *"I am the resurrection"* (John 11:25; even though He hadn't been resurrected yet)
- *"I am the bread of life"* (John 6:35).
- *"I am the good shepherd"* (John 10:11).

What the heart believes the mouth speaks. Faith is not only a matter of the heart, it is also a matter of the mouth. Our confession can imprison us, or set us free. Our mouth becomes the transportation of God's deliverance from heaven to man's need on earth. When we make our confession that our sicknesses were laid on Jesus and hold fast to that confession we bring the Holy Spirit on the scene. If you do not bring your words under your control, your life will be lived as a stumbling horse, directionless and accomplishing very little. A wise man will make sure his words are both positive and creative. A doctor looks at the tongue first to diagnose sickness in the body. The Holy Spirit looks at our tongue to diagnose a healthy heart; if we speak unbelief, poverty, sickness or evil, this points to a bad heart, a heart that needs to be renewed and healed.

Meditate on the Word

"My son, give attention to my words; Incline your ear to my sayings. Do not let them depart from your eyes; Keep them in the midst of your heart; For they are life to those who find them, And health to their flesh" (Proverbs 4:20-22).

The word "health" in original Hebrew means medicine. "My words are medicine to all their flesh". A life full of the word is a life full of health and prosperity. What you dwell on you dwell in. Dwell on the word of God and the promises of God daily and that is what you will dwell in, a day full of God's promises for healing hope and salvation for every area of your life.

You create the presence of God with your mouth. If you speak about healing, then healing comes. If you speak about a miracle-performing savior then you release the miracle working power of God. The Holy Spirit is bound or released by your words. If you have an inferiority consciousness, a poverty consciousness, a sickness or failure consciousness, God cannot work. We must be in agreement with God for God to work. Amos 3:3 states, *"Can two walk together, unless they are agreed?"*

2. Laying on of hands

When you lay hands on the sick and pray for them things happen just like it says it will in Mark 16:18-20, *"They shall lay hands on the sick, and they shall recover."* The key is "when" and not "if". The more people that you pray for to be healed, the more people who can be healed. There is no magic formula to this. Simply obey and pray. You are not the healer, God is. As you faithfully lay hands on the sick and pray believe what God says in his word.

3. Anointing with oil

James 5:14 asks, *"Is anyone among you sick? Let him call for the elders of the church, and let them pray over him, anointing him with oil in the name of the Lord."*

Just as water is in baptism, oil is a powerful symbol from the Bible. Oil is symbolic of the Holy Spirit. If you are sick the Bible says to call on the elders (leadership of the Church), and they will pray for you and anoint you with oil. Anointing with oil is in itself an act of faith. Faith filled leadership laying hands on you and praying for you and anointing you with oil in agreement is powerful.

4. Prayer of agreement

When praying you need to remember the truth of Matthew 18:19-20, *"Again I say to you that if two of you agree on earth concerning anything that they ask, it will be done for them by My Father in heaven"* and of John 14:14, *"If you ask anything in My name, I will do it."*

You need good faith-filled friends to stand by you and with you in times of sickness and hardship. When I was at Bible college I fell incredibly sick. It was the day of graduation and all my family was coming up to celebrate. But I was in bed, so sick I was unable to move, let alone stand. Four of my friends came to my bedside and prayed, not just for a few minutes but for over an hour. After about an hour of them praying and singing worship songs in my room I felt a rush of power come over me; because I had a very high fever it was like a cold rush (usually I feel heat with the Holy Spirit). I said to the guys, "I believe I am healed." I got up out of bed. I still felt weak, but I began to join them in worship and praise songs and even danced a little. I must say I didn't feel 100 percent that night, but I was able to enjoy the graduation because I had friends who stood with me in agreement and prayed for me until healing came!

5. Praise and Worship

Psalm 103:1-3 says, *"Bless the Lord, O my soul; And all that is within me, bless His holy name! Bless the Lord, O my soul, And forget not all His benefits: Who forgives all your iniquities, Who heals all your diseases."*

The Bible says that God inhabits the praises of His people (Psalm 22:3). God inhabits praise, not complaining, negativity or whining. I love the quote: "If you're a singer, sing; if you're a dancer, dance, but if you're a whiner, then take the day off."

I think one of the biggest problems is that most of our prayers start with please instead of thank you. When things don't look good, if sickness has come upon you, thank Him and praise Him for who He is and what He has done. Worship Him for all the good things He has given to you; thank Him in faith for great health. Refuse to let unbelief, doubt, fear

MY FRIEND, THE HOLY SPIRIT

and pity overwhelm you. Get overwhelmed by Him and his presence by getting lost in thanksgiving and worship.

6. Stepping out

I have found the miracle is in the stepping out. That is the majority of the battle, you will never see anyone healed if you don't step out, if you don't actually pray for anyone. Whether you feel like it or not it is in the stepping out and keeping your eyes on Jesus that brings God's favor.

I was on an outreach with my Bible college and they had organized for some of us to go to a hospital and run a chapel service. Sadly, only a few patients showed up. One of the guys spoke for a little while and then offered the opportunity for our team members to pray for patients who requested it. Pretty much everyone wanted prayer and I was paired with a very old lady called Dorothy. She was 86 and had a label on her top that said, "I am partially deaf please speak loudly." I looked around and everyone was praying really quietly with their patients. I mean, this was a traditional chapel service. I started to pray for her and she stopped me, asking me to speak up as she could not hear me, so I raised my voice a little louder, I could now feel a couple of eyes on me, no one else could see the label and must have wondered why I was drawing attention to myself. She looked at me and said young man you will have to pray louder and pointed to her label (like I hadn't already seen it). I thought, well here goes. I shouted and commanded the deaf spirit to leave and thanked God for healing. The whole room stopped praying and everyone was just looking at me, very quickly the chapel service leader brought the prayers to an abrupt halt. The lady I had been praying for asked if I would wheel her back to her room, I obliged. On the way back I started some very small talk with her as I felt a very awkward silence. I thought to myself here she is, 86, and I must have embarrassed her. But as I am speaking with Dorothy I realize that she is responding. I stopped in my tracks. I said, "Dorothy can you hear me ok?" She replied "Of course, when you prayed for me my deafness went and I can hear you perfectly." I was like well, yes of course, thank Jesus! The lesson I learned was never be afraid to step out, obey God, don't worry about what others may think.

Matthew 14:28-30: *"And Peter answered Him and said, 'Lord, if it is You, command me to come to You on the water.' So He said, 'Come.' And when Peter had come down out of the boat, he walked on the water to go to Jesus. But when he saw that the wind was boisterous, he was afraid; and beginning to sink he cried out, saying, 'Lord, save me!'"*

Peter stepped out and walked on water, and as long as he kept his eyes on Jesus and not the circumstances, he was ok. You cannot look

Gifts of Healings

at the circumstances and at Jesus at the same time; you must choose one. You must look at Jesus and step out in Faith to see the miraculous.

7. Rejoicing

Take careful note of the wisdom in Proverbs 17:22, *"A cheerful heart is good medicine."*

Did you know that if we are joyful, we release fluid that repairs cell damage or alternatively it breaks down if we are depressed? So get happy! The joy of the Lord is your strength (Nehemiah 8:10)!

In the mid '90s when the Holy Spirit was poured out fresh upon my church, many Christians experienced laughter. I was skeptical at the time, but you know what, that's what we all needed, to laugh our way to healing and renewed health.

"He who sits in the heavens shall laugh" (Psalm 2:4). You can laugh because you are seated in heavenly places with Christ (Ephesians 2:6). You are seated already in the place of victory.

Have you ever nervously watched your favorite sporting team as they played, hoping they would win? Your emotions going up and down like a rollercoaster as the game swings in the balance. How about watching your favorite sporting team when you already know the end score and that they have won. No matter what happens during the game, if they are behind, getting beat or not playing well for a time, you have no worry, no concern, because you know the end result; you know that they won, you know already that you have victory. Guess what, you are seated in victory. Jesus already won. You're seated with him and you can laugh at your circumstances no matter what is happening because you know the end result, victory! Laughter is healthy; laughter heals like medicine!

If a person is not healed when we have prayed for them they should not be told they are; let them walk in the level of faith they have, not all healings are instantaneous. Do not tell people to do away with their medicine and always encourage people who claim they are healed to see a doctor to verify healing. Luke 17:14 says, *"So when He saw them, He said to them, 'Go, show yourselves to the priests.'"* Healing can withstand any doctor investigation.

What about Paul's thorn?

One of the most prevalent objections raised today against the ministry of healing is Paul's "thorn in the flesh". Many believe that Paul had a sickness from God that He refused to heal. Let's look at some of the scriptures pertaining to this.

2 Corinthians 12:7: *"And lest I should be exalted above measure by the abundance of the revelations, a thorn in the flesh was given to me, a messenger of Satan to buffet me, lest I be exalted above measure."*

2 Corinthians 12:8: "*Concerning this thing I pleaded with the Lord three times that it might depart from me.*"

2 Corinthians 12:9: *"And He said to me, My grace is sufficient for you, for My strength is made perfect in weakness. Therefore most gladly I will rather boast in my infirmities, that the power of Christ may rest upon me."*

2 Corinthians 12:10: *"Therefore I take pleasure in infirmities, in reproaches, in needs, in persecutions, in distresses, for Christ's sake. For when I am weak, then I am strong."*

What was Paul's Thorn?

The expression "thorn in the flesh" is used in both the Old and New Testaments as an illustration. The "thorn in the flesh" never indicated sickness. In both, the thorns were personalities (Canaanites) creating problems for God's people.

In 2 Corinthians 12:7 Paul says it was a messenger of Satan (the angel of the devil or Satan's angel). Again it was a personality causing the problem not sickness.

This word "messenger" is translated from the Greek word angelos which appears 188 times in the Bible. It is translated 181 times as "angel" and seven times as "messenger". Without exception, in all 188 times, it is referring to a person and not a thing. Hell was prepared for the devil and his angels, or messengers (Matthew 25:41), and Paul's "thorn in the flesh" was one of these messengers of the devil.

CHAPTER 12:

Working of Miracles

Working of miracles defined: God's supernatural intervention into the ordinary course of nature.

It should be noted that there is a "work or working" involved in this gift and not simply a receiving of miracles. The key to the working of miracles is: "whatever Jesus says to you, do it!"

"A miracle is an event beyond the power of any known physical law to produce. It is a spiritual occurrence produced by the power of God, a marvel, a wonder" - Billy Graham

A person being born again is the greatest of all miracles. Every time a person invites Christ into their life and repents of sin, the miracle of regeneration is performed! Jesus' first miracle in the Bible was when He turned water into wine in John 2:1-5, *"On the third day there was a wedding in Cana of Galilee, and the mother of Jesus was there. Now both Jesus and His disciples were invited to the wedding. And when they ran out of wine, the mother of Jesus said to Him, 'They have no wine.' Jesus said to her, 'Woman, what does your concern have to do with Me? My hour has not yet come.' His mother said to the servants, 'Whatever He says to you, do it.'"* The line spoken by Mary is key! "Whatever He (Jesus) says to you, do it."

We identify another miracle Jesus performed in Matthew 14:15-16: *"When it was evening, his disciples came to Him, saying, 'This is a deserted place, and the hour is already late. Send the multitudes away, that they may go into the villages and buy themselves food.' But Jesus said to them, 'They do not need to go away. You give them something to eat.'"* Again the key to the miracle was doing whatever Jesus said to do. Jesus told the disciples that they were to give the people something to eat and they obeyed Him by finding five loaves and two fish. Jesus blessed and broke the food, distributed it to the disciples who then distributed the food to 5,000 men, not counting women and children, and they had basketfuls left over. Imagine being a disciple and Jesus is praying over five loaves and two fish before distributing it to you, and then you have to walk out amongst 5,000 men with only a small portion of bread and fish! But little is much when God is in it. And because they "did what Jesus said to do," the small portions were multiplied, and not only did they have enough food to feed the multitude, but there were leftovers!

The Greek word for "miracles" is dunamis, which means dynamite. Almost everywhere the word dunamis is mentioned in the Bible there is a reference to casting out demons such as in Mark 9:38-39, *"Now John answered Him, saying, 'Teacher, we saw someone who does not follow us casting out demons in Your name, and we forbade him because he does not follow us.' But Jesus said, 'Do not forbid him, for no one who works a miracle in My name can soon afterward speak evil of Me.'"*

I love this following example from scripture of Paul using this gift in Acts 19:11-12, *"Now God worked unusual miracles by the hands of Paul, so that even handkerchiefs or aprons were brought from his body to the sick, and the diseases left them and the evil spirits went out of them."* As we can see quite often, miracles only happened once demons left. This is not always the case as far as this gift goes, but almost every time the miracle is related to healing or restoration of some area of the physical body, demons are commanded to leave before the miracle takes place. Maybe this is why it is called "the working of miracles" as it takes work to get people set free to receive their miracle.

We hear the words "healed", "signs" and "wonders", and "miraculous" bandied around without much explanation as to their real meaning or purpose. So let me take a moment to explain each: to heal means to cure, make whole; signs are to indicate, signify, point-out; wonders are prodigious, causing wonder, extraordinary; and finally, miracles are miraculous power or a supernatural event. Have you ever wondered why there are healing, signs, and wonders? Simply put, it is the most effective form of Evangelism in today's world and is accompanied by manifestations of supernatural power.

In Matthew 11, two disciples of John were sent to inquire if Jesus was the promised Messiah, the Son of God. And when John had heard in prison about the works of Christ, he sent two of his disciples to ask Jesus whether or not he was the One or if he should be looking for another. *"Jesus answered and said to them, 'Go and tell John the things which you hear and see: The blind see and the lame walk; the lepers are cleansed and the deaf hear; the dead are raised up and the poor have the gospel preached to them'"* (Matthew 11:4-6). Jesus emphatically settled the issue that in fact He was the promised Messiah by pointing to the miracles that He had performed.

Working of Miracles

Many years ago I remember praying for a young girl after a youth meeting. She wanted to accept Christ but was not sure about Jesus. I went straight into my "Romans Road" evangelism presentation. Once I finished, she told me that she knew all these things and had heard them before, but what she wanted to know was whether or not God was real. At that moment I said, "Lift your hands to heaven." The moment I laid hands on her the power of God hit her like an electricity bolt, and she broke down in tears and wept and wept. She said, "Now I know God is real, not because I have heard it but because I felt his power and cannot deny him any longer." She gave her life to Jesus that night.

"It is the witness with evidence that convinces. One demonstration is worth a thousand lectures. One miracle is worth a thousand sermons" (author unknown).

The great promise of John 14:12 is that we would do greater works than Jesus: *"Most assuredly, I say to you, he who believes in Me, the works that I do he will do also; and greater works than these he will do, because I go to My Father."*

How can we do greater works than Jesus?

Because He has gone to the Father, and the promise Jesus gave was that when He went to the Father, He would send the Holy Spirit. We can do greater miracles because Jesus was confined to one body. He was one person that could be in only one place at one time. After He went to the Father, the Holy Spirit came to dwell in the body of Christ, which can be simultaneously performing miracles in many locations at the same time, 24/7, 365 days a year.

Imagine hell. Jesus does so many miracles per day, but at some point he finally sleeps. The demons get a break! But not so with the Holy Spirit baptism. The body of Christ is across different time zones, across the world. Stats show there are 1 billion Christians worldwide, but let's just pretend for a moment that the number is actually a mere 1 million. Even if there were 1 million Christians worldwide, the capacity of the Church in any given moment is one million miracles happening all at once. I've often heard the story of what would happen if everybody in China jumped at the same time, that the world would move. Let me tell you if all Christians everywhere released the miraculous power of God simultaneously the world would be moved! That is the greater miracle, the ability by the baptism of the Holy Spirit for the body of Christ to be releasing miracle power 24/7, 365 and simultaneously. No wonder the Devil hates the Holy Spirit and his gifts!

In Acts 20:7-12 we read about this type of power release when Eutychus was raised from the dead: *"Now on the first day of the week, when the disciples came together to break bread, Paul, ready to depart the next day, spoke to them and continued his message until midnight. There were many lamps in the upper room where they were gathered together. And in a window sat a certain young man named Eutychus, who was sinking into a deep sleep. He was overcome by sleep; and as Paul continued speaking, he fell down from the third story and was taken up dead. But Paul went down, fell on him, and embracing him said, 'Do not trouble yourselves, for his life is in him.' Now when he had come up, had broken bread and eaten, and talked a long while, even till daybreak, he departed. And they brought the young man in alive, and they were not a little comforted."*

What better way to turn your preaching around when someone falls asleep in your meeting, then falls out the window and happens to die and then you just go and raise him from the dead! Paul's preaching cannot have been that riveting, or perhaps this guy had gone without sleep for some time! Whatever the case note in this example the healing happened instantly. A miracle is an instantaneous healing or deliverance. But just like in the gifts of healings, unbelief can extinguish the workings of miracles also. In Mark 6:4 it says, *"But Jesus said to them, 'A prophet is not without honor except in his own country, among his own relatives, and in his own house.' Now He could do no mighty work there, except that He laid His hands on a few sick people and healed them. And He marveled because of their unbelief. Then He went about the villages in a circuit, teaching."*

You have to step out in faith. That is why it is called the "workings of miracles". Rarely do people receive anything by sitting passively. Stepping out in faith is a commitment, not an experiment.

In the church today there is too much leaning back and not enough pressing forward; we don't see enough miracles today because people do not want to "work" these miracles. This just breeds laziness and over time, unbelief. We become comfortable with our lack of miracles, and this then becomes the normal standard for the Church.

The Purpose of Miracles

1. To display the love of God

Matthew 14:14 says, *"And when Jesus went out He saw a great multitude; and He was moved with compassion for them, and healed their sick."* Jesus' love and compassion for the people continually moved Him to heal all who came to Him for healing. This should be the same for us, that deep down we are moved and motivated by love; godly biblical love does something, it does not just sit there and say nice words. *"For God so loved the world that he gave…"* (John 3:16).

2. To prove that Jesus is the Son of God

John 10:36-38 says, *"Do you say of Him whom the Father sanctified and sent into the world, 'You are blaspheming,' because I said, 'I am the Son of God'? If I do not do the works of My Father, do not believe Me; but if I do, though you do not believe Me, believe the works, that you may know and believe that the Father is in Me, and I in Him.'"*

Proof of the truth is not an unreasonable request. Scribes listening to Jesus demanded proof of His son ship in Matthew 9:2-7, and Jesus gave them proof. He proclaimed that he was the Son of God because he did the "works" of the Father.

Nicodemus even proclaimed in John 3:2 *"....for no one can do these signs that you do unless God is with him."*

Jesus stated that unless he did the "works" of the Father, then he was not the Son of God. What works did Jesus do? He turned water into wine, and then there was His miraculous provision for feeding the 5,000. He calmed the storm and seas. He raised Lazarus from the dead, as well as Jarius' daughter. John 21:25 reads, *"Jesus did many other things as well. If every one of them were written down, I suppose that even the whole world would not have room for the books that would be written."* Notice it says that Jesus "did" many other things and not that He just said them. So much of church life is about talk, more talk, more conferences, more three-point sermons, more big name speakers with the latest teaching and books; but where is the gospel power; where are the workings of miracles; where are the signs and wonders?

3. To prove that Jesus has risen from the dead

Without miracles today, there really is no way we can prove that Jesus has risen from the dead. Miracles today prove He is alive! When people get saved, healed and set free we know that Jesus lives today!

In Acts 3:6, Peter took a crippled man by the hand and said, *"In the name of Jesus Christ, rise up and walk!"* The man was miraculously healed.

When the crowds came to see the man, they seized the opportunity and preached about the risen Christ (Acts 3:12-16).

After Peter's testimony in Acts 4:16, the Sanhedrin's only response was: *"What shall we do to these men? For, indeed, that a notable miracle has been done through them is evident to all that dwell in Jerusalem, and we cannot deny it."*

There was no argument to the power of God. The miracle settled the issue. No argument, no discussion, the proof was right there. The miracle took the power of unbelief, false doctrine and deception away. The Sanhedrin realized that they could not speak against Jesus because the miracle was plain for everyone to see. If God is alive, then where is His power? Where is the evidence that He is alive? Surely if God is alive we must see evidence of this on the earth. This evidence is signs, wonders and the miraculous. A gospel void of this is a gospel of theology, not a gospel of relationship. With theology we know about someone, but with a relationship we experience that person.

4. To draw people to hear the Gospel

Why did the multitudes flock to hear Jesus? Luke 5:15 says, *"...great multitudes came together to hear, and to be healed by Him of their infirmities."*

John 6:2 says, *"Then a great multitude followed Him, because they saw His signs which He performed on those who were diseased."*

Churches try everything from sporting events to social activities to draw people in so they can proclaim Christ to them. We've tried to cover up our lack of power with plans, programs, and activities. Miracles draw the people to hear the Gospel, and miracles convince the people that the Gospel is true. Of course social activities can be powerful connection points to our community, but if that is all we do, then we have become just another social club in our community.

5. To bring glory to God

Psalm 96:3: *"Declare His glory among the nations, His wonders among all peoples."* We must understand that the gifts and miracles of God are not to make our own name famous, but they are to make His name famous. They are not for our gain but for His gain. Not for our glory, but for His glory.

Jesus healed a blind man recorded in Luke 18:43, *"And immediately he received his sight, and followed Him, glorifying God. And all the people, when they saw it, gave praise to God."*

Whenever the miraculous breaks out, people recognize that God is among us and glory is brought to His name.

6. To give credentials to the call of God

The credentials Jesus gave to prove His claim that He was the Son of God were not great sermons or great teaching, but miracles.

Working of Miracles

Acts 2:22: *"Men of Israel, hear these words: Jesus of Nazareth, a Man attested by God to you by miracles, wonders, and signs, which God did through Him in your midst ..."*

And the writer of Hebrews declared this about Jesus: *"God also bearing witness (of Jesus) both with signs and wonders, with various miracles ..."* (Hebrews 2:4).

When the prophet Elijah performed a miracle, raising the widow's son from the dead, it gave credibility to his ministry and the widow said, *"Now I know you are a man of God, and that the word of the Lord in your mouth is the truth"* (1 Kings 17:24). In the widow's heart, the miracle validated what Elijah had said.

I remember being in a meeting when the visiting minister said that miracles were going to break out all over the place. There was only a small gathering of people, possibly 50 at most. He went on to say that someone right at that moment was being healed of cancer and then proceeded to go on and on about all these different miracles that were taking place, and after that, he closed the meeting. I thought to myself, "Well, he didn't lay hands on anyone or call anyone up or even ask if anyone could notice a difference that they may be healed. He just listed stuff and closed meeting." I wanted to see the evidence. Where was the proof? I spoke to people after the meeting and not one person I talked to had the sicknesses he had described, let alone had anyone been healed of them. Of course this left the speaker with no credibility for anything he said and did not validate his ministry as someone who supposedly moved in "signs and wonders."

What Releases Miracles?

1. Prayer

Acts 4:30 says, *"By stretching out Your hand to heal, and that signs and wonders may be done through the name of Your holy Servant Jesus."*

The Bible says *"you have not because you ask not."* I have prayed for two people that were dead, and neither came back to life. But I have prayed for one person who was brain dead and in a vegetative state. The doctors wanted to turn off his life support, but God brought him back from the depths of death and he came back to life. The point is you will never see a miracle unless you ask, unless you pray.

2. Unity

Acts 5:12 says, *"And through the hands of the apostles many signs and wonders were done among the people. And they were all with one accord in Solomon's Porch."*

Psalm 133 states that in unity God *"commanded the blessing."* Unity creates an environment for miracles. If you have a body of people all together in one heart, mind and vision, then there is an environment of faith created for miraculous things to happen. In the Old Testament, God responded both to Israel's disobedience and obedience as a nation, not as one man. Quite often God would use one man to deliver Israel, but only after the nation had corporately sought the Lord and cried out to the Lord as one for help. During church prayer meetings, I have frequently perceived that there is not any unity. People come with their own agendas. Some people are engaged in prayer, others are silent; some just stand around looking bored while others have their hands raised and are crying out. Half the time during church prayer meetings, it is a struggle to get anything "prayed through" as half the meeting is disinterested or in unbelief. And you begin to wonder why some of these people even show up. If you come to a church prayer meeting, then come ready to engage, ready to pray with faith in your heart. And if you come into the prayer meeting disheartened and broken down, lacking faith, ask someone to lay hands on you and pray for you so you can be set free to engage with heaven.

3. Boldness

Acts 14:3 says, *"Therefore they stayed there a long time, speaking boldly in the Lord, who was bearing witness to the word of His grace, granting signs and wonders to be done by their hands."*

Notice that they spoke "boldly" and signs and wonders were done by "their hands." You have to step out and be bold. Nothing happens unless you are prepared to be bold and risk being a "fool for Jesus". In other words, what have you got to lose? Step out boldly and pray for someone. If nothing happens then they are just the same as they were before. You say I may look silly? Well, you were ok being silly in the world, boozing up and saying and doing things you regretted the next day; why not be bold and be prepared to be a fool for Jesus, you never know unless you have a go!

4. Perseverance (patience)

2 Corinthians 12:12 says, *"Truly the signs of an apostle were accomplished among you with all perseverance, in signs and wonders and mighty deeds."*

The signs of an apostle were "accomplished with all perseverance." Sometimes you have to persevere. A two-year-old boy named Kyle from our church was hooked-up on a life-support system. The doctors said he was dead and that the life support system should be turned off.

Working of Miracles

After his parents received a word from God, they dared to believe in God and fight for their son.

I prayed for Kyle on Saturday, along with his parents and our entire church. Nothing happened. People from our church came into the hospital every day and prayed. Nothing happened. Then one day while one couple was praying, his eye flickered and popped open. Then another day he started to move. The doctors denied these advances and said it was just reflexes. We all kept praying, and one week later Kyle was awake and alive. The life-support machine was turned off, not to end his life, but because he didn't need it anymore! When I first walked in there on that Saturday I prayed, I prophesied, I commanded life to come into his body; I spoke to the spirit of death and commanded it to leave. Standing over Kyle with Bible in hand, praying and declaring scripture of life and healing and hope over his body, I must have been a real sight to the doctors and nurses. Nothing happened in the physical realm that day, but in the spiritual realm I believe things began to shift.

Sometimes you just have to show real persistence, to keep praying and believing like when God commanded Ezekial to prophesy over and speak life into a valley full of dead bones that had been dead for some time (Ezekial 37). So Ezekial prophesied in verses 4 and 10, then again in verse 12. Not everything happened the first time Ezekial prophesied. He had to keep speaking to the bones. Repeated persistence and sticking with it, not giving up is what faith is all about. Look at Naaman. He had to wash in the river seven times (2 Kings 5). And there's the children of Israel; remember when they had to walk around the city of Jericho for seven days (Joshua 6). I like to say that faith is spelled p-a-t-i-e-n-c-e.

The two big P's of faith are what you need: patience and persistence. Hebrews 6:12 says, *"that you do not become sluggish, but imitate those who through faith and patience inherit the promises."* From these examples in the Bible we learn that when we pray and nothing happens, we should pray again, believe again, and step out again.

CHAPTER 13:

Gift of Prophecy

Gift of prophecy defined: A thought, impression, vision from the Holy Spirit to a believer to enable him to bring a word from God.

1 Corinthians 14:3 says, *"But he who prophesies speaks edification and exhortation and comfort to men".*

A prophecy is for edification, exhortation, and comfort.

Edification

Edify comes from word edifice, which means a building. To edify simply means to build up or strengthen.

Exhortation

The devil brings discouragement and depression, whereas to exhort means to stimulate, to encourage, to admonish, and to stir up.

Comfort

The third purpose of prophesying from this scripture is to comfort. The Greek word means consolation, to cheer up, or healing of distress, suffering, and persecution.

Prophesying is mentioned 22 times throughout 1 Corinthians, between chapters eleven and fourteen, which underlines its importance. We also learn that all can prophesy in 1 Corinthians 14:31-33, *"For you can all prophesy one by one, that all may learn and all may be encouraged. And the spirits of the prophets are subject to the prophets. For God is not the author of confusion but of peace, as in all the churches of the saints."* So it is clear that ALL can prophesy, however, this is does not mean you are a prophet.

Awesome in the Word

When I was at Bible college, not only was I the second youngest student there, but I was also the youngest Christian. I had only been saved for eleven months. I didn't know the Bible half as well as a lot of the students. For this reason, I sat at the back of the class so that none of the lecturers could see me or ask me questions. There was a guy in my class called Campbell who was phenomenal when it came to Biblical knowledge. He knew where all the scriptures were and could quote so many of them by heart.

One day in class Campbell must have been running late as he took a seat at the back table alongside me. The lecturer asked if anyone knew where a particular Bible verse was. Normally hands shot up all over the class, but on this occasion, no hands raised. Campbell even remained still. Wow, that verse I actually knew. It was probably the only verse I knew by heart, but I knew where it was. I checked again for lifted hands. Nope, no hands in the air, so up shot mine. Everyone's heads turned to face me at the back of the class.

"Yes, young man?" my lecturer said looking toward me.

I answered with the book, chapter and verse.

He replied, "Well done, that is correct."

Campbell whispered to me, "Awesome in the Word." Well, I was anything but that. One verse hardly constituted being "Awesome in the Word." But it encouraged me greatly.

Over the course of the next few months, every time he saw me, he called me "Awesome in the Word." To be honest, I felt kind of embarrassed. But after a while, I really liked it, and even more importantly, I felt the desire to live up to this. So I started to memorize scripture. But I just didn't memorize verses here and there, I tackled entire books of the Bible. I started with James, then 2 Timothy, Ephesians, Philippians, Colossians. In all I memorized 14 books of the New Testament between 1993 and 1994. All because of one guy who encouraged me. I believe, whether he knew this or not, that he was moved by the Holy Spirit to speak this prophesy over my life.

See, you don't have to be praying for someone to prophesy over them. You can "prophesy in normal every day conversation through a word of encouragement.

Prophesy is for edification, exhortation, and comfort. If it does not bring one of these or all three of these to the person receiving the prophecy, then you would be wise not to take on what is being said. While it is true the Bible says *"all may prophesy,"* it doesn't say that all will have the ministry of a prophet. A prophet speaks the future. A prophet is part of the body of Christ (belongs and is under spiritual authority in a local church) as a ministry gift (Ephesians 4:11). They function as members under authority and are recognized as such by the authority. If you are not recognized as a prophet in your own church, then you are not a prophet. It is the prophetic office that gives guidance for future events, but the spiritual gift of prophecy does not. The spiritual gift of prophesy never brings condemnation, rebuke, or correction. It is never directional like that. Directional prophecies are exactly that, to give direction for someone else's life using, "Thus says the Lord."

Brian Houston tells how his wife Bobbie was once prophesied over by a "so called" prophet, who prophesied that she should not marry Brian as he was not God's best for her life. Of course she rejected the prophecy and married him. He now says in jest that he wonders who God's best really was for Bobbie if Brian wasn't; I mean he is only the senior pastor of the largest church in Australia and responsible for the Hillsong music movement worldwide!

A prophecy is not to be used for guidance. What should you do if you have been given a directional kind of word by those who are not operating the ministry or office of a prophet? Don't base your life on it, and spit it out if it doesn't sit well with you. Or put it aside and let time test it. But don't go and act on it just because someone else said it! Too many people operate in directional prophesy when they should not. A prophecy is for encouragement, not foretelling. Yet when most people prophesy they start giving directional guidance when they are not in the office of a prophet. I do believe, however, that God can at times use those not in the office of a prophet to give a directional word—but only sometimes. A prophet who operates and is recognized in the office of a prophet brings; direction, correction, warning, encouragement, and instruction. They direct recipients to the ways of heaven.

Acts 20:29-31: *"For I know this, that after my departure savage wolves will come in among you, not sparing the flock. Also from among yourselves men will rise up, speaking perverse things, to draw away the disciples after themselves. Therefore watch, and remember that for three years I did not cease to warn everyone night and day with tears".*

So just because someone said, "thus say the Lord," doesn't mean it's from God.

Jeremiah 23:16: *"Thus says the LORD of hosts:*
   'Do not listen to the words of the prophets who prophesy to you.
   They make you worthless;
   They speak a vision of their own heart,
   Not from the mouth of the LORD."

Gift of Prophecy

1 Corinthians 2:15a: *"But he who is spiritual judges all things"*. This means to scrutinize, investigate, interrogate, determine and examine closely.

You can tell a false prophet because all they do is draw people to themselves; a genuine prophet draws people to the heart of God. The number one target for people who give false prophesies are those who are vulnerable, or easy to prey on. These are usually people who are wounded, hurt or offended. Even with the office of a prophet, what is prophesied will only come to pass if we engage this word. The Bible says that we are co-laborers with Christ. This means we work together. God's Word works together with you to bring the word to pass.

A prophecy is conditional and never automatic. If you run from it or don't obey it, then it won't come to fruition. Many people believe that simply because God said it, then it will come to pass. Now when speaking about the Bible, this is true. With other circumstances, it's about what we do on our part as it says in Isaiah 1:19: *"If you are willing and obedient, you shall eat the good of the land."* Notice it says, "if you are willing and obedient."

Some people just live their lives off words from others, always looking for a "word" rather than spending time with God via the Holy Spirit. The Bible doesn't say that as many as are led by prophesy or prophets, these are the sons of God. It says those who are led by the Spirit in Romans 8:14, *"For as many as are led by the Spirit of God, these are sons of God."* This means taking the time to listen and wait and fellowship with the Holy Spirit each day.

Does prophecy always confirm what's in your heart?

Not always. Jesus prophesied that Peter would deny Him; Peter didn't feel this confirmed what was in his heart at all! But generally speaking, prophesy usually confirms what is already in your heart. When that 10 dollar bill was set on the lunch table that morning after preaching and the host pastor said it was a sign of where God was taking us, this confirmed what had already been in Summer's and my heart. We had been privately praying about a possible move to the United States, and the pastor did not know this. Was this directional? To a degree it was, but more so it was encouraging and brought comfort about our pending decision. If a prophecy doesn't provide confirmation, test the word spoken and wait before acting.

How do you test a prophecy?

Ask God that if the word really is from Him that He will confirm it through other sources, one of these being God's word. We once had a man who wanted to leave our church and start a ministry in a different city, leaving behind his wife and kids (But since his wife had a great paying job, it would support him in this other city). He said he would eventually find a way to bring his wife and kids over. The problem was that for years he had been unsuccessfully trying to get this ministry started in his current city. If this pattern repeated, he would be separated from his wife and kids for a long period of time. The Bible states that the man who doesn't provide for his family is worse than an unbeliever (1 Timothy 5:8). When this was shared with him, he refused our advice, believing that he had received a word from God. Last I heard, he is still trying to get this ministry going in another part of America while his wife is still working and living in a different city. This is what happens when you don't "test" the word. The God who gave you that word to begin with is more than able to confirm that word in a number of different ways so you can be certain that word is from Him.

There's a phrase I love: "Eat the meat, and spit out bones." I cannot remember the first time I heard this or who even said it, but it has really stuck with me over the years. If you have someone prophesying over you, take what is good, what resonates in your spirit, and if something doesn't sit well, the Bible says to "test it" and "retain what is good." 1 John 4:1 it says, *"Beloved, do not believe every spirit, but test the spirits, whether they are of God; because many false prophets have gone out into the world."*

I know a lot of people who, if one thing in the prophecy doesn't sit well, criticize and throw out the whole prophecy. The Bible doesn't teach this way of handling prophecies, though. Take a look at what it says in 1 Thessalonians 5:19-21, *"Do not quench the Spirit. Do not despise prophecies. Test all things; hold fast what is good. Test it and retain what is good."* If 50 percent is good and 50 percent is not, keep the good part ("the meat") and put aside the part that doesn't resonate with you ("spit out the bones"). Remember that just because it might not resonate with you now doesn't mean it won't be accurate in five or even 10 years' time. I have prophecies that I wrote down 10 and 15 years ago that really didn't connect with me at the time. Thank God I didn't throw them out! Most of these words are starting to come to pass in my life now. Hang on to them because you just never know.

So should we always put a word we are not sure of on the shelf? Not always. As we see above the Word of God tells us to judge it first, not shelf it first. So deal with the word, if it is obviously false we need to deal with it, if demonic in nature, we would not shelf it. But if it is not demonic in nature, then putting it on the shelf can be harmless as time will test whether that word is of God or not; we just don't base our lives on it. The main thing to understand here is that the more spiritually mature we become the more accurate we will be in what we do. Over the years, I have heard people prophesy at inappropriate times and then use the excuse, "God made me do it. I couldn't help it." This is actually unscriptural. A prophecy is subject to the person prophesying as we read in 1 Corinthians14:32, *"And the spirits of the prophets are subject to the prophets."* This means you don't blurt out prophecies at inappropriate times, and if a church leader tells you to sit down and be quiet, you do it.

2 Peter 1:21 states that *"For prophecy never came by the will of man, but holy men of God spoke as they were moved by the Holy Spirit".* But God won't force you to prophesy, the prophecy is subject to the person prophesying.

Prophesying doesn't need to be complicated. I was prophesying over a girl many years ago and I felt that she was in distress and was discouraged. So I gave what I thought was one of my most powerful and anointed prophesies ever. I prophesied for about five minutes, and after I had finished, she seemed unmoved. One of the other guys on our team, then stepped in and said, "God wants you to know that you are beautiful." At this, she started bawling and did so for about a half-hour. Just goes to show how simple and "beautiful" a prophecy can be. God never placed the gifts of the Spirit in the Church to pull the Church down. Did it edify? Did it exhort? Did it build you up? If it didn't, then God was not the author of the prophecy.

Don't go looking for words, it may be a sign hard times are coming. Sometimes what God doesn't say is as powerful as what He does say. If God's happy with you, your spending time in His word and in prayer daily, then you may not need a word from a minister. His silence is like He's saying, "Keep going. You're doing great, Just keep flowing with me." Paul said to Timothy to use the prophecies to wage good warfare, so prophecies help us in tough times. When God speaks to us in prophecies we can use this word in prayer to fight the good fight of faith, to wage the good warfare, like it says in 1 Timothy 1:18, "This charge I commit to you, son Timothy, according to the prophecies previously made concerning you, that by them you may wage the good warfare."

How to prophesy

There are five key points you need to understand when learning how to prophesy.

All can prophesy, but there is an order. Let's look at the verse from earlier, 1 Corinthians 14:31-33: *"For you can all prophesy one by one, that all may learn and all may be encouraged. And the spirits of the prophets are subject to the prophets. For God is not the author of confusion but of peace, as in all the churches of the saints."* When broken down, this verse shows us three important factors regarding prophecies: we can all prophesy, one by one, that all may learn and be encouraged.

1. We can all prophesy, everyone.

Yes, that means you. But there is an order to it. We prophesy one by one. We don't do it at random times. We follow the church leadership that we are under.

There should be a learning environment where people feel it's OK to step out and maybe not get it right. As long as the heart is right and the prophecy is seeking to exhort, edify, and comfort, it is very hard to go wrong.

Everyone should feel encouraged, including the person prophesying. I love what it says in Proverbs 11:25, *"The generous soul will be made rich, and he who waters will also be watered himself."* This means that when you prophesy, not only are you building up the person you are prophesying over, but you are also building yourself up.

2. You cannot give what you don't have.

Another key to prophesying is that you cannot speak if you have not heard. The person who has never received anything into his spirit never has anything to minister out of his spirit. In Isaiah 50:4 we read, *"The Lord God has given me the tongue of the learned, that I should know how to speak. A word in season to him who is weary. He awakens me morning by morning. He awakens my ear to hear as the learned."* Do you get out of bed when the alarm wakes you up to pray? We cannot speak if we do not hear, and we do not hear if we do not listen. Prophecy flows from listening to heaven everyday; that is how you get "today's" word for someone. 1 Corinthians 14:24-25 states *"But if all prophesy, and an unbeliever or an uninformed person comes in, he is convinced by all, he is convicted by all. And thus the secrets of his heart are revealed; and so, falling down on his face, he will worship God and report that God is truly among you".* Is this experience missing from our churches today? I think for many churches it is, because we have put more faith in our fancy methods and programs than in the power of God. We don't flow in the power of God in our churches because we have not waited for the Holy Spirit or opened our churches up to him.

3. You can only prophesy in proportion to your faith.

Another thing to be careful of is trying to prophesy too big. We think that our prophecy has to be spectacular. As I mentioned earlier in this chapter, simple prophecies can be powerful, like when my friend told

Gift of Prophecy

that girl that God said she was beautiful. Sometimes the best prophecies are the simple ones anyway. But you can only prophesy in proportion to your faith as it tells us in Romans 12:6, *"Having then gifts differing according to the grace that is given to us, let us use them: if prophecy, let us prophesy in proportion to our faith."*

When I had only been saved about a year a friend and I was praying with a group over a guy named Derek, I could not get a word. I felt God wanted me to pray what was written on his T-Shirt. I thought, "Wow, that is too simple. I am conjuring this up because I have nothing else to pray." While I was pondering this, my friend in the group who was also praying started to pray about what was written on our Derek's shirt. He said that was what he had felt God was speaking to him about. Wow! I'd heard the same thing. Only he'd heard and obeyed while I tried to work it out in my mind because it seemed too simple. In that example I was lacking faith. The good news is we can build faith in our lives in many ways. Romans 10:17 says, *"So then faith comes by hearing, and hearing by the word of God."* Read the Word of God, pray the Word of God, speak the Word of God over your life and into your soul and over your circumstances. This is all seed planting. The more you speak, the more seed your plant and the greater the harvest of faith in your life. Faith grows through the Word of God. Be a student of the Word of God.

4. God only reveals "parts" in prophecies.

In 1 Corinthians 13:9-10,12, we read, *"For we know in part and we prophesy in part. But when that which is perfect has come, then that which is in part will be done away...For now we see in a mirror, dimly, but then face to face. Now I know in part, but then I shall know just as I also am known."* Prophecy mostly will confirm things to people that they already feel. So prophecy should confirm God's voice, it does not replace it. Prophesy always builds up it doesn't tear down. As we see from the verse above, the gift of prophecy is only "in part", it is not perfect or complete, it is open to human interpretation.

If we knew everything, we'd really be something. But the Bible says we *"see in a mirror, dimly."* Don't feel like you have to know everything. Some people ask me after I have prophesied over them, "what does that mean?" If I don't know, I tell them, "I don't know. Ask the Holy Spirit. If it doesn't sit with you, just put pray about it and put it aside." A prophecy is filtered through human interpretation. There is always going to be a measure of human element to every prophecy.

Let me give you an example, many times I have been part of a group who has laid hands on someone to pray. When someone else prays out a prophecy for the person we are praying for and it is the same word I had, I'm saying, "amen, amen" as they are praying because not only do I agree with the prayer, but I had the same word. Sometimes I will pray right after this and explain that I also had the same word and then add to it or prophesy it a bit differently, as it is impossible for it to be word for word as the previous prophecy. Other times I will stay silent just knowing I was there for prayer support. When God gives me the same word, I can support in prayer with greater faith. Either way, how this other person prophesied would not have been identical to how I prophesied it. It doesn't mean that is not of God, it just means that when we get the word it is filtered through us, the "dimly lit mirror." We only get the parts that God reveals to us and then we interpret these parts in a prophecy to the recipient.

Have you ever drunk coffee out of a Styrofoam cup? Regardless of what the coffee tastes like, good or bad, there is always a little bit of Styrofoam aftertaste mingled with the coffee flavor in every cup you drink. Some people say "Oh Lord it's all you it's not me" no it is God using you. So your gift is going to look and sound like you, like drinking coffee from the Styrofoam cup, you are always going to get a bit of a taste of the vessel. The same goes with prophesy, there will always be the "you" flavor to every prophesy that is given. I am not talking about the flesh here, I am talking about your uniqueness. The important thing to realize is that it is never perfect! We only know and prophesy in part. Jesus is the perfect one, and only when He has come to bring us all home to heaven will everything be perfect. So don't beat yourself up if you feel you have blown it when prophesying, but also don't take every word that you receive and base your entire life on it either.

5. Speaking in tongues leads to prophesying.

The more I pray in tongues, the more I flow in prophecy. I always wondered why, but then I read this verse in Acts 19:6, *"And when Paul had laid hands on them, the Holy Spirit came upon them, and they spoke with tongues and prophesied."* In fact I find the more I pray in tongues, the more I flow in the gifts of the Holy Spirit. The simple thing to keep in mind regarding prophesying is that as we act in faith. God will begin to bring words to our mind and heart. We just have to have the faith to step out and speak. When I was a brand new Christian, this seemed like the most fearful experience I could ever imagine, but "*God has not given us a spirit of fear, but of power and of love and of a sound mind*" (2 Timothy 1:7). Step out in love, release the power of prophecy, and don't be controlled by the fear of man. You never know unless you have a go. What have you got to lose?

CHAPTER 14:

Gift of Discerning of Spirits

Gift of discerning of spirits defined: A thought, vision, impression from the Holy Spirit given by God, which makes us realize that spiritual forces can be affecting a person or even ourselves.

The word "discern" may be defined as to recognize and distinguish between. Discernment is a form of direct perception. It is not the gift of suspicion.

There are four ways that the gift of discerning spirits can be beneficial:

1. To help us recognize the presence of the Holy Spirit and the ways in which God is working

A clear example from the Bible comes from John 1:29-32, *"The next day John saw Jesus coming toward him, and said, 'Behold! The Lamb of God who takes away the sin of the world! This is He of whom I said, "After me comes a Man who is preferred before me, for He was before me." I did not know Him; but that He should be revealed to Israel, therefore I came baptizing with water.' And John bore witness, saying, 'I saw the Spirit descending from heaven like a dove, and He remained upon Him.'"* John was able to recognize the presence of the Holy Spirit.

I have been in meetings where I can sense the presence of the Holy Spirit, and other times I've sensed Him leave due to something that happened that He didn't like. Sensing His presence gives us confidence as we minister. Luke 5:17, says *"Now it happened on a certain day, as He was teaching, that there were Pharisees and teachers of the law sitting by, who had come out of every town of Galilee, Judea, and Jerusalem. And the power of the Lord was present to heal them."* When we sense the presence of the Lord to heal, this gives us incredible confidence. I was in a hospital praying for a friend, and I sensed this overwhelming presence of God as I read a

MY FRIEND, THE HOLY SPIRIT

Bible verse. When I looked up everyone else in the room was in tears, as was I, I sensed that the Lord was present to heal and there was faith for a miracle to happen. I prayed that he would be healed, and the next day, he walked out of that hospital never to return. Below is his personal account of this story.

> "I was diagnosed with Acute Renal Failure after going to the emergency room for the third time. My stomach was constantly hurting so bad I could not sleep or find a comfortable position. The doctors first thought I was constipated, dehydrated, etc., but after my third time at the hospital, they finally took my blood and discovered my kidney's were failing. Immediately the doctor's demeanor changed when he read the results and asked me if I had a Living Will. Scary to think about, and my wife did not take it well.
>
> From that point they admitted me to the hospital for further testing. When your kidneys are failing, they measure your creatine levels. At a level 8 you are on dialysis or hooked up to machines to help your kidneys function. I was measuring over 4 and getting worse by the day.
>
> At this point, I was in the hospital now for a couple days and each morning they would take my blood to measure and see how I was progressing. I had hundreds of people praying for me and doctors were perplexed because I was young and healthy and they could not find a reason why this was happening.
>
> Finally my buddy Matt Hubbard called and said he was bringing a friend in to pray for me from his new church. I was pumped because I knew God could heal me. The next morning the kidney specialist had ordered a biopsy to try and figure out what was happening. I did not want that to happen, so I was believing I would be healed by that time.
>
> When [Pastor] Mark came in that night something shifted! When he got there my whole family was there (two sisters, mom and dad) and about 4 or 5 others. As he started to pray, the atmosphere in the room shifted. The presence of God fell in that room like I had never felt before. My family was crying, my friends were crying, and my heart felt like it was going to pump out of my chest. I got really warm and was almost sweating. [Pastor] Mark used a scripture in Isaiah 58 and declared healing in my body. He also prophesied that I would be used to reach others, as well as my wife. It was easily the most powerful time of prayer I had ever felt, seen or heard. Needless to say, the next morning my numbers had decreased and I was on the road to recovery. They did not do the biopsy,

and within two days, I was out of there and home as my numbers continued to drop back to a normal 1.0 during the following three or four days. I had my levels checked annually for the next two years and it was always perfect. Nothing wrong and my kidneys are fine to this day, five years later. Praise God!"

Another example of the gift of discerning spirits in action is found in Acts 14:8-10, *"And in Lystra a certain man without strength in his feet was sitting, a cripple from his mother's womb, who had never walked. This man heard Paul speaking. Paul, observing him intently and seeing that he had faith to be healed, said with a loud voice, 'Stand up straight on your feet!' And he leaped and walked"*. There is nothing more difficult than praying for someone who is in complete unbelief. But in this example, Paul, having the gift of discerning of spirits, could see that this man had faith to be healed. I love also how Mary was able to tune into this gift when she ran to the tomb of Jesus and saw angels, but Peter and John did not see the angels, they saw linen cloth (John 20:1-12).

Just because we don't see or feel God, doesn't mean that He is not there. Radio stations are out there everywhere, but when we don't have the radio on and don't hear them, it doesn't mean that they aren't there. If we tune into the right frequency for that station, we will experience it and know that it exists. The same is true with the Holy Spirit. Often times we must take the time to tune into what He is doing, tune into His voice to hear what He is saying. This will mean tuning out other things, things of the world. You can't listen to two radio stations at the same time (on the same device). One station has to be tuned out so the other can be tuned in.

I was asked to pray for a troubled young man once. We prayed hard but nothing happened. I asked God to show me what was preventing this man from being free. Through the discerning of spirits, I saw unforgiveness in the young man's spirit. Then the Holy Spirit gave me a word of knowledge (this is an example of the gifts working together) that this unforgiveness was toward his father. I asked him about this, and he explained that his father used to whip him with a jug cord (Dad's don't do that!). The moment he repented and forgave his father's wrong behavior, I was able to deliver him from the demonic spirit that held him in bondage. Through the Holy Spirit, I was able to discern a "spirit of unforgiveness," and this helped to set the young man free by the power of God.

2. To reveal character and motivations of human hearts

John 1:47 says, *"Jesus saw Nathanael coming toward Him, and said of* him, *'Behold, an Israelite indeed, in whom is no deceit!' Nathanael said to Him, 'How do You know me?'"* From this scripture we can observe that Jesus was able to see into his spirit. In fact, Nathanael wasn't even in front of Him and Jesus was still able to discern what kind of man that Nathanael was and what was going on in his human spirit. This can be helpful when looking to hire or promote someone, or even if you are trying to tell if someone is born again or not.

One day when I was street witnessing, I was talking about Christ to a guy who told me he had already been saved. But in my Spirit I could tell he was not, so I kept sharing with him. He did not repent and receive Christ as it is very hard for someone to receive the Gospel if they feel they are already righteous. As we progressed in conversation it was evident that he in fact was not saved and his whole idea of being saved was based on his own good works. The Holy Spirit had enabled me to recognize this in the man's life through the gift of the discerning of Spirits.

3. To indentify when evil spirits are the cause of sickness and strife

Mark 5:8-9 says, *"For He said to him, 'Come out of the man, unclean spirit!' Then He asked him, 'What is your name?' And he answered, saying, 'My name is Legion; for we are many.'*" When Jesus prayed for this man to be free from an unclean spirit, the demon did not come out right away. Jesus discerned there was another spirit at work and asked the demon to name itself. Once revealed, Jesus called it out by name and the man was set free. Another case in scripture where we recognize the gift of discerning spirits, particularly in identifying evil spirits is in Matthew 9:32-33, *"As they went out, behold, they brought to Him a man, mute and demon-possessed. And when the demon was cast out, the mute spoke."* Jesus discerned it was a demon causing the man to be unable to speak. I believe quite often we don't see healing because when the sick or disabled are prayed for, the cause of the sickness or disability is not discerned and dealt with. The discerning of spirits can help us minister to those that are sick as in Acts 10:38, *"...God anointed Jesus of Nazareth with the Holy Spirit and with power, who went about doing good and healing all who were oppressed by the devil, for God was with Him."* As the scripture states, Jesus, anointed with the Holy Spirit, healed those oppressed by the devil. Healing often comes only when we deal with the spirits that are the cause of the sickness which comes through the gift of discerning of spirits.

Quite often when the Holy Spirit gives me this gift, I can smell demons and sense them in other ways, such as heaviness around people. When I am around people or praying for or with others, sometimes I know exactly what kind of demon it is. This is similar to when Paul

Gift of Discerning of Spirits

named the exact spirit that was in operation in Acts 16:16-18: *"Now it happened, as we went to prayer, that a certain slave girl possessed with a spirit of divination met us, who brought her masters much profit by fortune-telling. This girl followed Paul and us, and cried out, saying, 'These men are the servants of the Most High God, who proclaim to us the way of salvation.' And this she did for many days. But Paul, greatly annoyed, turned and said to the spirit, 'I command you in the name of Jesus Christ to come out of her.' And he came out that very hour."*

One time during a prayer for a young man, demons were laughing every time I tried to cast them out. My prayer partners said he was free and that's why he was laughing, but I just felt something was not quite right. Through the gift of discerning spirits, I perceived that he was not laughing because he was free, but it was in fact the spirits that were holding him bondage who were laughing at our failure to properly deliver him. I asked the Lord what spirit it was and why he could not be delivered of this. I felt God tell me to ask him if there were any other sins he still had not come clean of and confessed. It took some time, but finally he shamefully admitted that he had been sleeping with prostitutes. The moment he confessed this and repented and renounced this sin, the demons came out and he was powerfully delivered.

Be careful, however, not to take this stuff to the extreme. Not everyone has a demon! I was once praying for a young man with a friend of mine (an overzealous friend). The young man was struggling with some personal stuff, and as we were praying for him, my friend suddenly yelled at the young man, "name yourself!" The young man calmly replied, "Karl." Karl was his actual name. It wasn't a demon's name, he wasn't manifesting, and he wasn't in need of deliverance.

4. To discern false doctrine and/or if someone is trying to deceive you

A prime example of this occurs in Acts 5:1-3, *"But a certain man named Ananias, with Sapphira his wife, sold a possession. And he kept back part of the proceeds, his wife also being aware of it, and brought a certain part and laid it at the apostles' feet. But Peter said, 'Ananias, why has Satan filled your heart to lie to the Holy Spirit and keep back part of the price of the land for yourself?'"*

When I was newly saved, I visited a friend's church that did not allow women to minister in any way at all. The men did everything and the women were expected to remain silent. In my heart I felt this doctrine was false. I didn't yet know about Galatians 3:28 that says, *"There is neither Jew nor Greek, there is neither slave nor free, there is neither male nor female; for you are all one in Christ Jesus."*

MY FRIEND, THE HOLY SPIRIT

At the time, I didn't know what to say but felt in my heart to ask questions. I spoke to one of the elders there, and he explained that they felt there were certain verses in the Bible supporting their doctrine for how they treated women. (For the sake of this book I am not going to go into this doctrinal debate, being that there are other great books out there for that.) I didn't know how to reply to his superior biblical knowledge and years of experience, because I had only been saved for six months. In my mind, I asked the Holy Spirit to guide me. I then felt the Holy Spirit ask me to look. "Where?" I thought. I looked at the walls and saw multiple pictures of missionaries with people of all different races in third-world countries.

I turned to the elder and asked, "So women in no way are allowed to minister in church?" The church elder said, "Correct." I then asked, "What is church?" He replied, "Anywhere God's people gather together." So I replied, "I notice all these men and women missionaries all over your walls. I see many pictures of women praying for people with different colored skin and with their children also. And there are other pictures of them with open Bibles teaching God's word." He nervously replied, "Yes." So I asked, "Why then are women allowed to speak and minister to people and children in third world countries?" He replied, "Ummm, well that isn't Church," and then he quickly excused himself before I could ask anything more.

The discerning of spirits helped me to see false doctrine and hypocrisy, even though I had been only recently saved. This certain church was not allowing women to minister to the people in their home town, but felt that it was OK for them to minister overseas. They also allowed women to minister in their church to children. So not only was there a great deal of hypocrisy but also false doctrine was masking this.

As with all of the gifts of the Holy Spirit in order to operate effectively in this gift, you must develop a sensitivity to the Holy Spirit and to His voice.

CHAPTER 15:

Gift of Various Kinds of Tongues

Various kinds of tongues defined: Speaking in a language you do not know.

The Greek word for tongues is "glossa", where we get glossary (which means language). Therefore speaking in tongues is speaking in a language that you do not know and have not learned.

Has there been more controversy over a gift of the spirit than the gift of tongues? For the most part, I believe that people are afraid of what they do not understand and there is little to no understanding due to little to no teaching on this subject. A manifestation of tongues establishes that God is real and at work amongst His people. When the Holy Spirit was initially poured out on the day of Pentecost (Acts 2) God used tongues when everyone was watching, and they heard the speakers talking in their own languages even though they had never learned them.

Notice it is not called the "gift of tongues" as I hear many people refer to it as. It is called "various kinds of tongues" meaning different genres of tongues.

This gift has both public (as a ministry gift) and private use (as a spiritual gift) as previously shown earlier in this book. In this chapter we will focus on the "spiritual" gift. All godly things are "spiritual" in nature. However, just because someone speaks in tongues, there is no guarantee that this person is living a spiritual life. Once God gives us a gift, he does not retract it.

Gifts were never given with the purpose of dividing believers. When those who speak in tongues misuse it so it becomes divisive it indicates a lack of love. And those who forbid it do the Church a disservice because they contradict the teaching of the apostle Paul. The Bible talks about the tongues of men or of angels (1 Corinthians 13:1). The various kinds of tongues we can see from scripture are listed below.

1. Other languages never learned, tongues of men (Acts 2:1-8).

On the day of Pentecost, the disciples spoke in foreign languages they had never learned; this does not require interpretation as it is speaking directly to the ears of someone else in their own language (while it may be foreign to you it is not to them).

2. Unknown languages, or New Tongues.

This is our personal prayer language. 1 Corinthians 14:2 says, *"For he who speaks in a tongue does not speak to men but to God, for no one understands him; however, in the spirit he speaks mysteries".*

This genre of tongues is for God, from man, by the Holy Spirit. It is not for others so no interpretation is necessary.

3. Angelic languages, which require interpretation.

This is a public tongue, a message from God to the people. These messages require interpretation as they are for man from God.

1 Corinthians 14:13: *"Therefore let him who speaks in a tongue pray that he may interpret."*

This is why the gift is called "various kinds of tongues," not "gift of tongues". Let's look at each of these genres of tongues.

1. Other languages never learned, tongues of men.

Speaking in a foreign language that you have not yet learned

Take a look at what it says in Acts 2:1-8:

> *"When the Day of Pentecost had fully come, they were all with one accord in one place. And suddenly there came a sound from heaven, as of a rushing mighty wind, and it filled the whole house where they were sitting. Then there appeared to them divided tongues, as of fire, and one sat upon each of them. And they were all filled with the Holy Spirit and began to speak with other tongues, as the Spirit gave them utterance. And there were dwelling in Jerusalem Jews, devout men, from every nation under heaven. And when this sound occurred, the multitude came together, and were confused, because everyone heard them speak in his own language. Then they were all amazed and marveled, saying to one another, 'Look,*

Gift of Various Kinds of Tongues

are not all these who speak Galileans? And how is it that we hear, each in our own language in which we were born?'"

1 Corinthians 14:22 says, *"Therefore tongues are for a sign, not to those who believe but to unbelievers; but prophesying is not for unbelievers but for those who believe."* These tongues that were poured in Acts 2 were not the same as the "personal prayer language" tongues, commonly referred to in the Bible as "praying in the Spirit." This is why the gift is called "various kinds of tongues." We see in this passage that those who received the baptism of the Holy Spirit spoke in languages that they had not learned previously. This leads to wonder and amazement and an incredible altar call of souls!

Rodney Howard Browne shares a story in his book about how a missionary woman who had been in India for some time and had returned home deeply discouraged. When she attended her home church, a message was given in tongues. The missionary then stood and shared that there would be no interpretation. She revealed that the message was for her because it had been given in the dialect of a remote Indian village that she had just come from. And since there had not been any other westerner that had ever been there, she knew this message was from God. The message was for her to return as her time there was not yet finished. There will be those who will be used frequently in this way as they travel as missionaries a lot. Personally I have not found very many occasions where God has used me in this way, and in the Bible we only see the one occurrence. This is not to say that it is not a powerful use of tongues.

2. Unknown languages, or New Tongues.

This is our personal prayer language. Much of this chapter will focus on this genre of tongues. Praying in the Spirit, or your personal prayer language, is a powerful gateway to the other eight gifts of the Spirit. The reason for this, I believe, is based simply around the law of second nature. When I played football our coaches would teach us things repetitively so that when it came to game time scenarios, we would react and do these things we had learned in training without even thinking because we had so immersed ourselves with these reactions in training that they had become part of our thinking.

Pray Always

Our personal prayer language is the one gift that we can operate in as often as possible as the Bible says we should "pray always". When we speak in our personal prayer language (praying in tongues) we are setting our mind and heart on the things of the Spirit. This familiarizes us to spiritual things. So when we are out in the world it becomes much easier to recognize when God is moving and what God is saying because spiritual things become second nature to us. If you are operating consistently in the gift of various kinds of tongues, it is much easier to operate in the other eight gifts.

Gateway Gift

Tongues has been mentioned and categorized by many as the "least of the gifts", however, in comparison with the other gifts, the most space has been devoted to discussing it in the Bible. Think of this, 3,000 Jews were saved through the gift of tongues, and this was the most difficult group to covert at the time.

If the "least of the gifts" can accomplish this amazing miracle, what amazing things can the greatest gifts accomplish? Meaning God has lowered the entrance point for us into the supernatural world to the lowest level of difficulty.

For this reason, I call it the gateway gift. It is the gift you first receive as evidence you have been baptized in the Holy Spirit. Some people teach that the tongues you speak when you are first baptized in the Holy Spirit is different than the spiritual gift of tongues. However, I do not see any biblical teaching to support this doctrine at all.

Paul prayed in tongues

In 1 Corinthians 14:18 Paul said, *"I speak in tongues more than all of you."* Paul did not make a claim like this about anything else. Here he is speaking about his personal prayer language.

The church in Corinth spoke to each other in tongues during everyday conversation, which he had to rebuke them for. So this means Paul would have spoken in tongues a lot of the time.

Paul said that he spoke in tongues more than the Corinthian Church (The Corinthian Church which spoke in tongues so much that they would bless the meal [say grace] in tongues which was not the proper use of tongues at all). Imagine going to eat at a friend's place. The time to eat has arrived and your host says, "Let's say grace", and then they proceed to speak in tongues for a few minutes. That is what the Corinthian Church had been doing.

Don't forbid speaking in tongues

Paul also taught that no one should forbid others to speak in tongues. In 1 Corinthians 14:39-40, it says, *"Therefore, brethren, desire earnestly to prophesy, and do not forbid to speak with tongues. Let all*

Gift of Various Kinds of Tongues

things be done decently and in order." I gather from this scripture that there must have been people who were preventing others from speaking in tongues, much like we see in some churches today where people are being taught not to speak in tongues or that tongues is not for today. Paul brought correction to this by telling the Church at Corinth, "Let people speak in tongues." Scripture plainly commands that we should not forbid speaking in tongues, yet there are churches that teach that speaking in tongues is from the devil (Which of course is a false doctrine and cannot be supported anywhere in scripture).

Knowing that speaking in tongues holds a high rank of importance is all the more reason to understand the three key purposes of this spiritual gift, which are:

1. A sign (The evidence of baptism of the Holy Spirit)
2. Edification
3. Praying God's perfect will

Let's examine these three purposes further.

A Sign

The first purpose, a sign, is talked about in the book of Acts. We will examine three different passages below in order to determine that the evidence of people being baptized in the Holy Spirit is speaking in tongues. This is how you know you have been baptized. Tongues are the "sign" or "receipt" that we have received the baptism of the Holy Spirit.

"And they were all filled with the Holy Spirit and began to speak with other tongues, as the Spirit gave them utterance" (Acts 2:4). Please note in this verse that it says all were filled and not some.

"While Peter was still speaking these words, the Holy Spirit fell upon all those who heard the word. And those of the circumcision who believed were astonished, as many as came with Peter, because the gift of the Holy Spirit had been poured out on the Gentiles also. For they heard them speak with tongues and magnify God" (Acts 10:44-46). From this passage you can see that they only knew that the Holy Spirit had been poured out on the Gentiles because they heard them speak in tongues and magnify God, showing that speaking in tongues is the evidence for the baptism of the Holy Spirit. But I love that the phrase "magnify God" is added, because everything we do should magnify God.

"And when Paul had laid hands on them, the Holy Spirit came upon them, and they spoke with tongues and prophesied" (Acts 19:6). Here they not only spoke in tongues after being baptized in the Holy Spirit, they also prophesied! One of the most beautiful things you will ever see

(along with a person receiving salvation and getting water baptized) is when you see someone receive the gift of the Holy Spirit. When I see people lined up ready to receive the baptism of the Holy Spirit, and then the Holy Spirit descends upon them, their countenance changes. It is quite magnificent to me. I feel my heart swell up with emotion in the same way it does when I see one of my children do something amazing. Then I lay hands on them and pray for them to receive the baptism of the Holy Spirit. Many times they are already speaking in tongues before I even get to do this. Other times they just need a little bit of encouragement, so I will pray alongside them in tongues until it starts flowing out of them so they don't feel so self-conscious. The stories of how much people's lives have changed once they received the baptism and started praying in tongues is incredible.

How long you should pray in tongues each day is up to you. If Paul, who wrote two-thirds of the New Testament, spoke in tongues more than everyone in the Church at Corinth, then I question how much more we need to be praying consistently in tongues every day. You can pray in the car, in the shower, when you exercise and when you have your daily time of prayer of course.

When I was first baptized with the Holy Spirit I could not stop praying in tongues (partly due to the fact that if I thought if I stopped that I may lose the ability to speak in tongues).

Edify

The second purpose is to edify. In Jude 1:20, it says, *"But you, beloved, building yourselves up on your most holy faith, praying in the Holy Spirit..."* And 1 Corinthians 14:4 says, *"He who speaks in a tongue edifies himself, but he who prophesies edifies the church."*

We understand that the above verses are referring to your personal prayer language (not a public message in tongues). So how do we build ourselves up? By praying in tongues. The more built up you are, the more you can build up others.

The Greek word for edifies is "charge." The best way I have heard this described is an example of charging a battery. If you have a digital camera (most have rechargeable lithium batteries), then you would charge this battery until it has the power to do what it was made to do (power a digital camera).

Praying in tongues charges you up so that you are enabled and empowered to do everything that God has called you and made you to do.

Gift of Various Kinds of Tongues

Remember Paul spoke in tongues more than everyone, so he was really saying, "I thank God that I build/charge myself up by speaking in tongues more than all of you!"

If Paul needed to speak in tongues more than the entire church to build and charge himself up, I know I sure need to do this daily, praying in tongues and charging my inner man, building and edifying my spirit so I can do what God has called me to do. When you feel your spiritual battery running dry, Jude 1:20 and Corinthians 14:4 tell you how to recharge!

How long should you speak in tongues each day?

As long as you want, really. The longest I have prayed in tongues is four hours (once or twice), and that was tough going. So I would just say until you are full.

How do you know when your full? How do you get full of water? By drinking until you are full. In order to recharge, you must keep praying until the burden lifts and you sense a note of peace in your spirit. The heaviness should fade and you should sense a lightness in your spirit. Something in your spirit will seem full, and it will feel like it's time to stop.

John 7:37: *"On the last day, that great day of the feast, Jesus stood and cried out, saying, 'If anyone thirsts, let him come to Me and drink."*

1 Corinthians 12:13: "*For by one Spirit we were all baptized into one body—whether Jews or Greeks, whether slaves or free—and have all been made to drink into one Spirit*".

Have you ever been at a restaurant, ordered a meal and ate, but felt cheated. You were still hungry. Likewise with prayer, sometimes we leave the Holy Spirit and the place of prayer too early, and we cheat ourselves.

The Bible teaches us to pray always in Ephesians 6:18. In fact "praying always in the Spirit" is part of putting on the armor of God. Let's pick up the passage from verse 17 of Ephesians 6 (Start from verse 10 to read the whole passage): "*And take the helmet of salvation, and the sword of the Spirit, which is the word of God; praying always with all prayer and supplication in the Spirit, being watchful to this end with all perseverance and supplication for all the saints—and for me, that utterance may be given to me, that I may open my mouth boldly to make known the mystery of the gospel, for which I am an ambassador in chains; that in it I may speak boldly, as I ought to speak.*"

So, pray in tongues "in the Spirit" always and whenever you can throughout the day when appropriate, without being a weirdo of course.

MY FRIEND, THE HOLY SPIRIT

When my oldest daughter Charlize was two, my wife and I went on our first trip without the kids to Hawaii. We did video chat with the kids a couple of times, which was a lot of fun. Summer returned home after four days, but I stayed there an extra two days for work-related stuff. The night I called home for a video chat, Summer left the room and it was just me and my little Charlize sitting by herself in my big black office chair. Well, we talked about all kinds of random things, from the lollipop she was eating to blowing kisses to each other, to pretend tickling each other and about what kind of puppy she would get for her birthday. After some time I felt it was time to wind it up and say goodnight, so I said to Charlize that I loved her and would see her in a couple of days. Charlize replied, "No, Daddy, we are talking. We are talking, Daddy." Her crave for connection just melted my heart. We spoke for a while longer, again mostly random comments of conversation (Isn't that what a lot of our prayers to God are, by the way?). And of course, when I tried to wrap it up and Charlize again spoke firmly, "No, Daddy, we are talking." I did eventually get finished with the call and blew lots of kisses. The point is the Holy Spirit is a lot like Charlize. He craves connection with us because we were created for connection with Him. Many times we seek to go and He is saying, "No, we are talking, don't go." But how often do we leave too soon, and we miss that intimate connection with heaven via the Holy Spirit. Stay in the place of prayer until you feel the urge from the Holy Spirit subside.

Perfect Will

The third purpose of praying in tongues is to pray God's perfect will as we learn from Romans 8:26-27, *"Likewise the Spirit also helps in our weaknesses. For we do not know what we should pray for as we ought, but the Spirit Himself makes intercession for us with groaning's which cannot be uttered. Now He who searches the hearts knows what the mind of the Spirit is, because He makes intercession for the saints according to the will of God."*

Praying in tongues is so powerful that when we do this, we are praying the perfect will of God every time! This perfect will of God is mentioned in Romans 12:2: *"And do not be conformed to this world, but be transformed by the renewing of your mind, that you may prove what is that good and acceptable and perfect will of God."*

How do we prove the good, acceptable and perfect will of God? If we persist only by praying in our own understanding, we may find ourselves asking only for the acceptable will of God and not His perfect will.

Gift of Various Kinds of Tongues

I believe the reason that Paul spoke in tongues more than anyone was that when you pray in tongues you are praying the perfect will of God. Praying in English (or your natural tongue) is important, but equally as important is praying in tongues. You do not know what things you may face today, this week, month or year, but the Holy Spirit knows and can help you to pray about such things.

If we pray and ask for things in a certain way, even if it is not God's best for us or His perfect will, God will often permit it as He did in 1 Samuel 8 when God didn't want Israel to have a King. But because they kept asking for one, He eventually gave in and said, "All right, if you want it that way, go ahead." And He permitted it. This is what can happen if we only pray out of our natural understanding for something we want.

Ephesians 6:18 says, to be *"praying always with all prayer and supplication in the Spirit, being watchful to this end with all perseverance and supplication for all the saints..."*

How can we pray for ALL the saints, unless we are praying in tongues? We don't know all the saints. It is simply not possible without tongues. The Holy Spirit makes intercession through us via the gift of tongues and enables us to pray about things that we don't know about. It's not possible to know "all the saints", but you can be praying for all the saints, and be praying the perfect will of God by praying in tongues.

What an amazing thought that you could be praying for a Christian brother or sister in need that you don't even know. I believe we will see the full result of all our praying in tongues when we get to heaven.

How often can we pray in tongues?

Whenever we want. God sets no limitations on prayer. In fact he commands us to "pray always" (Ephesians 6:18). Because speaking in tongues is prayer, we can pray in tongues whenever we want (within reason). This is not necessarily so with all the other gifts; although one could argue you could always prophesy over yourself.

This should not be confused with the ministry gift of tongues in a public assembly or praying in tongues in front of others where it is not appropriate, like at the dinner table (which is what the Corinthian Church was doing in 1 Corinthians 14:16-17). But as far as your personal praying in tongues, you can do this as often as you will.

Praying in tongues yields our life as a vessel for the Holy Spirit to pray for anyone and anything that is happening in the world. When you're praying in tongues, what you are really doing is saying, "Holy Spirit, I yield myself to you so that You can pray through me about anything you want."

In reality, this is another way of saying, "Not my will, but Your will be done."

Divine Secrets

1 Corinthians 14:2 says, *"For he who speaks in a tongue does not speak to men but to God, for no one understands him; however, in the spirit he speaks mysteries."* The words "speak mysteries" are actually better translated as "divine secrets." No man can understand you when you pray as you are talking "divine secrets" to the Father. It also means that Satan cannot understand either.

There are things that God wants you to pray that he doesn't want you or the devil to know. He doesn't want you to know so that you won't interfere with what the Holy Spirit is praying through you.

And He doesn't want the devil to know so he can't thwart the plans of the Holy Spirit. So I believe the primary reason the devil fights tongues as he does is because he cannot get in on the conversation. He cannot know what you are praying about if you are praying the divine mysteries (secrets) of God, the things only God knows. So the Devil fights tongues in every way he can.

Wheels of Prayer

Paul prayed in tongues and in his own language. He wrote in 1 Corinthians 14:14-15, *"For if I pray in a tongue, my spirit prays, but my understanding is unfruitful. What is the conclusion then? I will pray with the spirit, and I will also pray with the understanding. I will sing with the spirit, and I will also sing with the understanding."*

Obviously the words "in the spirit" refer to tongues, and "understanding" refers to your own language. You cannot get by on only praying in your own language. Paul said he prayed with tongues and with understanding. We don't know what we should always pray for (Romans 8:26), which is why we need both wheels of prayer. Our spirit can pray and our mind doesn't know what we are praying for; this is probably a good thing.

Now that you have good idea of the purpose of the gift of various kinds of tongues, I want to talk about some of the main objections people have about this gift.

Did Jesus speak in tongues?

One of the concerns is that Jesus did not speak in tongues and that there is no record of Jesus speaking in tongues or using the gift of

Gift of Various Kinds of Tongues

interpretation of tongues, even though the other seven gifts are evident in Jesus' ministry. Keep in mind, however, Jesus wasn't sent into all the world.

The disciple's were sent into all the world to share the Gospel. These two gifts are distinctive with the outpouring of the Holy Spirit on the day of Pentecost. Jesus even spoke about how believers would operate in these gifts after he left, where it's written, *"And these signs will follow those who believe: In My name they will cast out demons; they will speak with new tongues; they will take up serpents; and if they drink anything deadly, it will by no means hurt them; they will lay hands on the sick, and they will recover"* (Mark 16:17-18).

Jesus declared that there would be five supernatural signs that would follow all believers. Jesus did not say a few believers, but all. So it is clear that even though there is no record of Jesus speaking in tongues, He expects all of His Church to.

Tongues is from the devil?

The second objection is that some think speaking in tongues comes from the devil, which I have to admit is probably one of the most ignorant statements I have heard. Not only is this not supported anywhere in scripture, but I believe it is a "doctrine of demons" to attempt to try and rob the Church of one of its most powerful gifts. Think about this: if speaking in tongues is really of the devil, why isn't everyone who is unsaved speaking in tongues? If tongues were really that demonic, then everyone in the nightclubs, pubs, and strip clubs would all be speaking in tongues.

I've heard Kenneth Hagin recount a powerful story about a member of another church who got saved, but his pastor objected to his being baptized in the Holy Spirit and speaking in tongues. This new church member said, "Pastor, I know tongues is not of the devil because I had everything the devil could give me when I was a sinner, and if tongues were of the devil, I would have had it long ago. But I didn't receive this gift until I turned my back on the devil and got saved and filled with the Holy Ghost!"

Have tongues ceased?

Another objection is that some believe speaking in tongues has ceased. In my opinion, this objection is the most common about this spiritual gift. And the scripture used to back up this misconception has been misinterpreted. 1 Corinthians 13:8: *"Love never fails. But whether there are prophecies, they will fail; whether there are tongues, they will cease; whether there is knowledge, it will vanish away. For we know in part and we prophesy in part. But when that which is perfect has come, then that which is in part will be done away."*

While it does state tongues shall cease, it does not say they have. It also says prophecies will fail and knowledge will vanish. If tongues have now ceased, then prophecies and knowledge should have also. So tongues haven't ceased anymore than knowledge has vanished and prophecies have failed.

It is unfortunate that some Christians have taken a solitary scripture and based an entire false doctrine around it. This is the only scripture the objecting Christians quote to support such a false claim, whereas there are many scriptures supporting the use of tongues as a gift for today, as we have already seen.

Those who say tongues have ceased are spreading a false doctrine that has no scriptural backing. Do not be deceived by those who preach and teach this.

Tongues is only for the Apostles.

The last objection that I've heard is that only the apostles had the baptism and gifts. This is another inaccurate teaching. Clearly we see in scripture that this is not so. Nowhere in the Bible does it say that only the apostles can minister the baptism of the Holy Spirit. In fact we see the opposite from scripture. We see many other ordinary disciples and followers of Christ moving in the gifts of the Spirit who were not one of the original apostles.

Out of the 120 people there on the day of Pentecost, did only the 12 Apostles receive the Holy Spirit? No, all 120 did. What would be the point of the other 108 waiting for nothing?

The last recorded incident of people receiving the Holy Spirit happened about 20 years after the day of Pentecost, as recorded in Acts 19:1-6,

> *"And it happened, while Apollos was at Corinth, that Paul, having passed through the upper regions, came to Ephesus. And finding some disciples he said to them, 'Did you receive the Holy Spirit when you believed?' So they said to him, 'We have not so much as heard whether there is a Holy Spirit.' And he said to them, 'Into what then were you baptized?' So they said, 'Into John's baptism.' Then Paul said, 'John indeed baptized with a baptism of repentance, saying to the people that they should believe on Him who would come after him, that is, on Christ Jesus.' When they heard this, they were baptized in the name of the Lord Jesus. And when Paul had laid hands on them, the Holy Spirit came upon them, and they spoke with tongues and prophesied."*

Gift of Various Kinds of Tongues

The Holy Spirit was still being poured out then and people were still being baptized 20 years after the day of Pentecost, just like He is still being poured out today.

The closer we stay to the Word of God the more accurate we will be in whatever we do.

Not only are there objections to using the gift of various kinds of tongues, but there are also several common misconceptions amongst those who do use the gift. The most common misconceptions are listed and explained below.

- Speaking in tongues isn't for everyone.
- You can't pray in tongues at will.
- I can pray in tongues whenever I want, in front of whomever I want.

Speaking in tongues isn't for everyone.

This is the most common misconception and reason people do not speak in tongues. Those who believe this often quote (out of context) 1 Corinthians 12:29-30: *"Are all apostles? Are all prophets? Are all teachers? Are all workers of miracles? Do all have gifts of healings? Do all speak with tongues? Do all interpret?"*.

Paul is not talking about spiritual gifts but ministry gifts. He starts out by asking if all are apostles (ministry gift), if all are prophets (ministry gift), and if all are teachers (ministry gift).

In this passage, Paul is clearly not referring to the nine gifts of the spirit. If you read the two preceding verses (27 and 28), where it says, *"Now you are the body of Christ, and members individually. And God has appointed these in the church: first apostles, second prophets, third teachers, after that miracles, then gifts of healings, helps, administrations, varieties of tongues,"* Paul is speaking about ministry gifts. Therefore, the whole context of verses 27 through 30 is about ministry gifts, not the gifts of the Spirit.

If Paul was not talking about ministry gifts here, then why would he ask, "are all prophets?" This would imply that not all can prophesy? But Paul clearly states that all can prophesy in 1 Corinthians 14:31, *"For you can all prophesy one by one, that all may learn and all may be encouraged."* If he had been talking about spiritual gifts here, then he would have been contradicting himself.

This passage also shows that there are different rules for ministry gifts than there are for spiritual gifts. With a ministry gift not all are prophets but all may prophesy (spiritual gift); not all speak with tongues in a public assembly (ministry gift), but all may have a personal prayer language (spiritual gift).

MY FRIEND, THE HOLY SPIRIT

Diversity of tongues is also a ministry gift. Not all speak a public tongue (ministry gift) and not all interpret. But heed the instruction given in 1 Corinthians 14:27-28, *"If anyone speaks in a tongue, let there be two or at the most three, each in turn, and let one interpret. But if there is no interpreter, let him keep silent in church, and let him speak to himself and to God."*

The Bible clearly says that you must have someone in the office of an interpreter for the public tongue to function. There are those that are called to minister in diversity of tongues and interpretation in a public assembly, but not everyone is called to that ministry. God is the one who chooses who has this ministry gift.

You can't pray in tongues at will.

Of course you can, it is the one gift that you can function in at will. Pay close attention to what was written in 1 Corinthians 14:14-15, *"For if I pray in a tongue, my spirit prays, but my understanding is unfruitful. What is the conclusion then? I will pray with the spirit, and I will also pray with the understanding. I will sing with the spirit, and I will also sing with the understanding."*

Notice that Paul says, "I will". It is by his will that he prays with the Spirit (tongues).

God also commands that we pray always, and we already know that speaking in tongues is prayer. It does not get much simpler than that. Ephesians 6:18: *"praying always with all prayer and supplication in the Spirit, being watchful to this end with all perseverance and supplication for all the saints—".*

It's the big "S" in Spirit. It means praying always in the Holy Spirit, praying in tongues!

I would think it would be extremely difficult to pray constantly during the day in English. I would run out of things to pray for each day. But praying in tongues enables me to pray all through the day. I don't know what I am praying for, but I know I am praying the perfect will of God and somebody somewhere is the recipient of my obedience to pray. I pray in tongues in the shower, in the car, when I am walking, running, riding or swimming.

Does this mean that I should pray in tongues when I am at work? I once prayed in tongues all through my school day when I first got saved. I did so by quietly whispering and even then an unbeliever heard this and was confused. So we must use wisdom. The Bible says to pray always, but it also says that if we pray in front of others that they will not be edified. So we must approach the scriptures with balance. But speaking out in tongues at inappropriate times is not

Gift of Various Kinds of Tongues

scriptural (like weddings, meal times, or while the pastor is preaching, etc...). This leads us to the final common misconception about tongues.

I can pray in tongues whenever I want in front of whomever I want.

1 Corinthians 14:16-17 says, *"Otherwise, if you bless with the Spirit, how will he who occupies the place of the uninformed say 'Amen' at your giving of thanks, since he does not understand what you say? For you indeed give thanks well, but the other is not edified."*

In this passage, Paul explains that if you bless the food by speaking in tongues and someone else is present, it is not appropriate since they would not understand what you are saying and would not be edified. It would be selfish on our part to speak in tongues in this kind of setting because it would create confusion.

Kenneth Hagin shares this story about tongues being used at an inappropriate time and setting: "A certain minister's wife had a part to read during a wedding ceremony. After her husband spoke, she was to take her turn, but instead she fell to the ground, groaning and moaning in tongues, supposedly in travail for someone who needed prayer. People started leaving the wedding by the droves, which caused huge embarrassment to both families and reinforced the belief for those who don't believe in tongues, who probably left saying, "I knew those ignoramuses who speak in tongues were crazy."

If you ever do get that burden, excuse yourself by saying something like, "I am sorry I am going to have to leave," and go somewhere private. Or if those with you are Spirit-filled, it may be appropriate to get them to join you by permission. Always ask yourself this question before speaking in tongues out loud in front of others: I may edify myself, but is what I am about to do going to edify the people around me?

In my experience, I've heard many become confused about when it's appropriate to speak in tongues. Let me clarify this subject, by looking again at 1 Corinthians 14:27-28 where it says, *"If anyone speaks in a tongue, let there be two or at the most three, each in turn, and let one interpret. But if there is no interpreter, let him keep silent in church, and let him speak to himself and to God."*

It doesn't say that we cannot speak in tongues at church, but rather what is spoken in tongues is between the individual and God. So Paul was saying that the purpose of tongues was not for preaching and teaching but for personal edification only when he wrote, *"Yet in the church I would rather speak five words with my understanding, that I may teach others also, than ten thousand words in a tongue"* in 1 Corinthians 14:19.

If believers are all praising God together in tongues in church, it is acceptable, but it wouldn't be right for people to try and teach or preach or call out during preaching in tongues.

Praying together in a corporate setting

This is the question I receive the most from people when speaking, "Is it ok for many Christians to all be praying in tongues at the same time in a corporate setting?" Absolutely! Now this may ruffle some feathers, but think about this for a moment, why do you believe this? 1 Corinthians 14:28: *"But if there is no interpreter, let him keep silent in church, and let him speak to himself and to God."* But this is not referring to many people all praying together in tongues at once; this is specifically referring to someone speaking all on their own in tongues in front of a public assembly and then not giving an interpretation or there being no church ordained interpreter present. Paul rightly says if there is no interpreter then keep silent. Yet many people use that verse incorrectly to justify no corporate praying of tongues, which is taking this scripture out of context and twisting it to fit a theology that is not biblical. Remember the gift is "various kinds of tongues". So there is private use of tongues and public, you cannot take a "public tongues" verse and apply it to your personal prayer language. You must interpret the scripture in context, not out of context.

So when we are all speaking together in tongues in a corporate setting or in a prayer meeting, then it is fine and we don't need to interpret, because the tongues we are speaking is not for others since you are praying to God. It would be the same if I was in a corporate prayer meeting and someone was praying in German next to me. He wouldn't need to give me an interpretation because he was not praying to me, but to God. Imagine being at an international conference and everyone around you is praying in a different language, does anyone need to provide you with an interpretation of what they are praying? Of course not! Why? Because they are not praying for you or to you. Now if they had the microphone and prayed in their language and no one else there knew German, then would they need an interpretation for others to understand? Of course they would!

Yet there are some religious folk around who, in a corporate setting if everyone is praying and someone is praying in tongues, will be offended, but these same people wouldn't be offended if the person they were standing next to was speaking in French to God. So why get offended when someone speaks in a heavenly language? To me, this is hypocrisy. Elevating the human language of French or German

Gift of Various Kinds of Tongues

above the spiritual gift of tongues. Think of this incredible thought, what other way is there to have all the Church praying the perfect will of God at the same time? Praying in tongues in a corporate setting is beautiful and powerful. When all the people of God in one place are praying the "perfect will of God" this makes for powerful results. How else can you get everyone in the same place praying the perfect will of God in perfect unity? But as we learned earlier in Romans 8:26 that is exactly what happens when we pray in tongues, we are praying the perfect will of God, which is why the devil hates it when all the Church prays in tongues at the same time. But wait there is more! If the entire Church prays in tongues at the same time and the perfect will of God is being prayed for by all present then there is perfect unity in prayer and the devil also has no idea what is being prayed about!

1 Corinthians 14:2 *"For he who speaks in a tongue does not speak to men but to God, for no one understands him; however, in the spirit he speaks mysteries"*. We learnt earlier that "mysteries" is "divine secrets". If when we pray in tongues we speak mysteries, then you don't need to interpret because it is a divine secret, no one else is meant to know what you are praying about! That's why the above verse states "no one understands him", it is a divine secret between you and God, so when all pray together in tongues the perfect will of God is being prayed and the devil has no idea what the Church is praying about. So it seems that 1 Corinthians 14:2 and verse 28 contradict each other, but God does not contradict himself, one is referring to the public use of tongues, the other your personal prayer language.

3. Angelic languages, which require interpretation.

Bringing a message in a public meeting

This goes hand in hand with the gift "interpretation of tongues," so we will cover how this works in the next chapter.

CHAPTER 16:

Gift of Interpretation of Tongues

Interpretation of tongues defined: This is a thought, impression or vision from God whereby an interpretation (not a translation) of a public tongue message is given. A supernatural showing forth of that which has been said in an unknown tongue (language).

We gain considerable understanding about this gift from 1 Corinthians 14:27-28, *"If anyone speaks in a tongue (public), let there be two or at the most three, each in turn, and let one interpret (public). But if there is no interpreter, let him keep silent in church, and let him speak to himself and to God (private)"* (words in parenthesis mine).

First we learn that there should be a maximum of three messages spoken in tongues while meeting together and it must be followed with an interpretation. Secondly, we are taught that the church must have an interpreter or the one speaking the message must be able to interpret his own message.

We don't commonly see this gift in churches these days, and I believe that is because either churches don't believe in this gift or they have a poor understanding of them and their application.

Some people have taken from the above scripture that it is instructing us to remain silent in church and never speak in tongues in a corporate setting. But if you look at the context of this verse, it is simply stating that if you have a message in tongues but don't have the interpretation or there is no "church-ordained" interpreter present, then don't speak it out. This doesn't mean you can't sing or pray to God in tongues (as long as you are not the only one doing this), which is what the part in the verse, "let him speak to himself and to God" is referring to.

If you happen to be somewhere where there is no interpreter, you must be able to interpret before you speak out in a tongue. Be mindful that if there is no interpreter and the person wanting to speak out loud in tongues does not possess the interpretation, he should keep silent and only speak to himself and God.

1 Corinthians 4:13 says, *"Therefore let him who speaks in a tongue pray that he may interpret."*

The person giving message in tongues must always be prepared to interpret it. It is too easy to stand up, speak in tongues, and then sit down. Anyone can get up and speak in tongues, but giving the interpretation is an entirely different matter. So do not bring a public message in tongues unless you are prepared also to bring the interpretation if no one else does.

How this gift generally flows in a public setting

After a person has spoken out in an unknown tongue (heavenly language). This utterance is then followed up by a timely interpretation of the tongue in the language of the people who are present. This is given either through the original person used to give the message in tongues or usually by another person present.

The person giving the message and the person interpreting the message has control of the utterance. No one is ever forced by the Holy Spirit to give a message in tongues, rather they allow the Holy Spirit to freely flow through them to accomplish the mission of bringing a personal message that is directly from God. If the message is genuine; it will cause others in the room to acknowledge that it is so. It should bring encouragement to the believers that are present. I have found with this gift that the interpretation turns into the stand-alone gift of prophecy. So please refer to Chapter 13 as far as judging whether the interpretation is genuine or not. Note the gift is an interpretation, not translation.

Even when you've been given the ability to speak in a foreign language, someone still needs to interpret.

I heard a preacher tell a story once about when he was in a meeting in Washington, D.C. and a man delivered a word in tongues and another man interpreted it English. The interpretation was to get right with God and find God now. A Persian man came forward and was saved. He later revealed that the first part of the tongue was in his Persian language, the Farsi language, and the interpretation (given in English) was pretty spot on to the original message given in his native tongue. Obviously we can see how powerful an interpretation of tongues can be and how wonderfully it can be used in evangelism. Someone who did not know or had not learned the Farsi language spoke out a message from God and a Persian man was saved as a result.

MY FRIEND, THE HOLY SPIRIT

Regarding the interpretation of tongues, I have only been used once or twice and in the interpretation part only. But if no time is given in our churches to bring prophecy or a message in tongues, then there is never going to be an opportunity to move in this gift. I believe that small (house) group ministry settings are probably the most ideal places for this gift to function. It is still church in theory (as it is a body of believers gathered together for the purpose of glorifying God). This provides a safe and intimate place to move in the gifts of the Spirit.

CHAPTER 17:

Receiving the Baptism of the Holy Spirit

The baptism of the Holy Spirit is not for the secret disciple, but the for the open-confessed disciple. If you are even a little bit in doubt about the Holy Spirit, or pray with lukewarm attitude that God will baptize you with the Holy Spirit, you won't receive it no matter how long you pray. You must ask and receive by faith because *"it is impossible to please God without faith"* (Hebrews 11:6).

Jesus told His disciples to wait in Jerusalem Luke 24:49, "Behold, I send the Promise of My Father upon you; but tarry in the city of Jerusalem until you are endued with power from on high."

This was the last instruction that Jesus gave to His disciples before leaving them. It was not to go, but to wait. Yes He wanted them to go (Matthew 28:19-20), but first they had to wait.

1. The great commission was given to the whole Church
2. Every member of the Church has the obligation to fulfill it
How would this be accomplished? Answer: Power from on high.

Endued means to be clothed with power. Jesus told the disciples not to begin preaching at once, he told them to go into all the world, but to wait first. He told them that the preaching of the good news could not be done without the baptism of the Holy Spirit.

The primary purpose of the baptism of the Holy Spirit is efficiency in testimony and service, having to do with gifts for service more than nice feelings. In every passage of scripture in which the baptism of the Holy Spirit is mentioned, it is connected with testimony or service.

The Holy Spirit, our guarantee

When we receive the Holy Spirit, we do not receive a spirit of bondage, but a spirit of adoption. The Holy Spirit is our guarantee of adoption as it says in Romans 8:15, *"For you did not receive the spirit of bondage again to fear, but you received the Spirit of adoption by whom we cry out, 'Abba, Father.'"*

Via the power of Holy Spirit, we possess the promises and inheritance of God. The Holy Spirit is God's promise to us on earth as also written in Ephesians 1:13-14, *"In Him you also trusted, after you heard the word of truth, the gospel of your salvation; in whom also, having believed, you were sealed with the Holy Spirit of promise, who is the guarantee of our inheritance until the redemption of the purchased possession, to the praise of His glory."*

2 Corinthians 1:21-22: *"Now He who establishes us with you in Christ and has anointed us is God, who also has sealed us and given us the Spirit in our hearts as a guarantee."*

2 Corinthians 5:5: *"Now He who has prepared us for this very thing is God, who also has given us the Spirit as a guarantee."*

"By the Holy Spirit, believers are sealed, that is, separated and set apart for God, and marked as belonging to him forever" - Matthew Henry

So the Holy Spirit seals God's purchase of us. God places a seal on us when we receive Christ, the Holy Spirit. By the baptism of the Holy Spirit God gives us security of salvation and establishes His ownership over us.

How do you know you've been baptized in the Holy Spirit?

The Baptism of the Holy Spirit is a definite experience where you know if you have received it or not.

Acts 8:14-17: *"Now when the apostles who were at Jerusalem heard that Samaria had received the word of God, they sent Peter and John to them, who, when they had come down, prayed for them that they might receive the Holy Spirit. For as yet He had fallen upon none of them. They had only been baptized in the name of the Lord Jesus. Then they laid hands on them, and they received the Holy Spirit."*

In the above passage we can see that the believers in Samaria had not received the Holy Spirit; there was no grey area, not a maybe we have or maybe we haven't. Receiving the Holy Spirit is an experience so definite that one could easily answer yes or no to the question of whether they had received the Holy Spirit.

Receiving the baptism of the Holy Spirit is not done to make you happy. It is to make you useful. It is intended for efficiency in service of the

Receiving the Baptism of the Holy Spirit

Great Commission. Of course with the baptism of Holy Spirit, joy must inevitably be a result, because fruit of the spirit is joy. But it is joy that comes from doing His service.

I hear many people ask, "How can I get more of the Holy Spirit?" Really they should be asking, "How can the Holy Spirit have more of me?" The Holy Spirit is not someone we get hold of and use, like some power or influence. The Holy Spirit is a person of sovereign majesty, who uses our lives according to HIS will.

How does one know when he or she has received the baptism of the Holy Spirit?

A sure sign is speaking in tongues. Acts 2:4 says, *"And they were all filled with the Holy Spirit and began to speak in other tongues as the Spirit gave them utterance."*

As discussed earlier, they may be: tongues of men or of angels (1 Corinthians 13:1) which are other languages never learned (Acts 2:7), angelic languages which require interpretation (1 Corinthians 14:5), or unknown languages--our personal prayer language (1 Corinthians 14:2).

However, there are some of the circumstances that will keep you from receiving the baptism of the Holy Spirit

Blockages to receiving the baptism of Holy Spirit

1. Lacking in faith

Doubt or self-doubt is the enemy of faith. Therefore it is the enemy of God. Repent of doubt and unbelief, and believe in faith that the Holy Spirit is for you and that God will give you the Holy Spirit if you ask.

The Bible says, *"it is impossible to please God without faith"* (Hebrews 11:6). The promises of God are not automatic. They must be accessed and activated by faith. The Bible also says in Romans 14:23b that *"whatever is not of faith is of sin."*

I have prayed for people on the altar before and some were so open that I would pray and God would instantly move because of their expectation, their faith in God to bless them or touch them in some way was so great that it seemed as though I did not need any of my own faith to pray for them.

Jesus said in Luke 17:19, *"Arise, go your way. Your faith has made you well."* Notice Jesus did not say, "My faith has made you well"; rather He said, "your faith." When you come before God with faith and expectation, great things happen!

But then there are other times when I have prayed for people and they basically stand there and say, "OK, I'm not really into this but my wife has forced me up here; I'm only here to appease her, so go ahead and pray for me and get it over with." That is not faith. Sometimes, and this is the exception not the rule, God will still move and their lives are touched and changed, despite their disenchanted demeanor. Throughout scripture, though, the rule is the people who stepped out in faith were the ones that got the miracle.

You should also realize that you will receive according to your expectations. Every good and perfect gift comes from above as it states in James 1:17, *"Every good gift and every perfect gift is from above, and comes down from the Father of lights, with whom there is no variation or shadow of turning."*

You have to believe that if you ask God to give you the Holy Spirit and the gift of tongues, you are not going to get some other spirit. Take God at His word and believe what is promised, as explained in Luke 11:11-13, *"If a son asks for bread from any father among you, will he give him a stone? Or if he asks for a fish, will he give him a serpent instead of a fish? Or if he asks for an egg, will he offer him a scorpion? If you then, being evil, know how to give good gifts to your children, how much more will your heavenly Father give the Holy Spirit to those who ask Him!"*

If God says "how much more will your heavenly Father give the Holy Spirit to those who ask," then you can expect to get what God has said. But you have to expect to get because you get what you expect. According to your expectation that God will keep His word, you will receive like Jesus said in Matthew 9:29 *"According to your faith let it be to you."* Faith is the expectation that God will do what He says.

2. Sin

If we regard iniquity in our hearts, the Bible says God will not hear us (Psalm 66:18).

Every sin is an act of rebellion against God, therefore no sin is a small sin. People give the keys of ALMOST every closet in their heart over to God, but there is often some small closet's key they keep, causing the blessing not to come.

Resentment, bitterness and unforgiveness are probably the sins that restrict us the most in our walk with God. God cannot forgive us if we do not forgive others. We must release forgiveness to them in grace so God can release to us all that He has for us in grace.

Matthew 6:15: *"But if you do not forgive men their trespasses, neither will your Father forgive your trespasses."*

Renounce anything that could potentially block your receiving the gift of the Holy Spirit from any such involvement in the occult, witchcraft, palmistry, horoscopes, and/or freemasonry. James 5:16 says, *"Confess your trespasses to one another, and pray for one another, that you may be healed. The effective, fervent prayer of a righteous man avails much."*

I encourage you to talk with someone and have he or she pray with you over the renouncement of any of these past involvements with you or prior generations in your family.

3. Being unyielded

Yielding the tongue is the last thing our flesh wants to do when we come forward to the altar and give our lives to Christ. How do we do this? Just as Romans 10:9-10 tells us, it is by confession, *"That if you confess with your mouth the Lord Jesus and believe in your heart that God has raised Him from the dead, you will be saved. For with the heart one believes unto righteousness, and with the mouth confession is made unto salvation."*

Confession is one of God's spiritual laws. Confession brings salvation into every area of our life, but the wrong confession can just as easily keep God's blessing from coming over our lives. Salvation comes through confession. When we confess that we are weak or if we confess failure, doubt or fear, then we are not walking in the saving grace of heaven and are limiting God in our lives. Therefore we end up walking in fear and unbelief and not God's saving grace.

I find that when I am going through a trial or I have been mistreated, I try not to pray in English, because all I end up doing is whining and complaining to God about it.

The saying, "What you dwell on, you dwell in," is so true. This is why often when I am going through a trial I only pray in my heavenly language (tongues), worship and speak scripture. This way I am 100 percent certain that I cannot get into the flesh when I am praying in tongues, speaking the Word of God or worshipping.

The children of Israel cried out to God in the flesh because of an unyielded tongue that just brought out complaining and unbelief. Because of their confession, the entire generation never entered the Promised Land, and they died in the wilderness!

Paul said, *"I die daily"* (1 Corinthians 15:31). This means laying down the fleshly desires and being led by the Spirit. One way we can do this is by praying in the Spirit (praying in tongues), which yields our tongue, the most powerful member in our body, to heaven.

When we feel like complaining, we should pray in tongues instead. It's so easy to gossip, criticize and complain. Proverbs 18:21 says, *"Death and life are in the power of the tongue, And those who love it will eat its fruit."* What we say creates destiny, death, or life. Your mouth is like the rudder of a ship, steering your life. What you say sets the direction your life will go in.

I love what it says in James 3:2-5, *"For we all stumble in many things. If anyone does not stumble in word, he is a perfect man, able also to bridle the whole body. Indeed we put bits in horses' mouths that they may obey us, and we turn their whole body. Look also at ships: although they are so large and are driven by fierce winds, they are turned by a very small rudder wherever the pilot desires. Even so the tongue is a little member and boasts great things. See how great a forest a little fire kindles!"*

We create the world we live in by the words that we speak, so yield your tongue to heaven, and let the Holy Spirit take control and pray through you.

4. Believing in wrong doctrine

You don't try God and His gifts out. You will never receive what God has for you from heaven if you live in doubt. James 1:7 says, *"For let not that man suppose that he will receive anything from the Lord; he is a double-minded man, unstable in all his ways."*

You cannot be undecided about God and His gifts. You either believe that God is still moving in power and He is the same yesterday, today, and tomorrow, or you don't believe. Either you believe that the baptism of the Holy Spirit and the gifts are for you today, or you don't.

I am believing that if you had doubts before you read this book, you now no longer have these doubts and there is newfound faith in your heart to receive everything from heaven that God has for your life!

5. Refusing to make restitution

If you have ripped people off, you must do your best to repay people what you owe them. This includes the government, friends, family, old business partners, and anyone else that fits this category.

Follow Zaccaeus' example in Luke 19:8, *"Look, Lord, I give half of my goods to the poor; and if I have taken anything from anyone by false accusation, I restore fourfold."*

A friend of mine told once me a story of how he used to eat at Pizza Huts around the country and then skip the bill. Once he was saved, the Holy Spirit convicted him and he went back to each of those Pizza Huts to pay them the money he owed them from unpaid meals. That's real restitution.

6. Self-dependence

Being self-dependent is really just pride. God hates pride. In fact, in James 4:6 it says, *"God resists the proud but gives grace to the humble."*

You cannot be filled with the Holy Spirit and also be filled with pride. As we repent of our proud heart (which means that we surrender our will to His will for our life and we recognize and acknowledge our need for the Holy Spirit; that we cannot do life according our own strength) God gives us grace and we can receive the Holy Spirit.

The Devil wants to get you so full of yourself so that you can't be full of God. Thinking that it is by some great effort that we obtain this gift is really just pride.

7. Dishonesty

You may think that you are always honest, but do you exaggerate? Do you promise to do things and say yes but then never follow through?

But several examples are given in the Bible about keeping our word, like in Psalm 15:5, *"Keep your word even when it costs you, make an honest living, never take a bribe. You'll never get blacklisted if you live like this"* (The Message).

And from the New Testament we read in Matthew 5:36-37, *"Nor shall you swear by your head, because you cannot make one hair white or black. But let your 'Yes' be 'Yes,' and your 'No,' 'No.' For whatever is more than these is from the evil one."*

In other words, do what you say you are going to do when you say you are going to do it. We expect God to back up His word. We should be like God (Christ-like) and also do what we say. If our word holds no power with people because we never do what we say, then God's word will hold no power in our lives either.

8. Fearing the unknown

Another reason Christians don't grow in spiritual gifts is the fear of getting into error and excess. We can miss out on tremendous blessings because we interpret the Bible based on what we see in our churches rather than following what the Bible actually says. In order to operate in the gift of various kinds of tongues, the cord between our natural mind and our tongue must be cut. This is one of the biggest obstacles I see in people receiving the Holy Spirit and speaking in tongues. Their mind gets in the way. Our natural mind is against God just as we read in Romans 8:7, *"Because the carnal mind is enmity against God; for it is not subject to the law of God, nor indeed can be."*

So we must not initially focus on what we are saying because our mind will capture our words before our Spirit does and will hijack the impartation of the Holy Spirit to our lives. Do not let your natural mind get in between God and you. If your mind receives spiritual things, then it will filter doubt and unbelief. It will begin to think, "I can't speak in tongues. I will sound foolish. What is all this gibberish that I can hear everyone around me speaking?"

In 1 Corinthians 2:14 we read, *"But the natural man does not receive the things of the Spirit of God, for they are foolishness to him; nor can he know them, because they are spiritually discerned."*

Here Paul discussed how the natural man does not receive the things of the Spirit as they are spiritually discerned. If you let your mind receive before your spirit does, then you cannot receive because you cannot mix doubt and faith. Your natural mind cannot perceive or receive spiritual things, only your spirit can.

Don't try and work the gifts in your head, gifts don't operate in a natural realm (mental), they are operated on in the spirit realm. They manifest in the natural, but are accessed in the spirit realm; this is why many people cannot function in the gifts.

Some people are such perfectionists that they will never do anything unless they know they can do it right the first time. But striving for perfectionism cripples you from moving forward and receiving what God has for you. Let go and let God. You don't have to be a perfectionist or a control freak when it comes to the things of God.

God uses those that are yielded and available, and it is not just about your ability, it is about His ability and your availability. God is not going to keep coming to you if you don't yield and are not obedient. God would rather have a person step out and make a mistake, than have 100 people who are not yielded criticize someone who made a mistake. Mistakes can happen; the key is, are you yielded, are you teachable? If we want the Holy Spirit in our churches and in our lives, we will have to be prepared to do some clean up, some teaching and some correction.

Just because someone from church at a prayer meeting suddenly blurts out tongues over the microphone and then gives no interpretation doesn't mean they are a sinner or the church is in gross heresy. What is means is that person just needs a little teaching, and some adjustment on how to properly function in that gift. And if you are one of those that messes up, then if you're big enough to open your mouth, then you are big enough to take correction.

Proverbs 14:4: *"Where no oxen are, the trough is clean; But much increase comes by the strength of an ox."*

People will walk out of Church if they hear people speak in tongues without an interpretation, but this is not listed anywhere in the Bible as one of the things the Lord hates. There are things the Lord does hate as we see below.

Proverbs 6:16-19: *"These six things the LORD hates, Yes, seven are an abomination to Him:*

A proud look, A lying tongue, Hands that shed innocent blood, A heart that devises wicked plans, Feet that are swift in running to evil, A false witness who speaks lies, And one who sows discord among brethren."

Speaking in tongues without interpretation is not even mentioned as something that grieves the Holy Spirit. How do we grieve the Holy Spirit? When our conduct or speech is corrupt, not when someone blurts out tongues when they aren't supposed to.

Ephesians 4:30-31: *"And do not grieve the Holy Spirit of God, by whom you were sealed for the day of redemption. Let all bitterness, wrath, anger, clamor, and evil speaking be put away from you, with all malice."*

Let us not major on minors, let us have grace for those that may not be functioning correctly in the gifts but are stepping out with a right heart. Let us bring correction with love, not judgment and condemnation.

As we speak in tongues, the Holy Spirit rises up in us, comes on our tongue, and gives us a language to praise God, and out of our innermost belly will flow a river of living water (John 7:38)

You have to let go and be like a little child. When my daughter Charlize is standing at the edge of the pool and I say jump and I promise to catch her, she just jumps. She doesn't stand there and think it through in her mind. She doesn't have long discussions with me about gravity and trust. She just jumps when I say the word. In fact, Charlize prefers that I close my eyes when she jumps. Now that is real trust in me to catch her! (Of course I only pretend to keep my eyes closed.)

Trust God today, don't be worried about what other people think. We can spend our whole lives based around the thoughts and opinions of others and never enter in to what God truly has for us. Take a step of faith, close your eyes, and jump, only then will you see what God can really do through your life!

Ways to receive

1. Have desire

What does it mean to be thirsty? Think of that feeling after you've had a hard workout and your entire body and your thoughts are consumed with your need to quickly hydrate. In the same way, we must hunger for the Holy Spirit. If we are casual about the Holy Spirit and His gifts, then we put no value on them.

John 7:37-39 says, *"On the last day, that great day of the feast, Jesus stood and cried out, saying, 'If anyone thirsts, let him come to Me and drink. He who believes in Me, as the Scripture has said, out of his heart will flow rivers of living water.' But this He spoke concerning the Spirit, whom those believing in Him would receive; for the Holy Spirit was not yet given, because Jesus was not yet glorified."* Desire and pursue the Holy Spirit and you will find that anyone who truly seeks, finds.

2. Laying on of hands

Do you have to have hands laid on you to receive the Holy Spirit? Of course not. But this has been the way I have seen most people baptized in the Holy Spirit, as seen in Acts 8:17, *"Then they laid hands on them, and they received the Holy Spirit."*

The reason for this is that most times the receipt of the Holy Spirit takes place in a public meeting where there is a corporate anointing. When you are alone, it is just your faith. If it is you and someone else's faith, then there is a stronger anointing in agreement and the more people all in agreement, the stronger the presence of God can be.

3. Faith

As an opposite to unbelief, which is a repellent to the promises and presence of God, faith attracts and pleases God. Faith draws favor over your life. Faith obtains the promises of God. Faith is the language of heaven. When I am praying for people to receive the Holy Spirit, I figuratively see some like little children who simply and trustingly receive in faith. But others struggle in their minds, trying to rationalize God's power and ways in their limited and finite thinking. They allow doubt to creep in as they think about it too much. Their intellect does not allow them to receive in faith as they haven't yet learned to let go and let God be in control. But that is what faith is. It is letting go and letting God, even when we don't understand. We have to trust in faith by opening our hearts and banishing doubt and unbelief in order to receive all He has for us.

"So Jesus answered and said to them, *"Have faith in God. For assuredly, I say to you, whoever says to this mountain, 'Be removed and be cast into the sea,' and does not doubt in his heart, but believes that those things he says will be done, he will have whatever he says. Therefore I say to you, whatever things you ask when you pray, believe that you receive them, and you will have them"* (Mark 11:22-24).

4. Ask

The baptism of the Holy Spirit comes in answer to prayer. It seems too simple, but the Bible says that we *"have not, because we ask not"* (James 4:2). An example of asking for and receiving the Holy Spirit is recorded in Acts 4:31, *"And when they had prayed, the place where they were assembled together was shaken; and they were all filled with the Holy Spirit, and they spoke the word of God with boldness."*

Delving deeper into this wonderful gift the Holy Spirit gives us, it's crucial to fully comprehend a few more Biblical truths about it. For example, we must understand that the Holy Spirit does not speak in tongues through us. Acts 2:4 says, *"And they were all filled with the Holy Spirit and began to speak with other tongues, as the Spirit gave them utterance."*

On the day of Pentecost, the Holy Spirit gave utterance (enabled, prompting, or urge), but the believers did the talking. Notice that they began to speak with other tongues as the Holy Spirit enabled them. The Holy Spirit enables, we do the speaking.

Paul said in 1 Corinthians 14:18, *"I thank God I speak in tongues more than all of you,"* and not "I thank my God that the Holy Spirit speaks in tongues through me more than anyone else." A few verses prior, Paul wrote, "my spirit prays (by the Holy Spirit within me)." It isn't the Holy Spirit doing the praying. It is the Holy Spirit helping our spirits to pray. He gives the utterance, we do the praying.

The Holy Spirit will not force us to speak in tongues. The Holy Spirit never makes anyone do anything. If He did, He'd just go ahead and force everyone to be saved. But rather He directs, He prompts, He urges. That's what gives utterance means. It's the Holy Spirit who gives your spirit the ability to pray to God in tongues. You do the praying.

The miracle of tongues is not who is doing the speaking because we are the ones doing the speaking. The miracle of tongues is where the tongues are coming from and what is being said.

MY FRIEND, THE HOLY SPIRIT

You can't sit around waiting, though. Even if you only get a few sounds, hold onto that and expect more to come. Stay in faith as you learn to yield to the Holy Spirit. Otherwise you can fall back into the unbelief of "Well, I just spoke a couple of words, so I didn't really receive anything." Like a whistling kettle, as the water begins to get hot, it will let out a little bit of a whistle, but you don't take a kettle off the stove then, do you? You keep it on the burner until it's whistling longer and louder.

Commonly asked questions about the baptism of the Holy Spirit

Do I have to wait to receive the Holy Spirit like the disciples did?

It was only in the initial outpouring of the Holy Spirit that people had to wait. In all other accounts in the Bible, it was instantaneous. So you do not have to wait.

We are no longer required to wait for the Holy Spirit like at the day of Pentecost, He is waiting for us. You can pray and ask God for the Baptism of the Spirit right now, but you must do so in faith.

Some do not receive straightaway and this can be for the many reasons discussed above that you could be barricading yourself from receiving the Holy Spirit. But do not be discouraged. If you have prayed or been prayed for many times and still have not received the baptism of the Holy Spirit, talk to a pastor or someone you can trust.

What If I don't feel anything after I've asked to receive the Holy Spirit?

Well great news, you don't have to feel anything! For instance what if someone gave you a cashier's check for $1 million, would you say, "No I don't feel like receiving this gift? I don't feel it will work if I try and cash it." Your feelings don't have anything to do with the validity of the check; it's the authority behind the check that counts! The Bible doesn't say we walk by feelings, it says we walk by faith.

How can we receive?

We can receive the gifts of the Holy Spirit in various ways, but particularly:

1. By the laying on of hands (See 2 Timothy 1:6; 1 Timothy 4:14 and Acts 9:17-18).
2. By the sovereign act of the Holy Spirit (Psalm 115:3).

Receiving the Baptism of the Holy Spirit

3. By asking and believing to receive the gifts.

Luke 11:11 – 13: *"If a son asks for bread from any father among you, will he give him a stone? Or if he asks for a fish, will he give him a serpent instead of a fish? Or if he asks for an egg, will he offer him a scorpion? If you then, being evil, know how to give good gifts to your children, how much more will your heavenly Father give the Holy Spirit to those who ask Him!"*

What we can see by the scripture above is:

1. Any believer can receive
2. You don't have to wait
3. God has already given this gift we only need to receive

One day while driving back to Bible college from the shops I saw a guy on the side of the road hitch hiking. I felt in my heart to stop and pick him up, so I did. His name was Steve and it turned out he was newly saved. He confessed that ever since he decided to follow Jesus he had been struggling in his walk with God. I asked him if he had been baptized in the Holy Spirit and he replied he had not even really heard of the Holy Spirit. I shared my testimony and experiences with the Holy Spirit as well as some scriptures with him. The time came to drop him off and continue on to Bible college, but before we left him we asked if he would like to receive the baptism of the Holy Spirit to which he replied a resounding "yes". Right then and there on the side of the road we prayed for him. He lifted his hands to heaven and immediately started speaking in tongues. He was shaking from head to toe under the power of God. Tears streamed from his eyes and he gave me a hug and I then continued on with my drive back to Bible college. You can receive the baptism of the Holy Spirit anywhere and at anytime; you don't have to be at church or a special service, you can pray and receive the baptism of the Holy Spirit in your room and even on the side of the road.

Can people receive the baptism of the Holy Spirit immediately after salvation?

These events can happen almost simultaneously like in Acts 10:44, *"While Peter was still speaking these words, the Holy Spirit fell upon all those who heard the word. And those of the circumcision who believed were astonished, as many as came with Peter, because the gift of the Holy Spirit had been poured out on the Gentiles also. For they heard them speak with tongues and magnify God."*

MY FRIEND, THE HOLY SPIRIT

We can see that salvation and the baptism of the Holy Spirit took place at practically the same moment.

What is the difference between baptism and being filled?

The word baptism is never used or referred to in the Bible as a second experience. Even though it is a onetime experience, you can be filled over and over again with the Holy Spirit. All this means is that we need a new infilling for each new assignment every day. After they were initially baptized in the Holy Spirit in Acts 2:4, they were filled again in Acts 4:8: *"Then Peter, filled with the Holy Spirit,"* and again in Acts 4:31: *"And when they had prayed, the place where they were assembled together was shaken; and they were all filled with the Holy Spirit, and they spoke the word of God with boldness."*

So being filled with the Spirit should be a continuous reality of our everyday lives. Being filled with the Spirit is the measure that our daily activities are submitted to and controlled by the Holy Spirit. Being filled with the Holy Spirit meant they had a reputation of displaying traits and manifestations. If someone were to say that you were "full of rubbish", it would refer to a lifestyle where you speak and display a life of rubbish, so being filled with Holy Spirit means a life that displays the power of the Holy Spirit.

Acts 6:3: *"Therefore, brethren, seek out from among you seven men of good reputation, full of the Holy Spirit and wisdom, whom we may appoint over this business".*

What was the qualification for ministry? Being full of the spirit and wisdom, no mention of religious or college degree. Full of spirit means to not select people who are not full of the spirit.

Ephesians 5:15: *"And do not be drunk with wine, in which is dissipation; but be filled with the Spirit."*

The words "filled with the Holy Spirit" in the scripture above don't mean just a onetime filling, but a continuous or repeated action.

Don't be overly concerned about understanding the definitions of baptized, filled and endued. Rather be concerned about having the right experience by the wrong name than the wrong experience with the right name. What is important is that after the initial baptism in the Holy Spirit, we stay in touch with God every day and experience his presence every day. God is an "everyday God," not just a once a week or a twice a year at Christmas and Easter God. He wants to experience you every day, and He desires us to desire the same.

Receiving the Baptism of the Holy Spirit

What do we feel?

God's order is always as follows: first His Word, second belief in His Word, third experience and feeling. I have read of the wonderful experiences that men of history have had with the Holy Spirit and although I have had many of my own, there is none such given in the Bible that compares to the initial outpouring. There is no doubt that these apostles did have them, but they are not recorded, I believe, so that we will not get caught up in feelings and experience, otherwise we may look for the Holy Spirit a certain way. The only signs is tongues, boldness and power to witness and the outpouring of the Gifts of the Holy Spirit.

If you haven't already received that baptism of the Holy Spirit, then ask God right now by praying the prayer below (or your own prayer) and believe that you will receive what you ask for. But remember God won't force your mouth or shake your tongue. When you feel a stirring, you will have to choose to yield/obey by opening your mouth and moving your tongue to speak in tongues. Take a breath, receive in faith, and then make a sound.

"God, I yield my life afresh before you today. I open my heart to receive the Holy Spirit. I repent of all known sin and unbelief. I renounce the devil and all his evil practices. I thank you for Jesus, who died on the cross for me and my sins, and that I am made whole by the blood of Jesus that cleanses me from all wrong doing. Your word says that every good and perfect gift comes from above and that you will give the Holy Spirit to me if I ask you for Him. I ask you to baptize me now in the Holy Spirit, and I believe that I receive Him. Thank you for sending the Holy Spirit to empower me for righteous living, in Jesus name, amen!"

CHAPTER 18:

Moving in the Gifts of the Spirit

The first 33 years of the Church are recorded in the book of Acts. This is the Church in its infancy. By now, I believe the Church should be in full maturation. We should be mature in using the gifts, mature in knowing the correct doctrine and mature in moving in the power of the Holy Spirit.

But that's not the case because the accounts in the book of Acts show the Church in its infancy as having greater power and performing greater miracles through God than we see in most present-day churches.

For example, take a look at Acts 5:12, *"And through the hands of the apostles many signs and wonders were done among the people. And they were all with one accord in Solomon's Porch,"* and also Acts 8:5-8, *"Then Philip went down to the city of Samaria and preached Christ to them. And the multitudes with one accord heeded the things spoken by Philip, hearing and seeing the miracles which he did. For unclean spirits, crying with a loud voice, came out of many who were possessed; and many who were paralyzed and lame were healed. And there was great joy in that city."*

The Bible even says in Mark 16:15–18 that if we are believers, signs will follow: *"And He said to them, 'Go into all the world and preach the gospel to every creature. He who believes and is baptized (water baptism) will be saved; but he who does not believe will be condemned. And these signs will follow those who believe: In My name they will cast out demons; they will speak with new tongues; they will take up serpents; and if they drink anything deadly, it will by no means hurt them; they will lay hands on the sick, and they will recover.'"* For us believers, these signs should be a regular part of our lives.

Moving in the Gifts of the Spirit

Do you believe? Do these signs follow you?

1. Demons leaving. (Deliverance is always linked in the Bible to healing and the miraculous.)
2. Speaking in tongues. (So important we dedicated a whole chapter about it!)
3. Taking up serpents. (This speaks of having authority over the devil.)
4. Drink anything deadly, it will by no means hurt them. (This speaks of God's protection.)
5. They will lay hands on the sick and they will recover. (Do you lay your hands on sick people to see God's healing power?)

If we say we know God then where are the great exploits in our lives like it talks about in Daniel 11:32, *"But the people who know their God shall be strong, and carry out great exploits"*? It seems to me that when the Holy Spirit does move that some people are so quick to judge or critique other churches and ministers, but we really should be only critiquing ourselves.

We shouldn't reach conclusions about things we don't understand. People accused Jesus of having a devil (Mark 3:21), the disciples of being drunk (Acts 2:13), and of Paul being mad (Acts 23:24). In our lives there should be a supernatural element occurring that is unexplainable to the natural mind.

When you see something that doesn't fit how you think God moves, don't criticize it. If you remember in Mark 8:23, Jesus spit on a blind man's eyes to heal them. And just in case you thought spitting in a guy's eyes was enough to send you over the edge, he easily one-upped that when he spit in a man's mouth in Mark 7:32-35, *"Then they brought to Him one who was deaf and had an impediment in his speech, and they begged Him to put His hand on him. And He took him aside from the multitude, and put His fingers in his ears, and He spat and touched his tongue. Then, looking up to heaven, He sighed, and said to him, 'Ephphatha,' that is, 'Be opened.' Immediately his ears were opened, and the impediment of his tongue was loosed, and he spoke plainly."*

I have heard people say so many times, "The Holy Spirit is a gentleman. The Holy Spirit doesn't move in this way or that way". After a few times of hearing that sort of comment I would ask them, "Where is that in the Bible?" No one was ever able to show me because nowhere in the Bible does it say the Holy Spirit is a gentleman, nor does it dictate limitation on how He moves. This is not to say that sometimes when the Holy Spirit moves that He is not gentle, as indeed there is a gentle side to the Holy Spirit. But He is also much more than that. The fact is the Holy Spirit is God, and He can do as He likes.

MY FRIEND, THE HOLY SPIRIT

Gentleness is only spoken of a few times in the Bible (2 Corinthians 10:1 and Galatians 5:23) but never is the Holy Spirit referred to as a "Gentleman"; gentleness and being a gentleman are two very different things.

Let us not dictate to God. Many blessings have been lost because God did not move in the particular way that we wanted Him to.

Notice above it states that the people brought the deaf man to Jesus asking him to "put his hand on him". Did Jesus put his hand on him? Not at all, Jesus spat in his mouth and put his fingers in his ears! Some may have rejected Christ because of this, "Hey here's a guy that spits on people". Today a lot of people would leave the Church if a minister ever did that. They would brand him the "Spitting Minister!". If the deaf and dumb man had felt this way he never would have received his miracle. God is God and He can do what He likes!

"But our God is in heaven; He does whatever He pleases" (Psalm115:3).

"Whatever the LORD pleases He does, in heaven and in earth, in the seas and in all deep places" (Psalm 135:6).

"But He is unique, and who can make Him change? And whatever His soul desires, that He does" (Job 23:13).

So we should never just be focusing on the way God moves, the fruit is the main indicator of a true move of God. The Bible says by their fruits you will know them (Matthew 7:20).

Smith Wigglesworth was known to punch people with cancer, and these cancer patients would get healed. Should we all punch cancer patients in the name of Jesus? Should we all spit on people who are blind? Of course not, but at the same time we should not reject something just because it doesn't fit our theology on how we think God moves.

Punched in the face

One evening when I was with a friend driving home from having a "catch up" dinner, we were talking about going deeper in God and I had just finished a fast and was breaking it with a pizza. So there we were conversing in the car and out of the corner of my eye I saw a huge beast of a man beating a young teen with his fists on the sidewalk. I told my friend to stop, in an instant I had to make a decision. I had been fasting and praying all week about God taking me to deeper levels and using my life to touch the world and here I was witnessing someone in need. I jumped from the car and raced over to the scene; by the time I got there the youth was laying in the bushes groaning. I stepped in between the large hulk of a man and the youth. The man was surely over 300 pounds and over 6 1/2 feet, and at that time I was only 150 pounds (fasting had taken a few of those off and I was barely 6 feet), it felt like David and Goliath.

He looked at me in shock, here I was, someone about the same size of the youth he had just been pulverizing, standing in front of him. I looked at him and said, "Stop in the name of Jesus." Now in my mind I had not really known what to expect, but something along the lines of him being frozen, not being able to move, or running off at the mere mention of the most powerful name in the universe, but what happened next shocked me to the core, he punched me in the face as hard as he could.

I felt pain, and I could feel my face "ring". In my mind I was like, "What? Did he not hear what I said? How could this possibly happen? I said the name of Jesus!" So I looked at him again and shouted, "In the name of Jesus stop!" He looked at me again with a surprised look and then he did it again; he punched me in the face as hard as he could.

Now I was really in shock, before I could get a chance to say anything else, this look of disbelief is on this man's face. He spoke for the first time, "When I punched you the first time and you did not fall over I could not understand it", "I thought maybe I had not punched you hard enough, no one your size could withstand a punch like that and still be standing, so I punched you again, and when you did not fall down a second time, I realized that angels must be holding you up as you had mentioned Jesus." Now I was really shocked!

He kept speaking "I was brought up in a religious home and I know some of the Bible; particularly, I liked the angels." I was standing there, not knowing what to say, my face was sore and ringing and God had not come through the way I wanted Him to or thought He would. For the next 30 minutes or more I got to witness to this guy; he even gave me his phone number to call him, which I did. The other marvelous thing that happened is that even though my face was sore from where he punched me, when I got home to look in the mirror there were no signs of bruising at all; in fact my face felt just fine. I woke up the next morning and I couldn't even feel any pain, just a little stiffness.

This guy never ended up coming to church and to this day I don't know if he is saved or not, but all I know is God came through and saved me. And by the way, the youth in the bushes lived and also gave me the opportunity to share the gospel with him, but here is the interesting thing, what if I had run off after the first or second punch? I would have gone home upset, thinking God didn't come through, that he bailed on me! But God always comes through; we are the ones who bail on God. We expect Him to move this way or that and when He doesn't we throw in the towel and we miss the blessing God has for us.

MY FRIEND, THE HOLY SPIRIT

Revelation

One of the first steps in learning how to move in the power of the Holy Spirit and using the nine gifts is revelation. I won't spend a lot of time explaining this here because this is what the majority of the book is about: helping you obtain the knowledge, understanding, or in other words, revelation in your spirit, which was prophesied by Isaiah and repeated by Jesus, "the Spirit of the Lord is upon me."

Until you have that revelation, that certainty in your spirit, it is impossible to move in these gifts. You have to know that they are for you, that they are for today and that God wants to use you. You have to know unquestionably because without faith it is impossible to please God. It takes faith (certainty) to move in the spiritual gifts. This is revelation. One of the goals of this book is to impart to you the revelation that the Holy Spirit is for you, His gifts are for today and that God wants to use you to reach out to others and minister what He has given to you. If your doctrine or theology does not line up with the Word of God, your theology must change, not the other way around. I have seen verses that are twisted or taken out of context by those that try and explain a flawed theology that is void of the gifts of the Holy Spirit and the power of God.

When Jesus is giving his disciples instruction on how to pray he says this powerful statement in Matthew 6:10, *"Your kingdom come. Your will be done On earth as it is in heaven."*

God's will is to be done or reflected on earth as it is in heaven. If there is no sickness in heaven then God's will is that there be no sickness on earth. It means that if there was a condition in a person's life that was not in agreement with heaven's standard then it was to change. People are not tormented by demons in heaven, people are not sick in heaven, they are not poor in heaven, they are not hungry in heaven. The power that we have been given is to change what is contrary on earth to the way it is in heaven. Therefore whatever occurs on earth happens as a result of prayer and takes place in heaven first. Heaven wants revival, heaven desires miracles, and we are the vehicles through which the Holy Spirit works to bring heaven's standards to earth.

Preparation

After you obtain revelation, this certainty, then you need to begin preparing yourself and your heart. In 1 Corinthians 14:1 Paul instructs us to, *"Pursue love, and desire spiritual gifts..."* Spiritual gifts are not for complacent people. They are not "rocking chair gifts" but rather "battlefront gifts".

Moving in the Gifts of the Spirit

If you want God moving greatly through your life, you must prepare yourself. This means that you must spend time in prayer, in worship, and learn to wait on God. You will need to study and meditate on His word, which is also equally as important.

In addition to this, you can read books and listen to CDs in order to learn from other great godly men and women about God's anointing and power. The anointing comes by association, environment and influence.

Gifts are not going to flow in your life if you spend all your time feeding your mind with junk. Think of it this way, the size of the foundation determines the size of the building. Therefore, we need to have a big foundation. The anointing of God doesn't come cheaply. To be much for God, we must be much with God, every day, 24/7.

We can't sit around and wish for it because wishing will never be a substitute for prayer.

J Oswald Chambers once said, "A hurried glance at Christ, snatched after lying in bed too late, will never effect a radical transformation of character."

We need to have the mindset of preparing ourselves for God to move through us, as if we were training for the Olympics. An Olympic swimmer trains, and trains hard, every day, early, while everyone else may be sleeping. That's how Jesus "rolled". He was like the ultimate Olympic trainer, up early every morning. He prayed early and often. He prayed before anyone else was awake. Sometimes He prayed all night.

I love this quote, "Success is when 10,000 hours of preparation meets with one moment of opportunity" (author unknown).

We must develop faith if we are ever be all who God has called us to be. I believe this is the main reason many believers do not flow in the gifts and power of the Holy Spirit, they truly desire to and they read in the Bible that it is for them but they are never able to taste or touch it because they have not taken the time to develop faith and eradicate their lives of unbelief.

Proverbs 16:26: *"The person who labors, labors for himself, For his hungry mouth drives him on".*

The person who truly wants more of God, has to give more of himself to God, no more holding back the tithe, hiding secret sins or depriving God of daily devotional time, the power of God is for those that "labor", that are driven by hunger that can only be likened to a deep hunger for food, one of the most motivating forces God has given us, our need, desire and hunger for food."

MY FRIEND, THE HOLY SPIRIT

Proverbs 13:4: *"The soul of a lazy man desires, and has nothing; But the soul of the diligent shall be made rich."*

Too many people want the power of God but don't like the price tag; they think that it comes on the cheap, with no labor and no diligence to pursuing a life of faith. They do not want to take action and eradicate doubt and fear from their minds, they would rather the Holy Spirit be some wand they wave whenever they need God to do something miraculous.

The air is pregnant with unbelief; if we want to move in the gifts of the Holy Spirit, we must move in faith, we must develop faith. Hope is not faith, hope says I will get it sometime, faith says "I have it now". Hope is future, faith is now.

How much faith do you have? Only little faith? Then you will see little results. More faith equals more results.

Ephesians 3:20: *"Now to Him who is able to do exceedingly abundantly above all that we ask or think, according to the power that works in us."*

God is able to do for you more than you "ask or think"; God gives answers also through your thought life; you cannot be asking one thing and thinking another. Do you think about poverty, failure, sickness, impossibility or negativity? You cannot pray for one thing in the morning but all day be in doubt and unbelief about it, it is according to what you "ask and think". Your actions and thoughts must be in perfect fellowship with your confession.

The address of God, is your address. He dwells within you. If you are at home, He is there, if you are at work, He is there. God dwells with you and all His resources therefore are found in you. But God works through you; you are the channel. You have to develop your life to cooperate with God, if not, God will be limited. God is as big as you allow Him to be and as small as you confine Him to be.

If God showed you everything before you moved, you would not be walking in faith, you'd be walking by sight and that would not please God.

So you'll never see the full picture or know everything, that's why you need faith to step out without seeing the full picture. You do not require faith for what you can see or feel, but for what you cannot see and cannot feel.

Faith is not struggling or praying or crying, it is acting on what God has spoken; but you can only act if you hear, and you can only hear if you listen, and you can only move in faith if you have taken the time to develop that faith.

The power of God comes stronger when we put in a little extra prayer, a little extra waiting on God, a little extra word time and a little extra fasting. (I recommend Jentezen Franklin's book *Fasting* if you want to learn about the power of fasting.)

2 Timothy 2:15: *"Be diligent to present yourself approved to God, a worker who does not need to be ashamed, rightly dividing the word of truth."*

Therefore a worker (Christian) who doesn't study will be ashamed because how can he or she rightly divide the word of truth if they don't even take their Bible off the shelf? We grow the anointing by study of the Word and prayer.

Prevailing prayer is that which secures an answer. Saying prayers is not necessarily offering prevailing prayers. There is a "way" in prayer that secures answers, that way is the "way" of faith. True prayer is prayer in the spirit, prayer which the Holy Spirit inspires and directs.

All the gifts of the Holy Spirit work in the environment of faith. The Word of God is food for faith, faith lives when it hears the Word of God. Faith then speaks the Word of God, this is how it creates, through words. The miracle therefore is in your mouth.

We cannot pray and allow our minds to be filled with fear and doubts at the same time; only one can occupy our hearts, minds and mouth at one time. Either it is fear, doubt and unbelief or it is faith. Your mind cannot be thinking one thing (doubt) while your mouth is saying another (faith).

James 1:7-9 states, *"For let not that man suppose that he will receive anything from the Lord; he is a double-minded man, unstable in all His ways."*

Many people come into church and sing big songs then live small lives. We must seek to be consistent. They say, "Lord have all of me," then they don't honor God with their money, so really it is, "Lord have some of me, the parts I choose to give...." This is not a life of faith but a life of unbelief, thinking we can do a better job than God with our money by holding onto the tithe. A life of faith gives "all" to God, not some.

In my life, I have lived in many different places, and at each new place I had to find somewhere to pray, whether it was in my room, the beach, the park, or while walking the streets. When I was first saved it was "the cricket pitch" (which is like a baseball diamond). Every night I would go down there and pray; in rain, hail or shine, I was there. Then later I found a hill (which required a 15-minute climb) but looking out over the city turned out to be a great place for me to pray. Peter did even better, he prayed on a rooftop.

MY FRIEND, THE HOLY SPIRIT

Acts 10:9 states, *"The next day, as they went on their journey and drew near the city, Peter went up on the housetop to pray, about the sixth hour."* Now I don't know about you, but when I arrive in a new city, the first thing I do is check out the hotel, go for a swim, find a Starbucks, get something to eat and check out the sights. But not Peter, he went straight to prayer.

Escaped Lunatic?

Finding inspiration through Peter's commitment, I woke up at 6 a.m. to pray after staying at my friend Grant's house. I didn't want to wake up anyone else, so I decided to head outside, despite the fact that it was bitterly cold out. I borrowed a colorful jacket from the coat stand near the door and an equally vivid hat, which unfortunately happened to belong to Grant's sister. So there I was, headed out in my track pants and shoes, topped by girl's outerwear, to find a place to pray.

I spotted an empty parking lot next to a large building. Up and down the parking lot I marched, praying, crying out, lifting my hands in worship. I was having a really great time in prayer. About a half-hour into it, a police car pulled up. Two cops exited the vehicle, walked over to where I was praying, and asked to see my ID. Only, I didn't have it on me. The two policemen explained that the workers in the building had reported that there was some crazy guy in their parking lot. Reluctantly, I looked toward the building and all sorts of people were peering through the glass windows at me. How long had they been watching me? The cops asked again me for ID. I told them it was at my friend's house. But they insisted to see it, so I asked them if it was really necessary to go all the way up there and get it, being I hadn't broken any law. I was wondering why they needed to see my ID so badly anyway? They explained that there had been an escapee from the mental asylum, located only a few blocks away, and they thought that I was that guy.

I quickly resolved to head back to Grant's house, where he could verify that I was not an escapee from a mental asylum, even though that meant riding handcuffed in a police car. I'll never forget the shocked look on my friend's face when he answered the door to me in cuffs, escorted by two burly police officers who immediately responded to Grant's startled greeting by saying, "This guy claims to be your friend. Last night someone escaped from the mental asylum down the street, and we had complaints from workers in the building that this man may have been him. Can you verify that he is indeed your friend and is his ID inside?" Grant, being the great friend that he is, said, "I've never seen this man before in my life." My jaw dropped in disbelief, until he laughed and said, "Hold on. I'll get his ID."

Despite some of the interesting situations I've wound up in, it has always been my goal to rise early to pray. But this is a struggle at times. Why can this sometimes be so hard? I think there are a lot of reasons. But one thing I know for sure is that for each of us, it is a discipline that we must value above all else.

Mark 1:35: *"Now in the morning, having risen a long while before daylight, He went out and departed to a solitary place; and there He prayed."*

Luke 6:12: *"Now it came to pass in those days that He went out to the mountain to pray, and continued all night in prayer to God."*

Some people are "night people" and some are "morning people". I find the best time to ensure an incredible time with God happens every day is in the morning. If you are not a morning person, I suggest the following things that will help. I guarantee if you follow these three suggestions, you will always have a regular time with God in the morning.

1. Go to bed early. Turn off the TV, video game console, leave the party early, just do what you have to do to get a good night's sleep. I aim to be in bed before 10 p.m. each night, If I am going to get up at 5 or 6 in the morning to pray, I just have to.

2. Start with setting your alarm thirty minutes before you usually wake up. Once you have managed this successfully, you can start setting it an hour before you normally wake up. If you have been used to getting up at 8am every morning, don't suddenly start trying to get up at 5am every morning, take baby steps. Let your body adjust naturally and slowly.

3. Do not hit snooze. Try to have an alarm without a snooze button, if possible. Determine in your heart before the alarm goes off that snooze is not an option.

By now you understand that in order to move fully in the nine spiritual gifts, it is not enough only to understand and know about them, but you must also prepare yourself by prayer and meditating on His Word. And lastly, be ready to impart.

Impartation

Dwight L. Moody, the famous evangelist, was once told by an irate church lady, "Mr. Moody, I don't like the way you do your evangelism."

In reply, Mr. Moody said, "I don't necessarily like all of it either, but it's the best way I know how. Tell me, how do you do it?" "Oh, I don't," was the reply.

MY FRIEND, THE HOLY SPIRIT

"Well," said Moody, "I like the way I'm doing it better than the way you're not doing it."

Some people have asked me if I have the gift of healing or of faith. I have neither, I have the gift of the Holy Spirit and He is the one who has all nine gifts, but the Holy Spirit manifests himself through me, I just obey him and He moves through me.

Matthew 4:14 says, *"And when Jesus went out He saw a great multitude; and He was moved with compassion for them, and healed their sick. When it was evening, His disciples came to Him, saying, 'This is a deserted place, and the hour is already late. Send the multitudes away, that they may go into the villages and buy themselves food.' But Jesus said to them, 'They do not need to go away. You give them something to eat.'"*

Jesus instructed the disciples to give the people something to eat. It was their responsibility to provide, to give, to help, just like it is ours. You must have the expectancy for God to use you, otherwise how will you ever impart? You can have the revelation that God wants to use you to administer His gifts, you can prepare and pray until you are blue in the face, but it is the "giving", the impartation that defines what you carry as a gift.

> Acts 3:1–8: *"Now Peter and John went up together to the temple at the hour of prayer, the ninth hour. And a certain man lame from his mother's womb was carried, whom they laid daily at the gate of the temple which is called Beautiful, to ask alms from those who entered the temple; who, seeing Peter and John about to go into the temple, asked for alms. And fixing his eyes on him, with John, Peter said, "Look at us." So he gave them his attention, expecting to receive something from them. Then Peter said, "Silver and gold I do not have, but what I do have I give you: In the name of Jesus Christ of Nazareth, rise up and walk." And he took him by the right hand and lifted him up, and immediately his feet and ankle bones received strength. So he, leaping up, stood and walked and entered the temple with them—walking, leaping, and praising God."*

Notice that the miracle didn't happen on the way home from prayer meeting, but 3 in the afternoon, on way to the prayer meeting. They hadn't even been to the prayer meeting yet and they had their hearts in tune to the Holy Spirit.

We are spiritual conductors; we create an atmosphere through our lives. But we can only reproduce on the outside what is going on in the inside.

Moving in the Gifts of the Spirit

Imagine finding out that it is your close friend's birthday today (revelation). You go out and buy them a great gift that you know they will like and write a thoughtful card with meaningful words of friendship (preparation); but now imagine you never give this present or card to your friend (release/impartation). Revelation and preparation are no good without impartation. You have to release the gifts, release the power of God to others who need it. How do we know who needs it? We look, we pray, we expect. And then we take action. We have to be willing to do the work that God gives us to do.

Finding a wife

When I was single and felt it time to find a wife, I prayed and fasted for the first week of each month for a wife. Now how strange would it have been if I had only prayed and fasted but never talked to any females. And then one day I heard a knock at the door and on the other side stood a girl with lights coming down on her and angels singing as she said, "Thou hast been praying for a wife and here I am. Let us marry." That would have never happened. Instead, I had to meet Summer, get to know her, ask her out a few times, go on some dates. And once we had been friends for about a year, it was time to take it to the next level, so one night, to her great surprise, I kissed her. And the rest, as they say, is history. But the point is I had to take action. I couldn't only pray and expect. Yes, I had to have faith, but I also had to be ready to do the work. The Bible says, *"Faith without works is dead"* (James 2:20). I could have prayed until the cows came home and pigs grew wings and I could have fasted for 40 days and 40 nights, but at some point, I had to initiate human contact with a person of the opposite sex. I had to talk to Summer, get to know her, ask her out and risk facing possible rejection. In the same way, we need to approach all of life's adventures and challenges, pray and obey. Faith is giving prayer legs, and taking action. Some spell it R-I-S-K.

Pray and obey

One thing I have done is ask God for divine appointments and that He would use me to change lives. One evening, unexpectedly, as it often seems to be, He offered me one of these. I was on my way to have dinner at a friend's house, but I first stopped by the DVD store to return a rental. As I was returning to my car, I felt the Holy Spirit speak to me and ask me to look. So I glanced beyond my car toward the bus stop and saw a man shaking with his head in his hands. I felt straightaway the Holy Spirit prompt me to go and talk to this man. Now I'm thinking, "God this guy could have a knife or something or be dangerous. By the looks of him, he is mentally disturbed. Also you very well know, I have to be at this dinner and I don't want to be late." I paused for a moment and heard the prompt again, but this time I felt the Holy Spirit say to me, "What is the point of praying for divine appointments, if when I bring them to you, you ignore them?"

Well, that got me. I walked up to this man and asked, "Are you OK?" He (I later learned his name was Warren) looked up at me, shaking as if he was cold. I noticed he was only wearing shorts and a t-shirt. Tears streamed down his face over bruises and a cut lip. "No, I'm not," he muttered. Warren proceeded to tell me a tragic story, which had left him empty and depressed. Finally, I said to him, "Well I want you to know that God led me here to talk to you. I was just returning a DVD, and He told me to come and see you." And you are going to be as amazed with God as I was when I tell you what Warren told me next. "Moments before you came to talk to me," he said, crying, "I told God I was going to throw myself in front of the next bus that came past." Thankfully I was there and I had obeyed the Holy Spirit's prompting and Warren did not throw himself in front of the next bus. I took him in my car and got him some food, prayed with him and dropped him off at his house.

Warren required impartation. His situation required me to know that God would use me, that the Holy Spirit would guide me. It required me to have revelation, a certainty and conviction that God still moves today in power and in the gifts of the Holy Spirit. It required preparation in prayer and study of the Word on my part to learn and know, to recognize the voice of the Holy Spirit so that when He told me to talk to Warren, I would recognize His voice. And finally, impartation, which required me to step out in faith.

Too often we are looking for the "big" thing, the "big miracle", but if we are faithful with little things, the small acts of obedience, then He entrusts us with bigger tasks. This is ultimately how faith grows, through faithfulness.

I heard a preacher once say that the Church gets excited, it gets equipped, but then it never deploys. Be someone who gets excited by revelation, gets prepared and equipped in prayer and then deploys in faith to step out and move in the Spirit to touch a world that desperately needs to know and experience the power and love of God!

CHAPTER 19:

Hearing the Voice of God

Entire books have been and will be written about this subject, but I am only devoting a chapter to it. This chapter is not so much about steps to hearing the voice of God, but an exhortation to get a hold of God and allow Him to get a hold of you so you can position yourself to hear from God and walk in His supernatural ways by the Holy Spirit.

Hebrews 1:1 says, *"God, who at various times and in various ways spoke in time past to the fathers by the prophets, has in these last days spoken to us by His Son, whom He has appointed heir of all things, through whom also He made the worlds."* The key words in this verse are "God" and "has...spoken to us." God is speaking, so the question is, are we hearing? Are we even listening? Are we setting aside the time each day?

Too many Christians run around looking for someone to counsel them, but for most, what they really need to do is get on their knees and pray through their situation and take the time to wait on God, allowing the inner man to be renewed. You can receive the wisdom on high that you need and the Holy Spirit will guide you each day.

The problem is most people want their answers to prayer immediately (including me!). They want them fast and with the least amount of personal cost. But getting your answer may mean missing a few meals or waiting on God for hours. There are all these seminars and books on hearing the voice of God, but the key to hearing the voice of God is simply this: set aside time each day to spend in quality prayer and communion with God.

God's guidance is clear guidance

1 John 1:5 says, *"This is the message which we have heard from Him and declare to you, that God is light and in Him is no darkness at all."*

MY FRIEND, THE HOLY SPIRIT

We can ask God to make His will clear to us. Obscurity or uncertainty may arise from an un-surrendered will. I've heard people struggle over certain decisions in prayer. When I ask them what their dilemma is, quite often once I hear what is troubling them, I find the answer to their problem is actually in the Bible.

But some people run around from conference to conference hoping for a "word" from the pastor so that they will know what to do. And once again the answer to their problem is found in the Bible. These people don't need a word from the minister. They need to read the words from the Bible.

Read your Bible

One of my Bible college lecturers told a story that at the end of a service where he had been speaking in a church, ministering, and prophesying over people, he received a word from God for one particular lady who had been standing, waiting at the altar for prayer. The Lord spoke to him and said, "Tell this lady that this is the word of the Lord for her, 'Read your Bible.'" He promptly obeyed the Holy Spirit and shared this word. Of course this lady was none too pleased. But they later discovered that she had been going from church to church and conference to conference just looking for "words" from the minister, rather than getting on her knees in prayer and searching out the Word of God each day.

Proverbs 25:2 says, *"It is the glory of God to conceal a matter, but the glory of kings is to search out a matter."*

Some things are only discovered by the desperate. I believe God hides things from us not to withhold from us, but so we will seek Him. That is how we become a "king," by seeking out what God has hidden. God is a God of "hide and seek." He wants us to seek Him, and He wants to be found.

The key to having a regular time spent with God each day is actually setting aside the time to spend with God each day, sounds easy right? It isn't. Sometimes the things that are the easiest to do are also the things that are easiest not to do. For instance, if you try to set aside time in the evening before bed, all kinds of things can find their way to interrupt this scheduled time, like kids, birthday dinners, tiredness, and other social and church related events and of course your favorite TV shows.

Usually the best time to ensure that you get uninterrupted time with the Lord each day is in the morning. The main problem people have with this is that they struggle to get up in the mornings, leaving only enough time to shower, have breakfast, get dressed, jump in the car and arrive at work. For most people the main issue is a lack of proper planning. If I need to pray for an hour each day in the mornings, I have to get up around 5 or 6 a.m., but if I am watching TV, playing video games, on Facebook and Twitter and surfing the web until 11 p.m. or later, then the chances of me getting up at 6 a.m. are slim. There is a better chance that I will hit the snooze button seven or eight times!

The key is to turn off the TV, turn off the computer, turn off the video games, and go to bed early. That may need to be at 9:30 or maybe 10. That seems early to some of you night owls, but how important is hearing the voice of God to you?

Of course if you really are a night owl and can do the night prayer thing every night, all power to you! But for most we must go to bed early enough so when we wake, we are fresh and have time to seek God!

No wonder David said in Psalm 55:17, *"Evening and morning and at noon I will pray, and cry aloud, and He shall hear my voice."*

I think he prayed at three different scheduled times per day because he did not want to leave things to chance!

Trust me, try going to bed earlier, and then set your alarm for 30 minutes to an hour earlier for a week and see what happens. What have you got to lose? Nothing, but what you gain is a disciplined lifestyle of daily prayer for a lifetime. If you don't take the time to wait in the Lord's presence, to learn to listen to Him, you will never learn and know the secrets of heaven. You may say, "I don't even know what to pray for half the time!" That is what our heavenly prayer language (gift of tongues) is for. Praying the perfect will of God sensitizes your spirit to hear His voice with great clarity.

Try putting on some praise and worship music as you pray in your heavenly language each day. I pray every day in tongues, and I've found one the best places can be when I'm alone in the car. People may think you're mad, but who cares.

It's not just about us talking and praying. Prayer is not so much about what you say, but also what He says. Take time also to listen. In any relationship, it is difficult to grow unless both people talk in conversation.

In prayers too often we are taken up with our needs; in thanksgiving we are taken up with our blessings, in worship we are taken up with God himself.

John 4:23-24: *"But the hour is coming, and now is, when the true worshipers will worship the Father in spirit and truth; for the Father is seeking such to worship Him. God is Spirit, and those who worship Him must worship in spirit and truth."*

MY FRIEND, THE HOLY SPIRIT

God will always visit where there is true worship, regardless of where it is. God is not passive, the presence of God is always moving, it's active, God is seeking worshippers.

It goes the same way in any friendship; a friendship that just revolves around one person continually asking the other person for things is an unbalanced relationship, and one of the friends will eventually withdraw as the other friend is so caught up in themselves. But if we are conversing with our friend, thanking them and being grateful for them, if we are spending time with them just to be with them and praising them constantly, then we will find that friend will draw closer.

Listen

When I first got saved, someone gave me the best advice about hearing God's voice. I was encouraged to wait on God each day for at least five minutes, which does not sound like a long time, but it sure was! Have you ever tried sitting silent for five minutes? Time stands still.

But that is what I did. Day after day, for 5 minutes, I sat there and would say, "Here I am God, speak to me." I sat there with pen and notebook at the ready. Not a lot seemed to happen in the first few weeks and months. I think I even dozed off a couple of times. But I had always found that whenever I had needed guidance from God for a particular situation or decision that I would somehow know what to do or say. When I really needed for God to speak to me during the day, He would!

During that time when someone would ask me questions about God, at first I wouldn't know the answer. Then I would get a thought or an impression or hear a voice speak in my spirit, and I would then answer. The answers would amaze people (including me). Later on, I asked one of my leaders if that was the right answer and they would reply, "Yes, and here is where it is found in the Bible."

After a while the five minutes turned into 10, sometimes even 15 minutes or more. At first I just stared down at my blank notebook, but eventually I learned how to get myself so still and tuned into the Holy Spirit that I would begin to write. Sometimes I wasn't even sure if it was God, but I wrote anyway. Today, I pulled out one of those notebooks and read some of what I had written years ago, and they were spot on!

The Bible says it is impossible to please God without faith (Hebrews 11:6), and Jesus said that according to your faith (or expectation), it will be unto you (Matthew 9:29). What I realized was that even though I may not have heard God right then and there during that five or 10 minutes of listening for Him each day, I was activating faith by taking the time to sit and listen with a pen and notebook. I was initiating an expectation that God would speak to me. And you know what? Every time when I did need to hear Him, I did!

Be Expectant

I'm amazed at people who show up to church with no pen and paper. What this tells me is they either have a brilliant memory or that they have no expectation that God will speak to them through the pastor or minister or maybe they have placed no priority or little priority on hearing God speak to them. Perhaps in some cases, they had left their pen and notebook on the bench as they were trying to get the kids out the door and on time for church, which I have done a number of times, but I always found a pen and a church bulletin to take notes on when I arrived at church.

Roll the dice

I have to be honest, I didn't always obey those inner promptings, even today it is a challenge sometimes to obey when God asks. I remember once when I was newly saved that a really nice Christian girl invited me to go to a Bible study with her the next day, Tuesday evening. Now this seemed great to me, but I had football practice on that night. I was torn between the two, and I thought, Lord maybe this will be my wife what should I do? (I was only 17!)

To add to that dilemma, at lunchtime that day while I was playing tennis, one of the foreign exchange students from Finland (very attractive, I might add. All the guys called her the Finnish supermodel.) saw me playing. She asked if I would play tennis with her. "Wow!" I thought, "what a great opportunity to evangelize!"

When I asked what day she wanted to play, she told me that because of her swim training, she only had Tuesday evening free. Now I was really divided. I had to choose between football practice, the really nice Christian girl who had invited me to Bible study at her church, or play tennis with Anna Kournakova's twin sister. In my heart, I actually wanted to play tennis with this girl.

I prayed and prayed and could not decide what God wanted me to do. I see clearly today that honoring my commitment to the football team and keeping my word was the right decision. It's even clear in scripture concerning the importance of keeping one's word.

So what did I do? In a hat, I put three slips of paper, one for football, one for the Bible study and one for tennis with the unsaved Finnish exchange student. I prayed that God would guide me and picked one out...Football. I said, "I bind you, Devil, in Jesus' name" while I mixed up these slips again and slipped them back into the hat. I picked a second time, and again I plucked the football slip. At that point, I kind of got the message and heard God clearly say, "If you keep pulling out the paper slips, eventually you will get the one you want."

I'd like to say that I went to football practice that night, but I did what any 17-year-old male who had been recently converted, still battling the flesh, would do. You guessed it, I played tennis with the Finnish supermodel. I can't even remember if I witnessed to her or not as I was feeling so guilty about disobeying God.

Many of us struggle to hear God's voice because the Holy Spirit never forces us to do anything. Instead He will give us a prompting or an urge. But if we keep overriding those inner promptings or urges, at some point, we will not experience them any longer and we slowly become desensitized to the voice of God, like when we feel the prompting to turn off a movie we know is not appropriate.

Jesus did not say, "My sheep will know my book." It is His voice that He says we are to know. Don't get me wrong, of course God does speak through His word too. Anyone, though, can know the Bible as a book. The devil, himself, even knows and quotes scriptures. The Bible says *"My sheep know my voice"* (John 10:4,27). God actually expects you to hear, know and follow His voice (Read all of John 10). Only those whose lives are dependent upon the Holy Spirit will consistently recognize His voice whether through the Bible, that small still voice, through dreams (which by the way was the primary way God spoke to people in the Bible), or through all the other various ways God speaks. If you want to be close to the Holy Spirit and know the voice of God, then the key is this: love what He loves.

Love what He loves

In Jeremiah 30:21, it says, *"'For who is this who pledged his heart to approach Me?' says the Lord."* Some translations use the word "engage" or "devote" instead of pledged. When I read this verse one day it hit me like a ton of bricks. I thought to myself, "What am I doing to devote myself to being close to God?"

Think about this in a human relationship perspective. When I wanted to be close to my wife, Summer (before we were even dating), what did I do? Did I take her to a monster truck rally (Well, I would have if that was what she was into!) or invite her to sit in front of the TV all day to watch sports? Nope! Those things would have repelled her. Well, maybe not the monster truck rally. I am talking about a woman that went to the WWE on her 21st birthday! But I did things like buy her chocolates, go on dinner dates, movies, trips away, flowers, jewelry. These things drew us closer. Why? Because she loved these things.

So the way I devoted myself to be close to Summer was to love the things she loved.

The question then is, what does the Holy Spirit love? Worship, prayer, waiting to listen to Him with pen and notebook ready, being in the house with other believers, being in the Word, reaching out to lost ones, and the list goes on.

In the same way, we can repel the presence of God. What kinds of things repel the Holy Spirit? Cussing, dishonesty with taxes, gossip, a life that lacks holiness, being influenced by the wrong kind of people, watching movies or TV programs that offend Him, you know which ones.

Value His presence

We need to learn to host the Holy Spirit, not just as a onetime visitor when we need help, but as a permanent guest in our lives and in our homes. Have you ever visited somewhere and you are lavished on? Maybe the home of a friend or relative, where you are treated special, where there is plenty of love and hospitality. There are also nice restaurants like this. Conversely, there are places where we are made to feel unwelcome or the atmosphere is cold and inhospitable.

Which places are you more likely to return to? Of course the places you feel welcomed, honored and valued. Imagine if my guest came over and I acknowledged that they were there, but then ignored them. What if I didn't offer them a drink, spent no time with them at all. They can't even talk to me because the basketball is on. "Oh we will chat in the morning," I say as I head to bed, "oh you're still here", as I wake up in the morning rushing out the door because I slept through my alarm again. We have to put value on the presence of God for the presence of God to remain with us.

David cried out after sinning with Bathsheba 'take not thy presence from me'" (Psalm 51:11). Notice he didn't cry out "take not thy position from me", sadly this seems to be the cry of the modern day man of God after he is caught out, more concerned about position than the presence of God. But with David it was different, he put great value on the presence of God.

In the Old Testament only "special ones" had access to the presence of God, but in the New Testament we all have access. For thousands of years men wished and craved, but in one moment Jesus made everyone equal. Today sometimes I feel we take that privileged access we have to the presence of God for granted.

Psalm 22:3: *"But thou art holy, O thou that inhabitest the praises of Israel."* KJV

MY FRIEND, THE HOLY SPIRIT

The word "inhabitest" or inhabit, means to sit down, to remain. The Holy Spirit is not only attracted to praises but if you adopt a life of praise he promises to stay and abide always. The Holy Spirit loves and is drawn to praise and worship that truly glorifies God. (See 2 Chronicles 5:12-14.)

Romans 8:5 makes it quite clear, *"For those who live according to the flesh set their minds on the things of the flesh, but those who live according to the Spirit, the things of the Spirit."*

If you want to be spiritually minded and hear God's voice and walk in His ways, then it's very straightforward, engage in the thoughts and activities of heaven. Feeding yourself with a diet of movies or TV shows that engage in and promote things of a fleshly nature will only lead to a lifestyle of walking in the flesh.

There are two natures battling for mastery of our lives: The flesh and the spirit. The one we feed the most wins. If our spirit life is starved and we feed the flesh, then the flesh will rule. So sin (or the flesh) no longer reigns but it fights.

Hearing the voice of God is about loving what He loves and eliminating those things in our lives that repel Him. We can do things that either attract or repel the Holy Spirit. If you find that you cannot give up certain TV shows, then those things have become an idol in your heart.

Matthew 5:29: *"If your right eye causes you to sin, pluck it out and cast it from you; for it is more profitable for you that one of your members perish, than for your whole body to be cast into hell."*

So if cable TV or the Internet is causing you to sin, unplug it. It is better to unplug the TV set and cancel Internet and go to heaven without cable than to go to hell with a whole entertainment center around you. Declare war against every kind of evil, become a terrible enemy of sin.

It's important to remember that these things have zero eternal value and can get such a subtle hold on our hearts, diluting the presence of God and sensitivity to His voice. Just try shutting the TV off for one week. Spend that time in prayer and fasting and watch what happens. Sadly some people know more about football or celebrity gossip than they do about God and the Bible.

This is why so many people have become dull or desensitized to the voice of God, because it is according to what you "set" your mind upon, "what you dwell on, you dwell in." Movies, TV, Internet and other forms of media, etc...It's not that these worldly pleasures are always necessarily bad, the Bible states in 1 Corinthians 10:24, *"All things are lawful for me, but not all things are helpful; all things are lawful for me, but not all things edify."* But a person who has truly given himself over to the Holy Spirit loses desire for these things not because he thinks they are wrong, but because he now has something so much better that he loses taste for them. Of course media can be powerful in reaching others with the Gospel and equipping the Church for the work of the ministry. I enjoy a good football game and a good movie from time to time, but the question is what am I exposing myself to the majority of the time. If I always watched sports and never read my Bible then I am only building faith in my sports knowledge and when it comes time to impart the power of God knowing who had the most touchdowns in a certain season isn't going to heal the sick!

D.L. Moody was approached by a lady after a meeting where he had preached, and he thought maybe she had some encouragement for him. However, she said, "Mr. Moody, I do not like you." He asked, "Why not?" And she replied, "Because you are too narrow." He then said, "I did not know that I was narrow?" Nodding, she confirmed, "Yes, you are too narrow. You don't believe in theatre, you don't believe in cards, and you don't believe in dancing." He scrunched his brows and said, "How do you know I don't believe in theatre?" She said, "I know you don't." Moody replied, "I go to the theatre whenever I want to?" Her eyes widened. "What?" she exclaimed in surprise. "Yes, I go to the theatre whenever I want to," Moody repeated. She said, "Mr. Moody, you are a much broader man than I thought. I'm so glad to hear you say that," Moody replied, "Yes, I go to the theatre whenever I want to. It just so happens that I never want to."

Paul stated in Philippians 3:8, *"Yet indeed I also count all things loss for the excellence of the knowledge of Christ Jesus my Lord, for whom I have suffered the loss of all things, and count them as rubbish, that I may gain Christ."*

We must be careful, though, that we live life by the Spirit and not by legalism (letter).

In 2 Corinthians 3:6 it's written, *"Who also made us sufficient as ministers of the new covenant, not of the letter but of the Spirit; for the letter kills, but the Spirit gives life."*

A Christian's life, governed by the Holy Spirit, is not one with a long set of rules. But rather led by a living and ever present person with us, for you received not the spirit of bondage to fear. A life governed by rules is a life of bondage because there is always fear that we haven't measured up to the set of rules.

Like it says in Romans 8:15, *"We have received the spirit who gives us our place as sons."* Our lives should not be governed by a set of rules without us but by the loving spirit of adoption within us.

Many Christians believe if they are holy enough then they will please God and God will want to stay with them. This is like a child who believes his parents will stay with them because they make their bed and brush their teeth. Faithful parents stay with their kids whether the kids do these things or not. Out of secure relationships flow effective training, obedience, correction and love.

Holiness should not be our end goal. We are already the "righteousness of God in Christ Jesus". If holiness was our end goal then we should all just go to heaven now as that is the most holy place there is. This is like living on the defense, and having a "not sinning mentality", you cannot win with this mentality. You cannot win a basketball game by staying close to the hoop to protect it. But perfection is not behavior, it is relationship, it is not earned, it is received by faith. Our end goal should not be holiness but separation, yes separated from the world but separated to God for a purpose.

1 Peter 2:9-10: *"But you are a chosen generation, a royal priesthood, a holy nation, His own special people, that you may proclaim the praises of Him who called you out of darkness into His marvelous light; who once were not a people but are now the people of God, who had not obtained mercy but now have obtained mercy."*

The cycle of striving and performance based Christianity

This is a typical scenario that many Christians find themselves in. "Bill feels pressure, but he struggles to read his Bible regularly, he frequently misses devotional times altogether, he finds himself getting angry at his wife and kids, frustrated with his job and lack of appreciation or pay, troubled by lustful thoughts and pornography slip ups. Any time he loses his cool, lapses back into his lust addition or isn't praying he tells God he will "try" harder, every month or so he comes forward on altar calls, because he does not feel up to standard, he sees other people around him who seem like they have it altogether, he wishes he was more like his pastor or small group leader. So he comes forward on a particular altar call, gets a touch from God, prays a prayer, makes some promises but within a week or so he has slipped back into his old patterns.

His life over a period of time resembles this familiar pattern; promises, breakdowns, relapses altar calls, repentance, more promises, more vows followed by more breakdowns, more confessions, and you get the picture. The devil then comes along and says, "Bill you aren't cutting it, you are a hypocrite, you lead a double standard life, just give up, why bother?"

Galatians 3:3: *"Are you so foolish? Having begun in the Spirit, are you now being made perfect by the flesh?"*

What we have too often as we can see by Bill's example above is an Old Testament approach to serving and following God. It is the backward approach that will lead you on this same viscous cycle of performing for God to gain approval.

A gift is free

The first thing we must realize is that a gift is a gift, it is free. It cannot be earned or performed for. If you have to do something or pay something for it, then it is not a gift.

Get our eyes on Jesus

Secondly, we must get our eyes off ourselves and off our problems and onto God.

> Romans 7:15–25: *"For what I am doing, I do not understand. For what I will to do, that I do not practice; but what I hate, that I do. If, then, I do what I will not to do, I agree with the law that it is good. But now, it is no longer I who do it, but sin that dwells in me. For I know that in me (that is, in my flesh) nothing good dwells; for to will is present with me, but how to perform what is good I do not find. For the good that I will to do, I do not do; but the evil I will not to do, that I practice. Now if I do what I will not to do, it is no longer I who do it, but sin that dwells in me.*
>
> *I find then a law, that evil is present with me, the one who wills to do good. For I delight in the law of God according to the inward man. But I see another law in my members, warring against the law of my mind, and bringing me into captivity to the law of sin which is in my members. O wretched man that I am! Who will deliver me from this body of death? I thank God— through Jesus Christ our Lord!*

In this famous chapter, Paul uses the word "I" over 30 times. Therein lies the problem, he has an inward focus, instead of a God focus. You will always get what you focus on, whether good or bad, so if you are always focusing on what you don't want to do, you will just end up doing it. This is the point Paul is illustrating with his many "I's"

Now remember that Paul doesn't stop at Romans 7 on this issue of struggle, when he was writing this letter to the Roman's he did not stop at the end of Chapter 7 as there was no chapters, it was just one continuous letter, so in Chapter 8 (the next part of the letter) is the answer to his struggle from Romans 7.

In the eighth chapter of Romans "I" is mentioned only twice, whereas the Holy Spirit is mentioned throughout chapter. There is the key, don't keep thinking about what you don't want to do, stop beating yourself up by always thinking about what you do wrong and how imperfect you are, just focus on the God who is perfect and can do no wrong and the power of the Holy Spirit that he provides because what you focus on, you walk in. We spend too much time focusing on what we are not doing right, rather than what we are doing right

Flooding

Thirdly we must practice what I term the art of "flooding", what did God do when he wanted to get rid of wickedness on the earth and start with a clean slate? He flooded the earth. In the same way we must flood our minds with God's word and flood out the thoughts and strongholds of the flesh.

Flooding works in two ways, first it works by removing that which is there and then replacing what was there with something more desirable.

> Ephesians1:18: *"By having the eyes of your heart flooded with light, so that you can know and understand the hope to which He has called you, and how rich is His glorious inheritance in the saints (His set-apart ones), And [so that you can know and understand] what is the immeasurable and unlimited and surpassing greatness of His power in and for us who believe, as demonstrated in the working of His mighty strength, Which He exerted in Christ when He raised Him from the dead and seated Him at His [own] right hand in the heavenly [places], Far above all rule and authority and power and dominion and every name that is named [above every title that can be conferred], not only in this age and in this world, but also in the age and the world which are to come"* (Amplified).

That verse is amazing but have you really ever thought of how this actually happens, how do we get this light that is meant to flood the eyes of our heart? God wants our lives to be flooded by His light, the Bible says that "God is light" so He wants our worlds to be flooded with Him. In the above verse this is the only way you will truly know "the hope which he has called you" and "how rich is his glorious inheritance in the saints" that you can know and understand what is the immeasurable and unlimited and surpassing greatness of His power in and for us who believe".

How do we get flooded with God's light? The same way God modeled it for us from the very beginning, He spoke in Genesis 1, "let there be light" and light was. In the same way we get God's light in our lives by speaking His Word!

2 Corinthians 10:4: *"For the weapons of our warfare are not carnal but mighty in God for pulling down strongholds, casting down arguments*

and every high thing that exalts itself against the knowledge of God, bringing every thought into captivity to the obedience of Christ, and being ready to punish all disobedience when your obedience is fulfilled."

What are the weapons of our warfare for? Pulling down (flooding out) strongholds and bringing every "thought" into captivity to the obedience of Christ.

Build a wall in your mind so full and prepared with the Word of God, so when doubts, fear, depression or unbelief comes in, the wall of your mind is impregnable. So how does this work?

1. When these thoughts of fear or failure come in get a picture of you succeeding or overcoming, always picture success no matter how bad things are going.

I had to practice this recently when things looked grim regarding purchasing our dream home and negativity and unbelief was bombarding me every day. I had to prepare a mental picture in my mind which consisted of my family and me all playing in the pool (yes our dream home came with a pool).

"You've got to be aware of all the thoughts that flow in and out of your mind - that's the first thing. Many people just let those thoughts flow in and out without really knowing what they are thinking and without knowing the effects those thoughts have". -Lydia Lassila

We came up against delay after delay and obstacle after obstacle; what was meant to be a quick close was now turning into a battle to even get the house. But God had given me a promise that this was our house. So every time a negative thought or voice came into my head I immediately started thanking God for our new home and picturing all of us playing in the pool, I would imagine this scenario over and over every day for as long as I needed to until the negative thoughts went away. Today we all play together in our pool, in our new home, just as I had seen it over and over in my mind.

2. Whenever a negative thought comes in, have a scripture prepared to respond with.

When Jesus was tempted by the devil (Luke 4:1-14), He said "it is written" three times using three different scriptures, out there in the desert, with no Bible, no DVD series, no prayer partners or friends; but he had the Word of God and each time the devil spoke to Him he responded with the Word of God.

Once I had the picture set in my mind of my family and me all playing in the pool together I then got a word from the Holy Spirit. "The same God that parted the Red Sea is able to bring this house through to closing". I asked myself what was the harder miracle? The Red Sea being parted or us getting our home? In my mind the Red Sea seems the far more difficult but when it comes to God there are no degrees of difficulty; bigger miracles are not harder for God, they are harder for us to believe. It doesn't matter the size of your obstacles, or how big your mountain is or how insurmountable the giant is that you face; the question is how big is your God? Now you may think I'm crazy and that's just fine with me, call me the crazy man who got his house.

The old negative ways have lived in your mind so long that they feel at home there. It takes daily discipline of emptying and filling, of flooding your mind with the word of God. It's harder to get old thoughts out of your mind than new thoughts in. So every time that negative thought comes in, take it captive by speaking the Word of God. You have to know the Word of God to speak it, so take some time identifying the areas that the devil most attacks you in. What are the pervading thoughts that dominate your mind each day?

Jesus practiced eliminating the voices of fear and doubt from his mind in Mark 5:36 *"Overhearing but ignoring what they said, Jesus said to the ruler of the synagogue, "Do not be seized with alarm and struck with fear; only keep on believing"* (Amplified). I think sometimes we need to hear and then ignore. When we hear doubt, defeat or unbelief we need to ignore it.

Maybe you have a lack of peace; if so then you could memorize a scripture like Isaiah 26:3 *"You will keep him in perfect peace, Whose mind is stayed on You, Because he trusts in You"*. Anytime you sense a lack of peace or have thoughts that create a sense of anxiety, worry or turmoil, speak this verse over and over. What you set your mind on sets itself on your mind. Peace of mind is not complicated; just simply fill your mind with thoughts and scriptures that cause it to be peaceful. What you saturate your mind with is what your life will be saturated with.

Fill your heart with God's word, when you increase your word level, you increase your chances of hearing from God. Psalm 119:105 states, *"Your word is a lamp to my feet And a light to my path"*. The word of God brings clear guidance, it lights the path and shows your feet the way to go. Flooding your mind and life with the Word of God, God's voice and desires become easier to recognize. One of the best things you can do if you are a parent is when they are old enough, give motivation and reward for your children to memorize scripture, start the habit early.

The mind responds to teaching and discipline: you can make the mind give you back anything you want, but it can only give back what it was first given *"as a man thinks in his heart so is he"* (Proverbs 23:7).

Flooding proactively protects your mind and heart. The way we crucify the flesh is by living in the Spirit. Approaching life by focusing on what you don't want to do is a defensive and legalistic way of living; this is what Old Testament living looks like. Legalism focuses on what you can't have, rather than the amazing reality of what you do have. When we really realize what has been given to us the other loses its appeal.

A while back I read an article that stated that many, many years ago, before we had all this amazing technology, banks trained their staff to check for counterfeit bills by placing them in a room and letting them handle real money all day long. That way when a counterfeit bill was handed to them, they would know straightaway because they had spent so much time with the real thing.

I like this analogy as this is the same way it works with God. The more we spend time immersed in the real (purposes of God), the more in tune we become to hear and know His voice. This doesn't mean we shut off the world completely. We can be "in the world but not of the world."

You can be so engaged with God that hearing His voice becomes so natural to you that you know it's God, because you have devoted yourself to be close to Him, loving what He loves, spending time with Him and meditating in His word.

The Holy Spirit can give us guidance at every turn in life as He did for Paul, not permitting Paul to go to Bithynia as he had planned which we read about in Acts 16:6-7, *"Now when they had gone through Phrygia and the region of Galatia, they were forbidden by the Holy Spirit to preach the word in Asia. After they had come to Mysia, they tried to go into Bithynia, but the Spirit did not permit them."*

The Holy Spirit wants to give us guidance every step of our lives. If only we will yield to Him and follow His voice. So how do we hear His voice?

Do what it says to do in James 1:5-7: *"If any of you lacks wisdom, let him ask of God, who gives to all liberally and without reproach, and it will be given to him. But let him ask in faith, with no doubting, for he who doubts is like a wave of the sea driven and tossed by the wind. For let not that man suppose that he will receive anything from the Lord."*

We can see from this scripture that we do lack wisdom, so we need the Holy Spirit's guidance every day, but we must decide that God does want to speak to us and approach Him in faith knowing that He will speak to us, not hoping or wishing or striving.

Most often the Spirit operates as our spiritual conscience, directing us in ways that require us to follow and be led rather than to lead.

The Holy Spirit speaks in different ways: internal thoughts or impressions, His word, other people/leaders, desire or an urgency,

MY FRIEND, THE HOLY SPIRIT

restlessness, passion or circumstances that God uses to get your attention.

Too often we anticipate Him speaking and directing us a certain way but often He fails to conform to our expectations. Other times we just can't hear Him speaking to us over the noise in our lives; we are so distracted, focused on other things, we miss Him speaking to us. I recently read this quote "before we had video, God gave visions. Unplugged is the order of the hour".

God wants to give you a new vision just not what the Television (Tell-a-vision) gives you.

The devil has captured our attention, he has us busy doing good when we could be busy doing great. I think sometimes we miss God. We keep in our minds only what is natural and what we are used to and we tend to filter out what is different or "unnatural". So hearing God becomes difficult until we line our minds up with the way God thinks.

Isaiah 55:8 states, "'For My thoughts are not your thoughts, Nor are your ways My ways,' says the LORD." Which means our minds may not be used to His way of thinking.

How do we know it's God?

Of course, how do we know it is not the devil speaking to us? I mean, "What if it's not God?" This is the wrong question to ask; we should be asking, "What if it is God?" For instance if you feel a prompting of the Holy Spirit to speak to someone about Jesus, it is not the devil, nor is it your flesh as neither your flesh or the devil wants to tell someone about Jesus!

1. Seek it. We must seek the Holy Spirit and ask Him for guidance. But you will only seek after that which you desire. Pray each day, "Lord give me the desire according to your will". God will confirm desires, the best way is to screen your desire through scripture.

We need to move from seeking what we want to what "HE" wants, When we seek God we have to move from trying to get something from God to seeking what God wants from us. To realigning our hearts affections and priorities with His.

Seeking God's hands and His face are different, most of prayer is seeking His hands. Seeking His hands is because we need something, it's to do with us, seeking His face is to worship Him for who he is not what he can do for us. It is communicating love not thinking of what you will receive in return.

You can seek after and receive the anointing of God but not be led by the spirit (ie; Samson). Samson surrendered his spiritual rights in order to satisfy physical appetites. This is a scary thought, which is why our hearts should never just be solely focused on the gifts and power of God, but on seeking Jesus and His redeeming love which transforms our heart.

2. Wait for it.

We must be patient to set aside the time to wait and listen for the Holy Spirit. Let God know that your ears are open, that your heart is soft and that your hands and feet are ready for action.

Reduce your speed, slow down, sit still, learn to unplug, stop, and eliminate the noise in your life. Practice the art of silence daily. "Silence is the vehicle in which great things fashion themselves"

Luke 24:49: the word wait in this passage literally means "sit still". The cycle of waiting on God is followed by effective spirit filled service is the divine program for all time. Far more would be accomplished in our lives if each day we just practiced the art of waiting on God each day. Psalms 46:10 states, "*Be still and know that I am God*". That pretty much sums it up. "God cannot be seen by spiritual eyes that are shut, God cannot be heard by spiritual ears that are plugged, and God cannot be followed by a heart that stays stubbornly hard". -Bill Hybels

3. Expect it.

We must have faith and confidently expect that if we have asked that the Holy Spirit will speak to us and give us guidance, He will.

Matthew 9:29: *"According to your faith let it be to you."*

4. Follow it.

We must follow step by step as the guidance comes. Success in hearing from God is doing the next thing He tells you to do; in the Old Testament you hadn't heard until you had done. Be obedient in small things. Sometimes you will need to wait for God's timing. Pray until you have peace. God will confirm the right time.

1 Thessalonians 5:1: *"But concerning the times and the seasons, brethren, you have no need that I should write to you."*

Paul wrote this because God expects us to know and understand the season we are in, sometimes we may hear God or get a word from God, but is it for now?

MY FRIEND, THE HOLY SPIRIT

Over time you will learn to differentiate between the thoughts and impressions that are just yours and those that come from the Holy Spirit. But if you don't desire to really hear God's voice on a daily basis, then it will never happen. If you desire it, then you will seek after it. You seek after it by waiting for His voice and by expecting Him to speak to you, and then once the Holy Spirit has spoken, we must obey those promptings.

CHAPTER 20:

Closing Challenge

I hope that through reading the chapters of this book the Holy Spirit has stirred your heart like He has mine.

The Bible says in James 1:22, *"But be doers of the word, and not hearers only, deceiving yourselves."* This means if we are always just hearing but never doing we are in deception, ouch!

Ask yourself this question: of all the sermons that you have heard and all the songs that you have sung in the last year, have you really done anything for God, really? If you have been a Christian any length of time we have to ask ourselves whether over the last few years that we have been saved, all the conferences that we have been to, all the sermons that we have sat through and all the songs we have sung, has it really changed our actions? Are we moving in greater power, are more people being saved, being healed and set free through the power of God flowing through our lives? If the answer is no then we need to be deliberate about changing things in our world. We have to move from just believing that God has power to actual demonstrating that power.

James 2:14-19: *"What does it profit, my brethren, if someone says he has faith but does not have works? Can faith save him? If a brother or sister is naked and destitute of daily food, and one of you says to them, "Depart in peace, be warmed and filled," but you do not give them the things which are needed for the body, what does it profit? Thus also faith by itself, if it does not have works, is dead. But someone will say, "You have faith, and I have works." Show me your faith without your works, and I will show you my faith by my works. You believe that there is one God. You do well. Even the demons believe—and tremble!"*

MY FRIEND, THE HOLY SPIRIT

Corresponding action

Faith must have a corresponding action. As we see above, the Bible states, "faith without works is dead". So we can say we believe in miracles, that God raises the dead and the sick can be healed, but where is the corresponding action? The Bible says even the demons believe and tremble! So if all we do is believe, then we are doing just as much as the demons. If all we do is sing nice songs about how God can move in power and how mighty is He, and if we believe the Bible is true and believe the gifts are for today and the Holy Spirit moves in power, then where is it in our lives? Faith has to have a corresponding action in our lives. We believe, but the demons believe, so we must move beyond that and into what God has for us.

You are a byproduct of our expectations/beliefs

Most of us want 100 percent certainty before we will step out, but the problem is that it takes faith out of the equation. There is no such thing as "risk-free" faith. You can't experience success without taking the risk of failure, which reminds me of a story.

> One day a man fell off a cliff, but managed to grab a tree limb on the way down. The following conversation ensued:
>
> "Is anyone up there?"
>
> "I am here. I am the Lord. Do you believe me?"
>
> "Yes, Lord, I believe. I really believe, but I can't hang on much longer."
>
> "That's all right, if you really believe, you have nothing to worry about. I will save you. Just let go of the branch."
>
> A moment of pause, then: "Is anyone else up there?"

I am sure you may have heard this story before but it illustrates a powerful point, if the man really believed, he would have let go. If you really believe that God's power is for you and for today, it's time to let go of the branch of unbelief and step out in faith.

Armor of God

> Ephesians 6:10-18 states, *"Finally, my brethren, be strong in the Lord and in the power of His might. Put on the whole armor of God, that you may be able to stand against the wiles of the devil. For we do not wrestle against flesh and blood, but against principalities, against powers, against the rulers of the darkness of this age, against spiritual hosts of wickedness in the heavenly places. Therefore take up the whole armor of*

Closing Challenge

> *God, that you may be able to withstand in the evil day, and having done all, to stand. Stand therefore, having girded your waist with truth, having put on the breastplate of righteousness, and having shod your feet with the preparation of the gospel of peace; above all, taking the shield of faith with which you will be able to quench all the fiery darts of the wicked one. And take the helmet of salvation, and the sword of the Spirit, which is the word of God; praying always with all prayer and supplication in the Spirit, being watchful to this end with all perseverance and supplication for all the saints—"*

That's a lot of work just to get dressed! I mean I struggle to pick out a shirt in the morning, let alone getting dressed up spiritually for the day! What are these verses talking about? It's about preparing your entire person to be saturated with the very being, with the very power, with the very life of God! God isn't saying put on all this armor for nothing. You put on armor for battle, for doing, for stepping out and getting into it, not for sitting back.

Imagine the day of a big battle has arrived and a soldier is getting suited up with armor, but after putting on the helmet, breastplate and the other items, and picking up the sword and shield and singing some victory songs with the other soldiers and listening to a motivational speech from his commanding officer he then sits down. His commanding officer comes over asking him why he got dressed if he isn't going out to battle. He answers, "I believe we are going to win." That soldier would not last long in that army! But this is what the Church lives like today; we get suited up, we get excited, we sing victory songs (praise and worship) we hear a great motivational speech (sermon) from the pastor and then we...sit down.

Ezekial 47:3-5: *"And when the man went out to the east with the line in his hand, he measured one thousand cubits, and he brought me through the waters; the water came up to my ankles. Again he measured one thousand and brought me through the waters; the water came up to my knees. Again he measured one thousand and brought me through; the water came up to my waist. Again he measured one thousand, and it was a river that I could not cross; for the water was too deep, water in which one must swim, a river that could not be crossed."*

If you are only content with ankle-deep water, you don't need God. My daughters do not need my help in ankle-deep water, but in deeper water they need Daddy, they can't do it on their own. See, in ankle-deep water you don't need corresponding action because there is no faith, there is no faith in ankle-deep, or knee-deep or even waist-deep water; it's only when you get into "a river that cannot be crossed" because the water is too deep that you need God, that you have to

MY FRIEND, THE HOLY SPIRIT

activate faith. We cannot be content to stay in the shallow, we have to go to the deep; this means stepping out in the power of God in a practical and real way, not worrying about what other people think about you, having a confidence because you have heard the voice of God.

The cure for the fear of failure is not success. The cure for the fear of rejection is not acceptance. What is the cure then? Exposure to your fears; you have to expose yourself to what you are afraid of in order to overcome it, that is how you build immunity. If you never try anything because you are afraid of rejection or failure you will never overcome your fears.

"Twenty years from now you will be more disappointed by the things you didn't do than by the ones you did do, so through off the bowlines, sail away from the safe harbor, catch the trade winds in your sails, Explore. Dream. Discover". -Mark Twain.

Most people are one decision, one small act of courage between the ordinary and the extraordinary, one step from stepping into the supernatural, between you and your dream becoming a reality. Think about these characters from the Bible and how one act of obedience brought the power of God.

- Noah looked foolish building the ark in the desert.
- Sarah looked foolish buying maternity clothes at 90.
- The Israelites looked foolish walking around walls of Jericho blowing their trumpets.
- David looked foolish attacking Goliath with nothing but a slingshot.
- Peter looked foolish stepping out of a boat in the middle of a lake.
- Jesus looked foolish hanging half-naked on the cross after declaring himself to be God!

But...

- Noah was saved from the flood.
- Sarah had a baby.
- Jericho came tumbling down.
- David cut off a Giant's head.
- Peter walked on water.
- Jesus rose from the dead.

Fear and doubt blinds our vision; faith creates vision. We must choose faith, step out and obey God.

We must desire the Holy Spirit on a daily basis

You won't get anything you don't first desire. Matthew 15:28 says, *"Then Jesus answered and said to her, 'O woman, great is your faith!*

Closing Challenge

Let it be to you as you desire.' And her daughter was healed from that very hour." John 15:7 states, *"If you abide in Me, and My words abide in you, you will ask what you desire, and it shall be done for you."*

My wife was sharing one morning at the church staff meeting and was talking about how our daughter Charlize is so passionate and I thought about it and realized how intense my daughter can be. We got her a puppy for her birthday, "Soda". She just loves that puppy; she tells everyone about Soda, she shows her off to everyone, she walks around with Soda under her arm, she puts her on her bike (like standing on the seat with paws on the handlebars), she is passionate about that puppy! Then one day we come into the kitchen and she is on her knees licking the puppy; they are actually licking each other!

Another time, we bought her a bag for preschool and told her it was for taking snacks to preschool. Before we could even leave the store, Charlize had already filled the bag with tons of food without us noticing and we had to take it all out at the register! After we got home she was wheeling that bag around the house all day; at night she wanted to take it to bed and in the morning she wanted to drag it around the house with her again. We later found her in the pantry stuffing food into that bag!

I have to ask myself am I as passionate about God and the presence of the Holy Spirit as Charlize is about her puppy and her school bag? I want to be someone that devotes myself to being close to the Holy Spirit. Let's not be those that acknowledge Him, but then ignore Him each day. Let's set aside the time to be with Him, to know His word, invite Him to change our world so we can in turn change the world we live in. The more we live as citizens of heaven, the more heaven's activities should infect our lives and the lives of those around us.

Your first step is making the decision to devote your heart afresh to be close to God. Maybe you have drifted from that closeness you once knew. Maybe you just want more of Him. In other words, maybe your spiritual life feels stalled or you feel dissatisfied with where you are at. The fact that you even feel this means that God is stirring your heart to draw you closer to Him.

If you feel you need God to reignite your faith today, pray this prayer:
"I invite you, Holy Spirit, to come and fall afresh on me. Reignite my faith, draw me close to you, speak to me, and lead me as I open my heart to you. Do what you need to do in my life so that my life would be pleasing to you. I choose to honor you this day by acknowledging you and inviting you to take control of my life. Baptize me in your love and in your power and let the grace of God grant me closeness to you. May I bring glory to the name of Jesus all the days of my life! Amen."